CRE**A**TIVE
HOMEOWNER®

garden ponds,
fountains & waterfalls
FOR YOUR HOME

Kathleen Fisher

CREATIVE HOMEOWNER®

Dedication
In memory of Kathleen Fisher.

Acknowledgments
Many kind people were generous with inspiration and information.
Thanks to Al Short and his team at Harmony Ponds and Gardens; landscape designers Jeffrey Minnich, Sarah Boasberg, and Kibbe Turner; water gardeners Scott and Karen Nishioki, Sue Felley at Judith Resnik Elementary School, and Pandora Johns; horticulturist Larry Mellichamp; and for the suppliers, Charles Thomas and his crew at Lilypons, Allyson Handson at Picovs, and Dave Kelly at Aquascape Designs.
Thanks to Jim Lawrie for his review.

GARDEN PONDS, FOUNTAINS & WATERFALLS FOR YOUR HOME

SENIOR EDITOR	Kathie Robitz
PRINCIPAL AUTHOR	Kathleen Fisher
CONTENT EDITOR	Nancy T. Engel
CONSULTING HORTICULTURAL EDITOR	Elizabeth P. Stell
INTERIOR DESIGN CONCEPT	Glee Barre
GRAPHIC DESIGNER	Kathryn Wityk
DIGITAL IMAGING SPECIALIST	Mary Dolan
TECHNICAL REVIEWERS	Ken Badgley, Carole Ottessen, Mike Stoll, Brian Trimble
INDEXER	Schroeder Indexing Services
COVER DESIGN CONCEPT	Kathryn Wityk
FRONT COVER PHOTOGRAPHY	left Photos Horticultural, design: Paul Dyer/The Very Interesting Landscape Co.; top right Bluestock/Dreamstime; bottom right Lisa Turay/Dreamstime
BACK COVER PHOTOGRAPHY	top right Jerry Pavia; bottom left Photo Horticultural, design: Ash Parish Garden Club

Manufactured in China

Current Printing (last digit)
10 9 8 7 6

Garden Ponds, Fountains & Waterfalls for Your Home
Previously published as Complete Guide to Water Gardens, Ponds & Fountains
ISBN: 978-1-58011-506-3

We are always looking for talented authors. To submit an idea, please send a brief inquiry to acquisitions@foxchapelpublishing.com.

www.creativehomeowner.com
Creative Homeowner is an imprint of New Design Originals Corporation and distributed in North America by Fox Chapel Publishing, 903 Square Street, Mount Joy, PA 17552, *www.FoxChapelPublishing.com*, and in the UK by Grantham Book Service, Trent Road, Grantham, Lincolnshire, NG31 7XQ.

Safety First

Though all concepts and methods in this book have been reviewed for safety, it is not possible to overstate the importance of using the safest working methods possible. What follows are reminders—do's and don'ts for yard work and landscaping. They are not substitutes for your own common sense.

▪ Always use caution, care, and good judgment when following the procedures described in this book.

▪ Always determine locations of underground utility lines before you dig, and then avoid them by a safe distance. Buried lines may be for gas, electricity, communications, or water. Start research by contacting your local building officials. Also contact local utility companies; they will often send a representative free of charge to help you map their lines. In addition, there are private utility locator firms that may be listed in your Yellow Pages. **Note:** previous owners may have installed underground drainage, sprinkler, and lighting lines without mapping them.

▪ Always read and heed the manufacturer's instructions for using a tool, especially the warnings.

▪ Always ensure that the electrical setup is safe; be sure that no circuit is overloaded and that all power tools and electrical outlets are properly grounded and protected by a ground-fault circuit interrupter (GFCI). Do not use power tools in wet locations.

▪ Always wear eye protection when using chemicals, sawing wood, pruning trees and shrubs, using power tools, and striking metal onto metal or concrete.

▪ Always read labels on chemicals, solvents, and other products; provide ventilation; heed warnings.

▪ Always wear heavy rubber gloves rated for chemicals, not mere household rubber gloves, when handling toxins.

▪ Always wear appropriate gloves in situations in which your hands could be injured by rough surfaces, sharp edges, thorns, or poisonous plants.

▪ Always wear a disposable face mask or a special filtering respirator when creating sawdust or working with toxic gardening substances.

▪ Always keep your hands and other body parts away from the business ends of blades, cutters, and bits.

▪ Always obtain approval from local building officials before undertaking construction of permanent structures.

▪ Never work with power tools when you are tired or under the influence of alcohol or drugs.

▪ Never carry sharp or pointed tools, such as knives or saws, in your pockets. If you carry such tools, use special-purpose tool scabbards.

Metric Equivalents

All measurements in this book are given in U.S. Customary units. If you wish to find metric equivalents, use the following tables and conversion factors.

Inches to Millimeters and Centimeters

1 in = 25.4 mm = 2.54 cm

in	mm	cm
$\frac{1}{16}$	1.5875	0.1588
$\frac{1}{8}$	3.1750	0.3175
$\frac{1}{4}$	6.3500	0.6350
$\frac{3}{8}$	9.5250	0.9525
$\frac{1}{2}$	12.7000	1.2700
$\frac{5}{8}$	15.8750	1.5875
$\frac{3}{4}$	19.0500	1.9050
$\frac{7}{8}$	22.2250	2.2225
1	25.4000	2.5400

Inches to Centimeters and Meters

1 in = 2.54 cm = 0.0254 m

in	cm	m
1	2.54	0.0254
2	5.08	0.0508
3	7.62	0.0762
4	10.16	0.1016
5	12.70	0.1270
6	15.24	0.1524
7	17.78	0.1778
8	20.32	0.2032
9	22.86	0.2286
10	25.40	0.2540
11	27.94	0.2794
12	30.48	0.3048

Feet to Meters

1 ft = 0.3048 m

ft	m
1	0.3048
5	1.5240
10	3.0480
25	7.6200
50	15.2400
100	30.4800

Square Feet to Square Meters

1 ft² = 0.092 903 04 m²

Acres to Square Meters

1 acre = 4046.85642 m²

Cubic Yards to Cubic Meters

1 yd³ = 0.764 555 m³

Ounces and Pounds (Avoirdupois) to Grams

1 oz = 28.349 523 g

1 lb = 453.5924 g

Pounds to Kilograms

1 lb = 0.453 592 37 kg.

Ounces and Quarts to Liters

1 oz = 0.029 573 53 L

1 qt = 0.9463 L

Gallons to Liters

1 gal = 3.785 411 784 L

Fahrenheit to Celsius (Centigrade)

$°C = °F - 32 \times \frac{5}{9}$

°F	°C
-30	-34.45
-20	-28.89
-10	-23.34
-5	-20.56
0	-17.78
10	-12.22
20	-6.67
30	-1.11
32 (freezing)	0.00
40	4.44
50	10.00
60	15.56
70	21.11
80	26.67
90	32.22
100	37.78
212 (boiling)	100

Contents

Introduction

Adding a water feature to your yard or garden will reward you with endless hours of delight. If you're willing to invest the time, *Garden Ponds, Fountains & Waterfalls for Your Home* can be your guide to a beautiful water garden of your own creation.

Of all the things you could add to your landscape, a water feature has to be the most dramatic. What else could bring you sound, movement, reflections, and the opportunity to attract animals and use plants in entirely new ways? This book has been organized to both inspire you and provide practical, hands-on guidance.

Chapter 1 takes you on a historical tour of water gardening, where you'll probably discover that your motivation for building a pond or fountain isn't much different from those of the Moguls or Roman rulers of many hun-

A traditional Japanese garden may inspire you to adapt one or two elements and incorporate them into your own design.

dreds of years ago. You won't be able to copy the scope of most of these grand designs, but you will realize that you are indeed in very distinguished company. Chapter 2 talks about design considerations: where you will put your pond, how you will shape it, and how you will make it seem an integral part of the rest of your landscape. Thoughtful consideration of these factors, along with detailed knowledge of your soil, sun, wind, and weather, will ensure that your water feature brings you, your family, and visitors delight for many years to come.

Then you move on to the nuts and bolts of installing your new pond. Chapter 3 discusses the things you will need to build your pond and explains how to put pen to paper in planning it. Your pond's foundation, like that of your home, is the basis for all that will come later, so all of Chapter 4 is devoted to explaining what must be done to install it correctly. Thanks to modern technology that has made flexible liners and preformed shells affordable for everyone, you'll be surprised at how easy it is to do.

Once you have the foundation in place, you will find numerous options for adding frills. Chapters 5 through 7 describe fountains and lighting, bridges and stepping-stones, waterfalls and streams, and how you can add these features to your design.

If you have a naturally wet area in your landscape or if you enjoy collecting and growing unusual plants, you'll want to spend time reading Chapter 8. This chapter talks about bog gardens, which are often installed adjacent to a pond. This is where you can grow fascinating wetland denizens such as the carnivorous pitcher plants and Venus-flytrap or the terrestrial orchid called ladies-tresses.

Chapter 9 explains factors that affect the quality of your pond's water, which can mean life or death to your fish and make a difference in the way your water looks or smells. Chapter 10 is about the creatures themselves, from expensive collector koi to predators who might stalk them.

As a rule, water gardening brings pleasure far outweighing the work and expense it entails. Yet you do need to anticipate problems and do some periodic preventive maintenance. Chapter 11 goes over the few seasonal tasks you should carry out to keep your pond and its residents healthy.

Chapter 12 is the heart of the book. Sure, you can have a pond without any plants at all, but for most of us these features are water gardens. So this chapter is an encyclopedia of plants, from underwater oxygenators and water lilies to native wetland plants that look at home near a pond or stream. Choosing and arranging these plants will make your pond new to you every year.

Water gardening has something for everyone. If you're mechanically inclined, you may want to experiment with various sized pumps and filters. Artists will devote their time to shaping a stream, edged with perennials to bloom throughout the seasons. Nature lovers will plan and plant carefully to attract birds or even raccoons and snakes. Whatever your inclination, this book will help to get you off to a solid start on a fascinating hobby.

There's no better inspiration than nature. You can create a naturalistic look for your pond using freeform shapes, plantings, and stones.

Hardiness Zone Map

The Hardiness-Zone Map developed by the Agricultural Research Service of the USDA divides the country into 13 zones according to average minimum winter temperatures. Hardiness zones are used to identify regions to which plants are suited based on their cold tolerance, which is what "hardiness" means. Many factors, such as elevation and moisture level, come into play when determining whether a plant is suitable for your region. Local climates may vary from what is shown on this map. Contact your local Cooperative Extension Service for recommendations for your area. Or go to www.planthardiness.ars.usda.gov to find your hardiness zone based on your zip code. Mapping by the PRISM Climate Group, Oregon State University.

AHS Heat-Zone Map

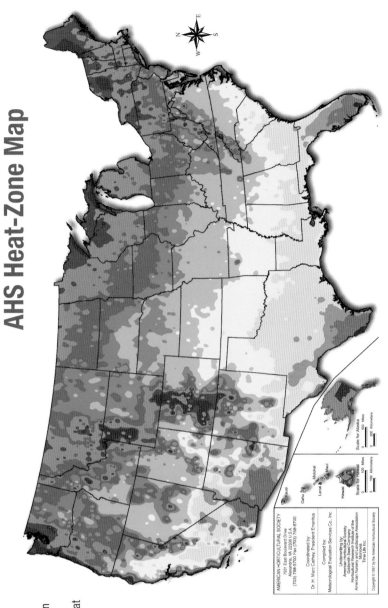

AMERICAN HORTICULTURAL SOCIETY
7931 East Boulevard Drive
Alexandria, VA 22308 U.S.A.
(703) 768-5700 Fax (703) 768-8700

Coordinated by:
Dr. H. Marc Cathey, President Emeritus

Compiled by:
Meteorological Evaluation Services Co. Inc.

Underwriting by:
American Horticultural Society
Goldsmith Seed Company
Horticultural Research Institute of the
American Nursery and Landscape Association
Monrovia
Time Life Inc.

Copyright © 1997 by the American Horticultural Society

The American Horticultural Society Heat-Zone Map

divides the United States into 12 zones based on the average annual number of days a region's temperatures climb above 86°F (30°C), the temperature at which the cellular proteins of plants begin to experience injury. Introduced in 1998, the AHS Heat-Zone Map holds significance, especially for gardeners in southern and transitional zones. Nurseries, growers, and other plant sources will gradually begin listing both cold hardiness and heat tolerance zones for plants, including grass plants. Using the USDA Plant Hardiness map, which can help determine a plant's cold tolerance, and the AHS Heat-Zone Map, gardeners will be able to safely choose plants that tolerate their region's lowest and highest temperatures.

Canada's Plant Hardiness Zone Map

Canada's Plant Hardiness Zone Map outlines the different zones in Canada where various types of trees, shrubs, and flowers will most likely survive. It is based on the average climatic conditions of each area. The hardiness map is divided into nine major zones: the harshest is 0 and the mildest is 8. Relatively few plants are suited to zone 0. Subzones (e.g., 4a or 4b, 5a or 5b) are also noted in the map legend. These subzones are most familiar to Canadian gardeners. Some significant local factors, such as micro-topography, amount of shelter, and subtle local variations in snow cover, are too small to be captured on the map. Year-to-year variations in weather and gardening techniques can also have a significant impact on plant survival in any particular location.

Plant Hardiness Zones

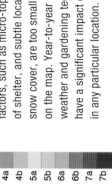
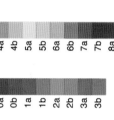

0a	4a
0b	4b
1a	5a
1b	5b
2a	6a
2b	6b
3a	7a
3b	7b
	8a

PART 1

Starting with a Plan

What inspired you to want to create a water garden or pond? Was it a feature you saw and admired at a friend's home, or did your inspiration come from something on a grander scale— a fountain, perhaps, in a public park or a photograph of a historic water garden? Whatever it was, enhancing your garden with a water feature will bring you many hours of delight. But first, you have to have a plan.

CHAPTER 1

Looking to the Past for Inspiration

From the beginning, human beings have venerated water. We know it as the sustainer of life and sense it as the source of our origins. Yet because it also holds fear for us, we need to control it. The earliest recorded water gardens reflect all of these things: the practical need for water to drink and to cleanse oneself, the necessity to irrigate life-sustaining crops, the desire for a sense of coolness and for comforting sounds in harsh surroundings, a need to control nature, and in many religious traditions, connection with the Creator.

This is where water gardens began—in the Cradle of Civilization, located between the Taurus Moutains of eastern Asia Minor and the Persian Gulf.

Fountains Abbey, in North Yorkshire, England, is the remains of a medieval Cistercian monastery.

Ancient Egyptians drew water from the Nile with a simple device called a shadoof.

Early Civilizations

The Cradle of Civilization was the birthplace of water gardens. The inhabitants of Mesopotamia, which extended from the mountains of eastern Asia Minor to the Persian Gulf, owed their success to their ability to control the Tigris and Euphrates rivers. That they succeeded in this is clear, although evidence of ornamental water gardens from this period is limited to a few artifacts—a carved water basin from 3000 BC and a stone fountain from about 1,000 years later.

The Assyrians, who inhabited the southern half of the Tigris and east, built vast hunting parks, and lifted water at least three stories high to plant the temple towers called ziggurats, the most famous of which were the Hanging Gardens of Babylon.

The Egyptians were able to harness the Nile with a device called the "shadoof," consisting of a horizontal pole attached to a pivot, with a bucket on one end and a counterweight on the other. (Employing elementary physics, it is still used today.) Carvings and relics in their tombs show us that they had elaborate pleasure gardens, where these desert dwellers could escape the heat among water birds and fish.

In a tomb built in Thebes around 1400 BC, archeologists found plans for a garden entered by canal and divided into four main areas with a rectangular pond in each.

This cross-shaped motif was often centered with plantings of lotus. Egyptians revered the lotus as both medicine and a religious symbol. Another early water garden plant was the bulrush, famous for hiding the abandoned infant Moses, but also used to fashion ropes, mats, sails, and even to construct rafts solid enough to transport stone obelisks.

In the middle of the eighteenth century, the Landscape Movement in Great Britain inspired a naturalistic style that emphasized water rather than heavy planting. Here, the reflection of the house in the water enhances the overall landscape.

PERSIA

The citizens of Persia (now Iran) also divided their gardens with cross-shaped channels, a form they called "chahar-bagh." Cyrus the Great, in the sixth century BC, fed his garden through underground channels called "qanats," made by drilling a shaft to the source of water, then sloping a channel to its destination. About a century later a descendant, Cyrus the Younger, is credited with coining the word "paradise" (although certainly not the concept) for a garden. He named his garden "Pairidaeza," from the Persian words meaning "around" and "wall." Persians loved their gardens so much that they wove their designs into rugs in order to enjoy them in winter.

When Islamic Arabs invaded Persia in 637 AD, it wasn't the end of this garden tradition, but in fact, launched its spread throughout the Islamic world for at least a millennium. These road-and-dust-weary nomads were enchanted by the walled gardens and further inspired by the Koran, in which Mohammed described paradise as a garden complete with fountains.

Moorish water garden. The Generalife is a sensual garden near Granada and was a summer residence for Spanish rulers.

The Generalife. In the thirteenth century, the Moors—descendents of Arabs and Berbers who invaded Spain in 711 AD—built two exemplary gardens still in existence in the hills overlooking Granada. The Palacio de Generalife was the summer residence of their rulers. This garden is romantic, intimate, and sensual. Particularly so is Court of the Canal, a long narrow space with three-level pavilions at each end. A pool that runs its length is flanked by lush plantings. Water jets arcing over it and bubbling basins shaped like lotus pads provide the water music.

Alhambra. Gardens of the more poetic-sounding Alhambra (Red Castle), on the other hand, are massive and expansive as befits a fortress, which it was. In the Court of the Lions, a dozen carved King of Beasts spout water into a hexagonal pool and hold aloft a 12-sided fountain basin. Around the edges of this court, alabaster columns support ornate arcades. In comparison, the Court of the Myrtles has a single rectangular pond with closely pruned myrtle hedges.

Some 7,000 miles away in Mogul India (captured by Asian warlords such as Tamberlane and Ghenghis Khan in the thirteenth and fourteenth centuries), gardens reflected the Persian influence in their canals and geometric shapes. They harnessed rivers to fuel water features, notably the chute called the "chadar."

In the late 1500s, hundreds of Mogul gardens were built at the foot of the Himalayas in Kashmir, where water flowed down the mountains and into Lake Dal. One of those surviving is Shalamar Bagh, as famous for its name, meaning "place of love," as for its series of pavilions surrounded by water. The nearby Nishat Bagh is made breathtaking by a central canal descending over 12 levels, each linked by a broad chadar. Over these falls, water plays over indentations in the rocks, which are angled to capture sunlight.

Taj Mahal. The Moguls are also famous for their tomb gardens, particularly The Taj Mahal, built between 1632 and 1654 by the last Mogul emperor, Shah Jahan, in memory of his favorite wife, Mumtaz Mahal. He broke tradition by positioning the tomb at one end of the cross-shaped canal, rather than in the center, so that the entire structure is reflected.

The Taj Mahal, the most famous of the Indian tomb gardens, honors the memory of a Mogul emperor's favorite wife.

ASIA

The earliest Chinese gardens, like those of the Assyrians, were sprawling hunting parks. Their emperors, beginning at least with the Han dynasty (206 to 220 AD), built lakes covering hundreds of acres as centers for boating and socializing. But even though most of these lakes were artificial—and in winter, sometimes the flowers were, too—nature was the ideal in these as well as in small private gardens. Many of the latter have been reconstructed in Suzhou, sometimes called the "Venice of the East," where canals and enclosed courtyard gardens lap at the foundations of homes and other buildings.

Confucius set the tone for Chinese gardens in 500 BC, with the axiom that "the wise find joy in water, the benevolent find joy in mountains." These two elements—the water representing the female, or *yin*, and rocks the male, or *yang*—have been central to Asian gardens ever since. Just as *feng shui* is the art of creating interior spaces with positive energy, the goal of shanshui (the word for landscaping that means mountains and water) is to bring energy to gardens.

Western gardeners often remark that plants play a secondary role in Asian gardens, although this is less true than it was for the Islamic or Italian Renaissance gardens, where the majority of plantings were evergreens. In China, the favored plants were the three friends of water (plum, bamboo, and pine), and peonies, chrysanthemums, and of course, lotuses. Lotuses were especially sacred to Buddhists, who believed that Buddha was born in the heart of a lotus.

In 612 AD a missionary from Japan described the Chinese imperial gardens to his own empress, who adapted the lake-and-island motif for her gardens. Although the basics of Asian gardening have changed little over the centuries, as they have in the West, there are some distinct periods of influence that changed garden design:

■ **The Heian period (795–1195),** which further emphasized reproducing natural beauty in small landscapes, with specific suggestions for the diversion of streams and placement of rocks. Ponds were to be shaped like a crane in flight and islands like a turtle, both symbolizing eternity.

■ **Momoyamam (1573–1603),** when the tea garden came to the forefront, with the introduction of water basins for that ceremony and stepping-stones across lakes.

■ **Edo (1603–1867).** Edo was the name for Tokyo until 1869, and this burgeoning city saw the development of wealthy estates with attendant large lakes.

Some Japanese gardens are stroll gardens, intended to take visitors on a contemplative journey, while true contemplation gardens are to be viewed from indoors or a terrace. When bringing water to a garden is impossible, the Japanese suggest water with the placement of rounded stones.

Egyptians and Chinese revered the lotus flower, here depicted by Yum Shou-Ping (1633–1690) in Album of Flowers.

Garden design is an artform that has existed in Japan for centuries. This traditional design is located in Kyoto.

ANCIENT GREECE, ROME, AND THE RENAISSANCE

The ancient **Greeks** did not create artificial water gardens around their homes, but rather, revered natural areas endowed with springs, which they believed were homes of gods and nymphs. Later, these were embellished with statuary, and in time evolved into elaborate nymphaea, or water theaters.

Romans. The Romans were considerably more ambitious. Pliny the Younger (62 to 113 AD) left detailed records of his hillside garden, where a pool with a tall water jet alternately filled and emptied and water gushed from a stone cistern under a semicircular marble bench into a marble basin below. Pliny's villa also featured a hippodrome—a structure for horse races— as did that of Hadrian, emperor from 117 to 138 AD. Hadrian's, at Tivoli, contained a central canal longer than 5 football fields. His circular Marine Theater contained a pool with an island, on which stood a pavilion large enough to have its own garden and several rooms. Surviving still is the Canopus, a curving colonnaded canal in an excavated valley. That more modest private gardens did exist we know courtesy of Mount Vesuvius' eruption in 79 AD. It preserved for all time the city of Pompeii, where small open spaces, surrounded by colonnades, often contained basins with fountains. It was during the Renaissance in the sixteenth century that Italy and then France developed the ornate classical-style water gardens and fountains.

The Greeks believed springs were home to gods and embellished them as elaborate water theaters.

Italian Renaissance. Many Italian Renaissance water features evoked scholarly subjects. There were the massive stone fountains carved by great artists of the time such as Andrea del Verrocchio (Boy with a Dolphin), frequently depicting goddesses such as Venus or January shivering in the cold. But these artisans had an equally playful side. They devised grottos to frighten visitors, whimsical beings animated by water (automata) to amaze them, and water games (giochi d'acqua) to play tricks on them.

Tivoli. Considered the ultimate example of this creativity is the Villa d'Este at Tivoli. Designed by Pirro Ligorio for the Cardinal Ippolito d'Este, it was sited at the top of a steep slope with views to Rome and the Sabine Hills. The fountains are powered by diverting water—over 300 gallons a second—from a nearby river. Its most famous feature is the Terrace of One Hundred Fountains, where terraces hold three rows of spouts punctuated with carvings of eagles and obelisks.

The towering geysers of its Organ Fountain are indeed reminiscent of a mighty organ's pipes, but in fact the fountain was named for its sound, as were the Owl and Dragon fountains. Elsewhere, stair rails are also water chutes, and water spurts from the breasts of a sphinxlike creature.

Villa Lante. At the Villa Lante, the sides of a narrow canal called a catena d'acqua are scrolled to look like a chain. While the more reverential Muslims raised the sides of water channels as an invitation to sit and contemplate the heavens, here architect Giacomo Vignola built a long table with a trough in the center with more earthly intent—cooling wine.

Grottoes. These water features had their origins in the nymphaea of ancient Greece. In the classical world, they evolved into ornate terraces or rooms with statues, columns, and balustrades. The grotto, on the other hand, retained a pretense of being a rough-hewn cave while becoming ever more elaborate and fanciful. Like the Haunted House at an amusement park, grottoes combined bits of lore with special effects, with the same results—squeals and nervous laughter. Some went for glitter, with crystal stalactites and high ceilings encrusted with semiprecious stones and imported seashells. One that Bernardo Buontalenti created for the Medicis at Boboli featured a sculpture of slaves by Michelangelo and was lit by a crystal fish bowl inserted in its roof.

At the Villa Pratolino, a Medici garden that no longer

exists, he gave free reign to his playful side, in some cases combining automation with classical figures such as the Apennine (January), pressing his hand on the head of a sea creature to squeeze water from its mouth. A washerwoman appeared to wring water from a marble cloth. Guests who weren't soaked by squirting benches were drenched by jets on staircases. Water-activated whistles imitated numerous bird species.

On a purely grand scale were the baroque water theaters, most notably the one built at Villa Aldobrandini for Pope Clement VIII. Created as a semicircular amphitheater behind the villa, its balustraded wall is punctuated with huge niches inhabited by statues. In the central cove, Atlas stands atop a hill of stones hoisting on his shoulders a globe that releases a curtain of water. But the show continues above him, where a steep water staircase, flanked by two spiral-dominated pillars, is cut into the wooded hillside.

The most famous feature of this Tivoli garden is the Terrace of One Hundred Fountains, with three rows of water spouts.

This scroll-sided canal, the Catena d'Acqua (chain of water), was designed for Cardinal Giovanni Francesco.

FRANCE

As the Italian influence flowed to France, its style was first copied and then adapted, with the baroque flourishes and aquatic playfulness displaced by emphasis on tying architecture to the formal landscape on a sweeping scale. In many cases, these grand gardens were extensions of the moat-surrounded French chateau. Because the landscape sites were often much flatter than in Italy, cascades gave way to reflecting pools and parterres, gardens with paths between features. Italian Renaissance style moved most literally across international lines via the Francinis. One of them, Thomas, had been at Pratolino before he and two brothers came to France to work for King Henry IV (whose wife was Marie de Medici) in the 1590s. (Thomas's sons would eventually work for Louis XIV at Versailles.)

At Saint-Germain-en-Laye, the Francinis filled the royal garden with fountains, grottoes, and automata. But it was the garden of Cardinal Richilieu at Rueil, begun in 1610, where the brothers made their biggest

splash (so to speak). Bringing water a mile and a quarter by aqueduct, they powered among other things an immense cascade and two grottoes. In one grotto, satyrs and nymphs spouted water from their genitals, and visitors could manipulate a water spout to form flowers, umbrellas, stars, and other shapes.

Seventeenth-Century France. Another hallmark of this period was converting shallow muddy areas into lakes or canals by giving them a new artificial edge. At the royal gardens at Fontainebleu southeast of Paris, for instance, a marsh was shaped into a triangular lake. The chateau was further surrounded by moats on other sides. Later, Thomas Francini's brother Alexandre would add his famous Tiber fountain. But it was Andre Le Notre who, after putting the finishing touches on Fountainebleu, created the three gardens considered to be exemplary of seventeenth-century France: Chantilly, Vaux-le-Vicomte, and Versailles.

Chantilly. A relatively small chateau, Chantilly was surrounded by large moats but positioned so that Le Notre chose to open vistas in two directions. Andre Le Notre edged an existing river to form the Grand Canal more than 100 yards across and extending a mile before turning a half mile in a second direction. Chantilly also is characterized by a water parterre, long vistas, and a series of rectangular, round, and oval reflecting basins. The chateau there was destroyed during the Revolution 200 years after its constuction, but has been rebuilt.

Vaux-le-Vicomte. Owned by Louis XIV's finance minister, Vaux-le-Vicomte is an example of the moated chateau. The garden, surrounded by woods, descends slowly past an immense parterre of swirling greenery. The main canal, some 1,100 yards long, is concealed from visitors by a terrace, but far in the distance they can see a grotto with seven immense arched niches, topped by a balustraded terrace, then a hillside sweeping up toward a statue of Hercules. Between the house and main canal is the Grand Miroir d'Eau, a square pool that reflects the entire water-surrounded chateau. The effect has been compared to that of the Taj Mahal, which was completed two years before Le Notre began work here. A buttressed cascade tumbles down from the platform on which the chateau seems to float, but there are few fountains. Instead, this garden is famous for the exquisite proportions and perfect relationship of its elements.

Temple of Venus. Le Notre used water to bring life to the Temple of Venus and the sprawling landscape of Versailles in France.

Peterhof. At the palace of Russia's Peter the Great in Peterhof, a canal flows to the sea between jets of water.

Versailles. Of course, Versailles is the most famous of the three, possibly linked more in the minds of non-gardeners with the Treaty ending World War I, but for gardeners symbolizing the ultimate in (depending on their tastes) elegance or ostentaciousness. While the major design of the garden was carried out in the mid-1660s, both structure and landscape saw expansion over several decades under the Sun King, Louis XIV.

Individual features may sound like echoes of other Le Notre designs—a cross-shaped canal (5,900 by 4,920 feet), a water parterre, numerous reflecting basins—but what sets it apart are both the sprawling site and the skillful way he used water to make it vibrant, rather than an outdoor museum. Like many Renaissance gardens, its sculpture focused on a classical theme, in this case Apollo the sun god. In one of Versailles's most photographed images, Apollo rises from a pool on his horse-drawn chariot. In the water parterre are two pools that reflect the palace façade; beyond the vast orange grove is a lake 765 yards long. On cross axes with the grand canal are bosquets— groves of trees—each framing a fountain that continues the Apollo legend. Unlike Chantilly, water resources were not up to the task, and it was a constant struggle to pressurize the 1,400 water jets.

The Sun King's grandson Philip V was more fortunate in this regard when, as King of Spain, he tried to copy Versailles at La Granja, where two reservoirs collected water from surrounding mountains. That garden in turn inspired the Palazzo Reale near Naples, the home of Philip's son Charles III and site of what is considered the grandest of all cascades, stretching almost two miles up a hillside and fed by an aqueduct almost 25 miles long.

Peterhof. In Russia, a Le Notre pupil orchestrated the construction of an aqueduct about half that long to supply Peterhof for Peter the Great. Here, a double cascade flows down a water stair from the palace's balustraded terrace into a semicircular basin and through a canal to the sea. On each side of the canal are small circular basins with single jets and bosquets with their own water features. The Grand Cascade has 64 different fountains and over 200 statues, bas-reliefs, and other decorations. Behind it, The Grotto contains the pipes that feed it.

Neptune fountain in Versailles. The fountain represents Neptune, the ancient god of seas and oceans.

ENGLAND

Elsewhere in Europe, gardens were relatively austere. The Dutch and Germans preferred formal canals, jets rather than fountains, and relatively little sculpture. An example is Herrenhausen in Germany, begun in 1680, where water adds movement to rectangular patterns of tall trees and hedges.

Chatsworth. A notable exception to this restraint is Chatsworth, developed over two centuries beginning with the first Duke of Glouchester in the late seventeenth century. From a domed "cascade" house built by baroque architect Thomas Archer, a 24-foot-wide water stair tumbles down a hill toward the house. A pupil of Le Notre designed other waterworks. In the eighteenth century, the grounds would take a step toward the future with the work of Capability Brown, who altered the course of the nearby Derwent River to give the home a more picturesque approach.

Beginning in 1826, under the sixth Duke of Devonshire, head gardener Joseph Paxton attempted to link artifice and nature, shaping rocky cascades and woodland water features. The Duke, wanting to impress Russiar's Czar Nicholas I on a planned visit, had Paxton build the single-jet Emperor Fountain. Powered by gravity from a lake 381 feet higher, it was then the tallest jet in the world at 290 feet. (The czar became ill and never saw it.) Paxton also designed the famed Crystal Palace, built to house the temperate world's first giant waterlily, Victoria amizonica, with pads more than six feet across.

Landscape Movement. Beginning with the first half of the eighteenth century, the Landscape Movement led a trend away from enclosed outdoor rooms and toward gardens that linked architecture to the world beyond. As in Asia, nature was the model to emulate. Fountains and jets were considered gauche. "Only the vulgar citizen...squirts up his rivulets in jettaux," wrote one critic. Instead, designers created waterfalls, bubbling streams, rocky ravines, or rills—narrow channels that wound among trees or hillocks. By 1819, even the ingenious design at Villa Pratolino in Italy would be replaced by an English-style garden. Somewhat ironically, those who espoused the natural landscape often altered both wetlands and historic gardens in ways that would be unthinkable or even illegal today.

Blenheim Palace. This French-influenced water parterre was built for the Duke of Marlborough at Blenheim, his Oxfordshire, England, estate, in the 1920s.

Monet's Garden. The artist Monet broke from tradition by damming a stream to create his romantic and heavily planted pond.

Mid-to-Late 1800s

By the mid-1800s, there were fewer grand private estates where landscape architects could move even miniature mountains or streams. Public parks became a more frequent subject for water-garden designers. Joseph Paxton's design for Birkenhead Park near Liverpool, with two labyrinthine lakes and an island, inspired American Frederick Law Olmsted's work in New York's Central Park, Brooklyn's Prospect Park, and Boston's Back Bay.

Monet's Garden. In the 1890s, artist Claude Monet made a radical move at Giverny by damming a stream to create his famous pond. Divorced from any reference to the surrounding architecture, it was lushly and sensuously planted, inspiring most of his late work—and many romantically inclined gardeners today. In the early twentieth century, architect Edwin Lutyens and plantswoman Gertrude Jekyll were a famous pair, billed as collaborators but often disagreeing about whether structure or plantings should get top billing. One of Lutyens's favorite water features was the dipping well: an arched alcove where a basin was fed by a spout. Adapted from Renaissance designs, it nevertheless fit beautifully in small landscapes.

Jekyll, known for her lavish perennial borders and use of flower color, recommended restraint in the number of species planted adjacent to a pond. She recommended planting the garden leading away from the pond to segue into natural areas beyond with spring wildflowers, then larger perennials and shrubs leading toward water-loving trees.

Modern Water Gardens

We can thank modern technology for making water gardens available to anyone with a shovel and an electrical supply, rather than just to royalty and others who could afford teams of engineers, architects, and artisans.

In Victorian times, the steam pump brought water to some gardens, but even then, most relied on gravity. When soil wouldn't hold water, it had to be "puddled" by stomping straw into clay. The first rubber liners came along in the late nineteenth century, and have steadily become both more durable and less expensive, as have pumps and filters.

Modern Perspective. What hasn't changed much are our motivations for creating water gardens. More imperative for many of us now, perhaps, is the recognition that our natural environment is shrinking.

Longwood Gardens. The fountain garden is a famous feature of this Pennsylvania estate built by Pierre du Pont in the early 1900s.

Seattle Center. The Dandelion Fountain, at Seattle Center, an entertainment complex, exemplifies modern public water features.

CHAPTER 2

Plan from the Start

What inspired you to create a water garden? In this chapter, you'll find other questions to ask yourself along with some possible answers. Your own answers will help you to plan your project. Planning will help prevent first-time mistakes and ensure that your water feature will bring you pleasure, not problems. Good soil is essential for your plants to grow properly. For a garden to flourish with healthy plants that are strong enough to resist pests and diseases, you must first invest in improving the soil. Unless your property drains sufficiently so that rainwater doesn't cause flooding or erosion, you may need to improve the drainage.

Considering Your Lifestyle

When professional landscape designers begin a project, they ask about your lifestyle and goals. What do you want to do in your garden? Do you spend a lot of time outside the house enjoying your property, or is your yard more of a backdrop for your house? Do you want your pond to beautify the view from inside the house or to dress up your entryway for the pleasure of your guests?

If your time outside is limited to sitting on the patio reading the newspaper or discussing the day's events with your spouse, a small container garden or independent fountain may be all you need or want to deal with.

Entertainment. If a patio or deck is the focus of your outdoor life and entertainment is your game, water gardens offer great potential as both mood setters and conversation pieces. A small water feature softly bubbling in a corner may be relaxing and stimulate quiet conversation, while a big splashy one may heighten excitement and joviality. Place a raised pond along one side of a deck or even in the middle of it, and give the pond a wide edge so that you and your friends can sit and watch the fish or admire the plants unique to a water garden. If you have a patio that looks out over a long, narrow garden, you can make the space look even deeper if you install a long formal pool or place a pond at the far end to create a focal point. Keep the lines of a more remote water feature clean and bold so that the design can speak from a distance.

If you have young children, you may want a pond where they can explore nature for hours. Even shallow ponds pose a safety hazard for toddlers, however. Safer alternatives include a small fountain burbling in a shallow circle of pebbles or a waterfall that empties into a shallow stream.

Landscaping. If you enjoy puttering in your garden, you can allow a water feature to be as demanding as you like. As with any other part of your landscape, a pond offers endless possibilities for adding plants or rearranging those you already have, plus the added enticement of fish and other pond animals. Or you may make your pond secondary to all of your existing plants. For example, one gardener used a backhoe to dig a half-acre pond as the centerpiece of a collection of unusual trees and shrubs; the beautiful colors and shapes of which are now reflected in the view from his sunroom window.

The hardy water lily's beauty, above, and the colors and fragrance of some varities, can be the inspiration for creating a lush water garden. They bloom by day and by night, so you can enjoy their pleasure for hours.

Alongside a pond is a peaceful place to relax. You can see the reflection of the sky in this lily pond, opposite.

Siting Your Water Feature

Even on the smallest property, you may discover several spots for a water feature. In selecting the site, consider where the water feature will give the most pleasure while still being practical. You also need to make sure the water garden will look as though it belongs where it is, a task that involves both siting and additional landscaping.

AESTHETIC CONSIDERATIONS

Your view of the pond will greatly determine how much you enjoy it. Ideally, you want to be able to watch it change throughout the seasons from as many vantage points as possible. From indoors, you can enjoy your pond even in inclement weather: the reflection of scudding clouds, the splash of raindrops, the formation of ice. If your region has long winters or if you spend relatively little time outdoors, think about where you might be able to see the pond from one or more windows.

Before you dig, make sure you'll be able to see the water feature from your intended viewing location. For example, if you want to view the pond outside a breakfast nook, make sure you'll be able to see it when sitting down. When siting the pond, look for something you can use as a mock pond, such as blue plastic drop cloths or some old sheets, and lay the material in various places in your garden to experiment with positioning and size.

If you have a relatively large garden, you may want to make the water feature a pleasant destination or even a surprise for someone who is walking through the landscape to admire other plantings, or is sauntering toward a gate or a dock.

All children love being around water. A shallow, natural-style pond can be both educational and safe.

If you position your pond where you can glimpse it through a window, you'll multiply the hours you can enjoy it.

HIDDEN WATER FEATURE

You can employ a landscape-design trick known as evoking a sense of mystery. Instead of putting the pond in full view, hide it so that just a teasing glimpse beckons and invites strollers to investigate. Between the path and the pond, plant tall grasses or a hedge of lacy conifers—or erect a bamboo screen or vine-covered trellis—allowing just a shimmer of water to hint at what lies beyond.

A completely hidden water feature offers other advantages. You can still create a sense of mystery by beckoning a viewer toward a camouflaged pond with a curving path. Such a concealed pond can be a welcome retreat where you can be alone with your thoughts, enjoy the sights and sounds of nature, and forget the chores that await you in the study or laundry room for a while. To make this area even more of an outdoor "room," add decking (or a flagstone or gravel floor), a dining table, and lighting so that you can enjoy it at night. Total enclosure of a water feature is especially appealing if you are surrounded on all sides by sights and sounds that you want to block out: heavy traffic, nearby neighbors, or a less-than-beautiful toolshed, for example.

Make sure that the plants you choose are suited to the amount of sunlight they will receive in a particular spot.

This beautiful tropical garden contains a decorative bridge over a waterfall that empties into a large pond.

Reflections. In considering views from your pond, remember that you will want to look not only across it but also into it. What will be reflected in the pond, and how will those reflections change throughout the day and throughout the seasons? Can you capture sunrises or sunsets? The full moon in June? What about azaleas in spring or maple leaves in autumn? Some experts suggest placing a large mirror on the prospective pond site to give you some idea of how water might reflect light and color. If you're a photographer, you know it's easier to see the image well if you keep the sun behind you, and this is true of ponds as well. If you're staring straight across at the sun, all you'll see is glare.

Existing Features. Another important aesthetic consideration when choosing a site is how easily the water feature can be integrated into the existing landscape. De-

BORROW VIEWS

When picking a spot for your pond, see whether there are any views worth "borrowing" for your design. Borrowing a pleasing but more distant view is like adding a window to your garden room. It makes a small enclosure seem larger without sacrificing privacy. Decide which elements of the wider world to allow into your cozy spot. Consider the potential view from each side of the pond to see what pleasant vista you could incorporate—the corner of a neighbor's lot with a perennial bed or expanse of green lawn, or a view back toward your own house where you have plantings you enjoy. A hedge of just the right height can capture the top of a church steeple or tall trees while blocking out less-attractive lower views. If there is a nice view from only one side of the pond, draw attention to it with a small area of stone, brick, or wood decking. A bench or a lantern will suggest a place of welcome. It doesn't need to be functional; the bench can be a rustic child-size seat, and the lantern can be stone or a battered antique.

Concealing your pond on one or more sides can evoke an exciting sense of mystery.

A bench or other seating sends a visual message that "this is a nice place to be." Place it to capture the best view across your pond.

termine which existing yard features will complement the pond and which will detract from it. Before deciding on a site, examine the views from all angles. For example, siting the pond in one area of the yard may mean that you would need to remove one or more large trees or shrubs to allow you to see the pond from the house. Or you may find eyesores such as an old shed that will need to be razed or a bare house wall that should be disguised with vines.

Factor in reflections when siting your pond. Water lets you double your visual enjoyment of the landscape's existing features such as trees and rocks.

For a small pond, a little shade reduces algae and evaporation, and keeps visitors cool.

If you have decided on a particular size for your pond, you'll need to take that into consideration when choosing the site. For example, a small pond can get lost next to an immense deck. A large pond stuffed into a small side yard may look out of proportion.

Many ponds look like a hole in the ground with a necklace of stones, and gardeners don't solve the problem by adding a starched collar of plants. Ponds look more natural anchored to an existing feature such as a large boulder or a small specimen tree or tucked into the curve of a perennial or shrub border.

If you don't have such an existing feature, you may need to create one. Or you can connect the pond to the rest of the garden by echoing other elements in the landscape. Incorporate bricks in the pond's design to complement a brick house, a deck surround to mimic the deck on the house, a shape similar to that of the planting beds, or plants of the same species (or shape) as planted elsewhere.

Paths. Paths are another way to tie your pond to the rest of your landscape and to your home.

Practical Considerations

Beauty isn't all you need to think about in choosing a place for your pond. Climate, existing structures and trees, and the general lay of the land can all determine whether your pond is heaven or a headache.

Sun and Shade. If you want flowering plants to be an important part of your water garden, you need to place the pond where it will get at least six hours of sunlight a day. Water lilies in particular don't bloom well with less sun (although there are a few varieties that will perform in partial shade).

There is a downside to too much sun, however. Water will evaporate quickly from a pond in full sun in hot climates. Sun encourages algae and, if the pond is small, can heat the water too much for fish. (See "Controlling Algae," on page 177, for some helpful tips.) For this reason, small water features—and especially tub gardens—need shadier sites. For larger ponds, provide shade with floating plants or situate small trees to give dappled shade across at least part of the pond's surface. Use rocks to create overhangs where fish can cool off, as well as hide from predators. Remember that nature creates inviting pools even in the heart of heavily shaded woodlands, and you can, too, by choosing appropriate plants.

If you've only recently moved to your property, keep records through each season the first year on how much sun different parts of the yard receive. Use this information to judge whether a site will meet the needs for your water feature.

Wind. Ponds should have some degree of protection from wind, which like sun will hasten the rate of evaporation. Wind can also blow leaves and other debris into your pond, spoil the grace of fountains, and knock over tall plants in containers. If possible, choose a sheltered site, one protected from wind by a hill, woods, building, or fence. If your yard is windy and has no sheltered spot, you'll need to create some type of a windbreak. Surprisingly, a barrier that lets some wind through is more effective than a solid windbreak such as a close-board fence, which allows wind to blow across its top and resume full force a few feet beyond it. Depending on the style of your pond, you can create an effective windbreak by installing an open-board fence, a screen of native evergreens, or an attractive flowering hedge.

If you decide to use trees to create shade or a windbreak, select and site them carefully. For example, Leyland cypress (×*Cupressocyparis leylandii*) is often recommended as a fast-growing screen, but with a growth rate of 3 feet a year and a mature height of 65 feet, it frequently outgrows its welcome. Don't be overeager to remove existing trees. But when adding any new trees near your pond, choose species that will stay small, and avoid willows and other species with thirsty roots that can damage your pond's liner.

Trees can add to your cleanup chores by dropping twigs, berries, nuts, and leaves into the pond, where this debris may decompose and change the water 's chemistry. Some plants that otherwise make attractive windbreaks—such as yews, hollies, rhododendrons, and mountain laurels—have toxic leaves that can harm fish if allowed to accumulate. Pine needles contain tannins that can turn water brown and sicken fish. A willow's thirsty roots can punch through pond liners that have even minute leaks.

This pond's location, opposite, offers a perfect view and just the right amount of sun and shade.

COMPLYING WITH LOCAL REGULATIONS

Make sure your plans comply with local building codes. Depending on where you live, regulations may deem a pond beyond a certain depth a safety hazard and, just as they do with swimming pools, require that you fence it. Fencing may be required for ponds as shallow as 2 feet. Most zoning boards consider a pond a structure, and as such there may also be rules pertaining to its placement and size.

If you intend to redesign a natural water feature, such as a pond or stream, you would be altering a wetland. In that case, find out if you need to apply for a permit, usually with your local conservation commission, department of natural resources, or other environmental review agency. But keep in mind, this process usually involves preparing a complex and legally demanding environmental impact statement.

Make sure that the plants you choose are suited to the amount of sunlight they will receive in that particular spot.

Microclimates

Wind and trees are just two of the factors that can create what are called "microclimates" in your garden. Your house also creates microclimates—cool and shady on the north, warm and sunny on the south, with gentle morning sun on the east, and hotter afternoon sun on the west. The same is true for outbuildings, fences, or a solid line of trees or shrubs.

A large paved area, such as a driveway or a patio, may create a hot spot. This can mean faster evaporation from a nearby pond and require more frequent watering of plants. The bottom of a slope is often a frost pocket, several degrees cooler than the top, so your pond and plants will freeze earlier and thaw later there.

If summers are short, you can extend your water-gardening season by looking for sites on your property that get the greatest sun exposure. If summers are long and hot, you can reduce evaporation and protect fish and plants by giving the water some protection from the sun at midday or in the afternoon.

Many factors have an impact on your pond's water, plants, and fish. Study your property's little idiosyncrasies to maximize success.

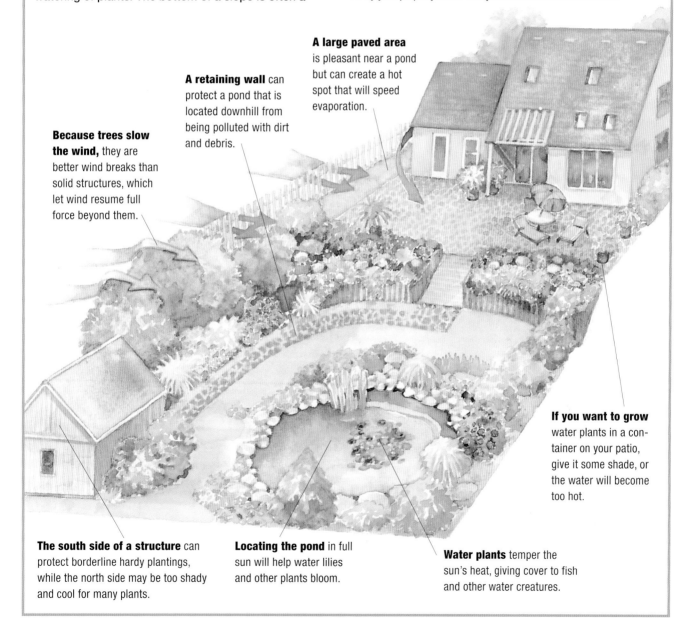

A large paved area is pleasant near a pond but can create a hot spot that will speed evaporation.

A retaining wall can protect a pond that is located downhill from being polluted with dirt and debris.

Because trees slow the wind, they are better wind breaks than solid structures, which let wind resume full force beyond them.

If you want to grow water plants in a container on your patio, give it some shade, or the water will become too hot.

The south side of a structure can protect borderline hardy plantings, while the north side may be too shady and cool for many plants.

Locating the pond in full sun will help water lilies and other plants bloom.

Water plants temper the sun's heat, giving cover to fish and other water creatures.

Slopes and Runoff. Slopes create an array of possibilities as well as challenges for water gardeners. A steep slope lends itself easily to waterfalls and natural-looking rock terraces. A gentle slope presents an opportunity to create a stream. Even though nature creates ponds at the bottoms of slopes, this can be the worst place for an artificial pond. Runoff from a slope can wash dirt and debris into the pond, as well as pollutants such as lawn chemicals. Even if you don't use fertilizers or toxins in your garden, neighbors uphill may.

It's possible to divert runoff with retaining walls or ditches on either side of your pond. (See "Special Sites" on page 66 in chapter 4.) But there are still other problems with a slope. As previously noted, the bottom of a slope may be several degrees cooler than other parts of your yard. And the bottom of a slope is also where you are most likely to encounter problems with the water table.

Convenience. While you don't want your pond on top of your electrical line, you do need access to power. In order to hook up pumps for a waterfall, aeration, or cleaning; mechanical filters; and fountains. Lighting likewise requires electricity.

You should also locate your water garden near a water source because midsummer droughts, leaks, and natural evaporation will require that you occasionally top off your pond's water level. (See "Maintain Pond Levels Automatically with a Float Valve" on page 99 for a handy gadget that will top off your pond for you.)

Of secondary concern, depending on your stamina, is convenient access to tools you will need to clean your pond and tend your plants. You will also need a shed or garage to overwinter delicate tropical water plants. It isn't much fun to lug sopping-wet lilies a long distance when fall's first norther is blowing.

Underground Surprises

If you dig a pond below the water table, flexible pond liners can balloon up and rigid liners can heave out of the ground, or the soil around them can erode. Determine the depth of the water table under your potential pond site by digging some test holes.

These test holes will also tell you about the composition of your soil—an important factor when you are planning. Soil texture can vary from one area of your property to another. Good garden loam is easiest to

work. Other soil types require a bit more work. Clay soil is heavy, making it harder to excavate, whereas sandy or pebbly soil can collapse along the edges.

Rocks and a high water table may not be the only surprises you'll hit with your shovel. Hitting underground utilities can be a nasty shock, literally. Most areas now have a single agency with a memorable name such as "Miss Utility" that will come out to your home and mark any underground lines.

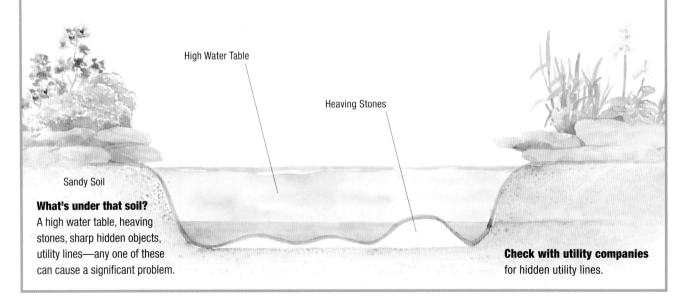

High Water Table

Heaving Stones

Sandy Soil

What's under that soil?
A high water table, heaving stones, sharp hidden objects, utility lines—any one of these can cause a significant problem.

Check with utility companies for hidden utility lines.

WATER GARDENS IN CONTAINERS

One of the easiest ways to try your hand at water gardening is to create a miniature pond in a container. You can use something as elegant as a ceramic planter or as rustic as an old horse trough, kettle, or half a whiskey barrel. Choose a container at least 18 inches in diameter—24 inches is better.

Locate your container garden where you can enjoy it often, such as on a deck or a patio. Because it will overheat more quickly than a pond in the ground, situate the container so that it gets some shade during the hottest part of the day. It will also need frequent topping off and cleaning, so consider how you will drain the container and refill it; a spot within reach of a hose works best. Keep in mind that the planter will be heavy when filled.

To keep your container from rusting or leaking and to deter any toxins it might contain from harming plants or fish, you should line it. There are now fiberglass shells specially made for half barrels. For other containers, use a piece of PVC liner.

Although you shouldn't cram the container with plants, it's possible to enjoy a half dozen species in even a small one. In Chapter 12, you'll find many water lilies that adapt to tub gardens. Try to include an upright plant or two, as well as one that will hang gracefully over the side. If the container is too deep for a marginal species, grow one in a pot set on one or more bricks.

A few small goldfish or mosquito fish will help keep your minipond free of mosquito larvae. Unless you live in a warm-winter climate or can sink the container into the ground for the winter, you'll need to transfer the fish to an indoor aquarium for a few months each year. Plan on re-placing most of the plants. If you have a sunroom with a tile floor, you may be able to move the whole display indoors. (In the case of a particularly large container, you may want to have a contractor do an inspection and verify that your floor will support its weight when filled with water.)

A more complex pool design could include a fountain and container plantings.

A small gazing pool can be created at the edge of a pathway or garden.

Size and Styles

Once you've picked a spot that's breathtaking and not back-breaking, you need to think about the size and style of pond that you want. You need to give these decisions a lot of long and careful consideration. Although you may easily reshape and replant a flower bed, you'll find it difficult to reshape or move a water garden.

Your best bet is to visit as many other ponds as possible before finalizing your plans. Some water-garden suppliers have demonstration ponds, as do public gardens. Although many public water features will seem too huge and expensive to relate to your home garden, focus on the details: the overall shape and setting, the plants, and the material used for the edge and the surround. If nothing else, you will gain a sense of what you like.

Traditionally, ponds have been divided into formal and informal styles. The style you choose will guide your choice not only of pond shape but also of plants, decorations such as fountains and statues, and other materials that you use around your pond. The design guidelines for a formal style are not as flexible as those for an informal style. The style tips that follow are merely suggestions. In the end, you'll need to make the choices that please you.

Visit as many ponds as possible to get a feel for what you like. This one would probably excite a plant lover.

With an informal water garden, you have the greatest design latitude and the opportunity to create something truly unique.

POND SIZE

Most people err with a pond that is too small. A small pond in the middle of an open lawn can look lost. In a typical, sparsely planted suburban backyard, a pond up to one-third the area can be pleasingly balanced. The more heavily your garden is planted, the more charming a tiny pond can be as an element in a busy bed or along a landscaped path. Use a rope or a hose to mark the pond outline, and live with the layout for a few days.

Consider 18 inches the minimum depth for an inground pond. The colder your climate, the deeper your pond will need to be to keep the roots of water lilies and other hardy water garden perennials from freezing in winter. A local water-garden supplier or an Extension Agent can advise you on your area's frost line, the depth at which your soil freezes in the average winter.

Even in relatively warm climates, koi ponds are an exception to the usual depth recommendations. These large fish need water at least 3 and preferably 4 feet deep. Ponds designed to attract wildlife should have variation in depth, including some shallow ledges or a tapering beach area, inviting different aquatic creatures, birds, and mammals. (More detailed information on depth is covered in "Designing the Pond Configuration," in chapter three on page 60.)

Most people err by creating a pond that is too small. One-third the size of your yard isn't too big.

FORMAL STYLES

Generally, formal pools are geometric—square, rectangular, circular, triangular, or some combination—and have a clearly defined edge. They typically include features such as fountains or statues but rarely bridges or stepping-stones. Plantings are minimal. Surrounding plants are often those commonly used in formal gardens, such as pruned boxwood hedges, topiaries, or rose standards. But today there is a trend toward more relaxed-looking plants (especially ornamental grasses) in the landscape surrounding formal water features. Some designers believe that only formal pools are appropriate in urban gardens and even most suburban yards. Formal pools can be dug into the ground, be of a raised or semiraised style, or be sunken into a patio. Raised pools may be less of a safety hazard for small children. They are also easier to tend without bending and stooping, and they can be built with a wide edge that allows you to admire goldfish without having to drop down to your knees.

Formal water features are generally defined by their geometric shapes, above. They needn't be big to be elegant.

Geometric shapes are sometimes paired with lush plantings, blurring the lines between formal and informal styles.

Choose a design that will coordinate with the architecture of your house, opposite. Classical motifs and ornaments are consistent with formal designs.

Statuary and ornamental furniture complement formal water garden design, below.

Hardscape and Ornaments. The lines of a formal pool need to be kept plain and simple. The crisp edges are built with regularly shaped materials such as bricks, machine-cut stones, tiles, or landscaping ties. If you want to create a patio or a path beside the pool, consider using a material similar to that used for the edging. Within or adjacent to a deck, the same wood decking can be used to create a pool that is formal in shape yet relaxed in feel. For benches, look to classic designs such as stone or park benches; to create shade, consider a wisteria arbor of white columns or something similarly elegant.

A fountain can serve a practical purpose: if you have fish and don't have a waterfall, a fountain will aerate the water for them. In a small pool, though, a fountain may disturb the water too much for water lilies. (See pages 110–123 for more about fountains.)

Some statues are designed to highlight water by appearing to walk on it or to chase fish. Others double as fountains by pouring or spraying water. Remember that one such arresting figure is generally enough for a pool.

Bridges and stepping-stones can work in a formal design if they are geometric. Waterfalls and streams for a formal pool are normally highly stylized with water falling in a curtain over a sheet of acrylic, or down a series of stone steps.

Softscape. As for plantings in and around a formal pool, the species of plants are less important than the manner in which they are employed. Formal pools are usually planted with restraint so that the clean outline of the pool and its edging remain apparent. Some small formal pools with fountains are not planted at all. A single dramatic tree—such as a weeping pear or a bonsai on a pedestal—or a matched pair of containers holding rosemary will complement the emphasis on hard materials.

Around the pool, consider using conifers and other plants that lend themselves to pruning. Some of the most famous formal pools are surrounded on three sides only by a clipped, U-shaped hedge. Some contemporary pools in country settings have what amounts to a "hedge" of ornamental grasses. Adjacent flower beds, when present, are often geometric in shape, like the pool, and are planted with a limited selection of species.

Within the pool, water lilies and lotuses will look beautiful if they aren't disturbed by the splashing of a fountain. Restricting yourself to water lilies and other low, horizontal plants can make the garden seem larger. But if you find this effect too static, consider adding individual clumps of ornamental grasses, a tub of cattails, or margins of irises, lilies, or daylilies. Their more vertical shapes will add visual interest.

A formal water garden may be integrated into the landscape through the use of materials, such as stone, used in other structures.

Even around the most informal pond, use restraint in varying plant species, and group them in bold masses.

Most designers agree that just one arresting statue is generally enough for a pool.

INFORMAL STYLES

An informal pond can range from one that is a bit more playful in shape to one that mimics nature with a carefully planned mini-ecosystem of native plants and adjacent bogs. In addition to being irregular in outline, most informal water gardens are built into the ground with their edges concealed by natural-shaped stones, pebble beaches, or tall native grasses. They are unlikely to include fountains and more likely to be complemented by waterfalls or streams. You can keep plants to a minimum and employ rather traditional cultivated annuals and perennials, or you can surround the pond with so many subtropicals or wetland species that the water surface almost disappears under such a vast assortment of floaters, creepers, and waving grasses.

Informal ponds can be appropriate for many styles of homes and gardens, from old farmhouses to ultramodern designs, rich with natural woods and windows. If your home is in a natural setting of fields or woods or if you can picture it in such a setting, it probably deserves an informal pond.

Hardscape and Ornaments. The edging of informal ponds is usually quarried or hand-cut stone intended to mimic nature. Similar stones may be arranged in tiers to serve as the foundation of waterfalls. Islands are sometimes included in large ponds; boulders serve that purpose in smaller ponds. Paths and surrounding areas are of natural materials, such as bark, pine needles, or gravel.

Architectural elements are kept to a minimum, but they might include arbors of grapevines or bent willow. Seating can be of almost any style that beckons the viewer to stop awhile and relax. For accents, possibilities could include a simple birdhouse, boulders, or sculptures. Wood is the most appropriate material for bridges. In keeping with the level of informality you choose, options range from a span of decking to weathered planks to a single fallen tree across a stream. (Flatten the undersides of the ends so that it doesn't roll, and cover the top with hardly noticeable chicken wire to provide traction for walking.) Handrails of rustic timber with bark still attached will add to the informality and safety of these choices.

Stepping-stones, like edging, should be natural shapes rather than cut, and arranged in an uneven line. A single slab of weathered stone may do for a small pond or a narrow stream. The most informal ponds are not a place for fountains, except those that bubble just above the surface like a natural spring. A simple spray or geyser is good for slightly more formal ponds.

Softscape. Even though there are fewer guidelines for planting informal water gardens than for formal pools, resist the urge to plant one of every variety you can get your hands on. Strive for a minimum of three plants of each variety. An uneven number of plants in clusters or masses will keep your design from looking stiff and formal. The edges of your planting areas should be big bold curves, not little squiggles or straight lines.

In addition to taking design cues from your home's architecture, you might want to choose a planting style that is regionally appropriate both in terms of style and plant material. For example, rock gardens often become an adjunct to water features through serendipity, when gardeners with a mound of leftover dirt or rocks put two and two together. Gardens such as these look right at home in arid mountain climates because many traditional rock-garden plants flourish in the bright sun and dry climate there.

If you live surrounded by deciduous woodlands, fill your rock garden with plants that grow naturally in this environment. Good bets include ferns, native ground covers, or ornamentals such as creeping bellflower that droop gracefully over embankments.

If you live in the subtropics, an appealing option is to strive for the jungle look, cramming your pond with tropical water lilies, parrot's-feather, and giant papyrus, and planting the surrounding area with huge-leaved green taro, hibiscus, and giant chain fern. But if you have a Zone 7 garden with a warmer Zone 9 spirit, capture a tropical feel with lush-leaved perennials such as ligularia and hosta, evergreen shrubs such as acuba, and a hardier species of papyrus.

When hardscaping, combine natural elements, such as stone slabs and boulders, with ornament. Arrange elements in tiers.

POND SURROUNDS AND PATHS

The style of the walkways and paths around your water feature should match the style of the pond. For informal ponds, create paths of loose materials such as gravel or bark chips; you can install edging to keep the material in place. Try large, irregular stepping-stones or wooden rounds around the pond edge to provide access. Formal pools may incorporate walks of brick, patio tiles, wood blocks, concrete, cut stone, or similar paving materials.

Extend the path around the perimeter of the pond to encourage strollers to view the pond from different vantage points. If the pond is large enough, extend the path or stepping-stones into or even across the pond itself.

Pondside seating areas can be as simple as a wooden garden bench or as elaborate as a wood deck or a masonry patio with table and chairs to accommodate a sit-down dinner for 20. Be careful, though, not to let features overwhelm the pond itself. They should be in scale with the size of the pond. Regular trimming and pruning activity may be needed to retain the look.

JAPANESE GARDENS

The Japanese garden is by far the most popular non-European style imitated by North American gardeners, and water—sometimes actual, other times only suggested by stones—plays an integral part in such a garden.

The Japanese style may be appealing because it contains both formal (stylized) and informal elements. Its goal is to echo nature with rocks, water, and plants, but in a controlled way. A Japanese pond may be accented with a formal stone lantern, but the pond itself is irregular in shape. Landscaping may include carefully pruned topiary along with softly waving grasses and bamboos. The arrangement of elements is more dynamic than in other formal styles, while still creating a relaxed and peaceful feeling.

Hardscape and Ornaments. A water feature in a Japanese garden doesn't need to be big. It could be as simple as a stone basin. Basins are valued for both form and function—for instance, as a place where you can wash your hands or birds can bathe. In Japanese culture, a tsukubai is a basin where guests wash before tea; the water is fed into the basin through a bamboo pipe, called a "kakehi." A more specialized variation is the shishi odoshi, or "stag scarer," in which water flows into one end of a bamboo pipe that is suspended in a seesaw fashion. When the pipe is full of water, it tilts and dumps its water into a basin or pond (or stream), and then it swings back to its original position.

The pipe makes a hollow clack at one or both ends and is sometimes sold in catalogs as a "deer chaser." (Directions for building a shishi odoshi appear on page 114.)

Often a Japanese pond is edged with boulders of different shapes and interesting textures. Islands are a common feature in larger ponds; they can consist of a single large boulder or a berm of earth for a small Japanese maple. Koi, the beautifully colored carp, are classic additions, but they require more attention and deeper water than do other fish.

Softscape. One reason Japanese-style gardens are so popular is that the plants they employ are well suited to North American gardens. Many plants native to Japan—including ferns and dogwoods—have close relatives in North America and are easily adaptable to the region's growing conditions. A lot of the favored plants—mosses, camellias, azaleas—are shade lovers, which makes this style ideal for a gardener who wants a water feature but doesn't want to give up beautiful old trees. You can have a wonderful Japanese garden in the sun as well, by leaning toward a collection of unusual conifers.

Foliage plays a more important role in this garden style than do flowers. Evergreens are essential and generally make up a majority of the plants. Boxwoods and conifers are often meticulously pruned, although broad-leaved flowering shrubs may be allowed a more natural form. Simplicity, balance, and calm are hallmarks of Japanese garden design.

A stone pagoda, opposite, is a feature that often graces a Japanese garden.

Meticulous manicuring imparts formality, but materials are chosen with the goal of echoing nature. The resulting mood is both dynamic and peaceful, right.

Japanese maples are one of the most popular plant choices. A single specimen may be used as a focal point, or several may be planted in a grove to create a small-scale echo of a large woodland. There are Japanese maples with red or variegated leaves; most have brilliant fall color. Shapes and sizes range from ground huggers to those that will grow 30 feet high and wide.

Plants included for flowers should also provide interest at other times of the year. A weeping cherry offers eye-catching form even when not in bloom; classic shrubs such as azaleas, rhododendrons, and camellias contribute both an elaborate burst of spring bloom and handsome evergreen leaves. Because their foliage provides interesting shapes and textures when they are not in bloom, good perennials include Japanese or Siberian irises, astilbes, and daylilies.

Texture. With fewer flowers in the planting, textures assume even more importance. Ferns and mosses are encouraged at ground level; rocks have special value if they are covered with lichens.

Hostas with strongly ribbed or variegated foliage are not planted in rows or en masse but are instead tucked singly and discretely at the foot of a stone or the bend of a path. Tall grasses such as Japanese Silver Grass (*Miscanthus sinensis*) provide vertical interest and rustle in the wind. Bamboo is almost a requirement; it is included as living

Rocks have an important role in Japanese ponds, sometimes serving as islands. All are carefully chosen and placed.

clumps and in architectural elements such as fences and fountains. But if you grow bamboos, you will want to restrain them. Planting in a 2- to 3-foot length of culvert pipe sunk vertically in the ground would not be overdoing it.

Accents. Most large Japanese gardens you may have visited or seen in photographs probably included a camelback, lacquered footbridge, possibly bright red. But less elaborate

A MOSS MILKSHAKE

Moss needs shade and humus-rich, moist soil with a low pH to thrive. If you're lucky enough to have moss growing in your yard, you can transplant it. Dig up a tuft of moss with soil attached, and crumble it into a blender. Add equal amounts of water and buttermilk, and process the mixture until completely blended. Add water, if necessary, until the finished product is the consistency of a cream soup. Spread the resulting moss shake where you want a new colony of moss. Keep the area constantly moist until the new moss is established.

In choosing plants for Japanese gardens, left, foliage and form are as important as bloom color.

footbridges are more appropriate to a small garden; these include granite slabs to span a small stream, stepping-stones, and zigzag wooden bridges. Stepping-stones may be flat, naturalistic rocks or rectangles of granite or concrete.

If your garden still seems unfinished, it may need an accent. Popular choices include a stone basin, a boulder, a stone lantern, or a pagoda. Once functional, Japanese garden lanterns are now usually just decorative.

Although a Japanese-style garden appears the very epitome of calm and relaxation, don't be misled about the work involved in its upkeep. A great deal of pruning and tidying is required to maintain the restrained appearance and to keep these gardens in peak shape.

Large gardens may employ an elaborate footbridge design. Smaller gardens may do with something less sophisticated.

ENHANCE YOUR DESIGN WITH LIGHTING

Lighting can extend the hours you enjoy your pond or water garden and add entirely new dimensions. Lights can give star status to plants or features that have only supporting roles during the day. You might focus a spotlight onto a contorted willow on a well-planted berm, use uplighting to exaggerate the rough texture of tree bark, or highlight a small statue partly concealed by pondside growth. Or use a spotlight to emphasize a waterfall or the branches of a tree. (To get the best effect, hide the lamp behind a clump of grasses; tuck it behind stones; or place it high in a tree.) If you have a fountain, an underwater light at its base will allow you to admire its play from a window after dark.

Lighting is easily overdone. Harsh spotlights may deter burglars, but they detract from the magic of nightfall. A bright light directly on the pond can cast everything in an artificial glare or—even worse—let you see nothing beyond the reflection of the light fixture. When in doubt, start with fewer lights. A strictly utilitarian design might use low downlights to outline the path to the pond, position a low-wattage yard lantern near a bench, or directly illuminate a dining area with a light pointed away from the pond. Carefully positioned lights will allow you to feel safe while still catching the moon and stars in the water's surface or marveling as a night-blooming water lily unfolds.

If your pond is situated some distance from your house, consider a system that will let you turn on the lights from the house and then turn them off when you arrive at the pond. That way, you can enjoy the natural darkness when the mood strikes you. This is particularly important if you have a wildlife pond. Keep lighting dim, and turn it off when you go to bed to reduce energy consumption and avoid scaring off creatures of the night. Also consider using solar light fixtures. For more about light installation, turn to page 124.

CHAPTER 3

Pond Liner and Edging Choices

Will you use a flexible or preformed pond liner? What other materials are available? How will you configure the pond? How will you create the pond's edging? Do you need a site plan before you begin? Before installing a pond you must decide on some preliminary issues. These subjects and more are covered in the following pages.

Liners

You can't expect to simply dig a hole in the ground and have it hold water. You'll need to provide a watertight foundation. Most ponds today are built using flexible liners or preformed shells. Either material can be used to create a formal pool or an informal pond. You'll also need to provide an edging to mask the rim of the liner; edging can be a visual asset by clearly delineating a formal pool or helping an informal pond blend into the landscape.

FLEXIBLE POND LINERS

Although they're called flexible because of their physical malleability, the big selling point of these liners is their design flexibility. From a small and shallow splash pool for toddlers to a raised koi pond for fish hobbyists, or a multi-acre fishing hole to a winding creek, you can make a flexible liner adapt to your design. Flexible liners are also relatively inexpensive and easy for do-it-yourselfers to install. You lay the liner in the hole, fill the pond with water, trim the liner, and install the edging.

Polyethylene liners resemble the black plastic sheeting sold in hardware stores, but they're much thicker. Polyethyl-

If you want to create a naturalistic water feature such as this one, above, a flexible liner may be the best choice.

A meandering stream, opposite, may be your inspiration for the shape of your pond.

ene sheeting isn't particularly durable, though, so don't use it for a pond unless you want just a small, temporary one with which to try your hand at water gardening for a couple of years. You can, however, use it successfully for a wetland or bog garden, because in such situations it doesn't need to be watertight.

Liners made especially for ponds are either PVC (polyvinyl chloride) or synthetic rubber—either butyl rubber or EPDM (ethylene propylene diene monomer). English gardening books usually talk about butyl, which is made only in Sweden, but EPDM is more readily available in North America. Be sure you get a liner *made for ponds;* EPDM rubber sheeting that is intended for use on roofs and other purposes can contain toxins harmful to plants and fish.

Naturally, the best liners cost more. Rubber liners last longer than the best of the less-expensive PVC liners because they are stretchable and more resistant to ultraviolet light. Thicker liners of any type generally last longer, too. Butyl or EPDM rubber liners are available in thicknesses from 30 to 45 mil and will typically last from 20 to 30 years. PVC liners are available in thicknesses from 20 to 32 mil.

At the bottom end of the scale, a 20-mil PVC liner can be expected to last from 5 to 7 years; a 32-mil PVC liner will last from 10 to 15 years.

Flexible pond liners come in stock sizes ranging from about 5 x 5 feet to 30 x 50 feet. Some manufacturers offer custom sizes. By joining the edges of the sheets with seam sealer, you can create any size or shape.

Because flexible liners are susceptible to punctures from rocks, gravel, broken tree roots, or other sharp objects, cushion it with an underlayment. A carpet pad is one choice. Other options include 2 to 3 inches of sand, fiberglass insulation material, or layers of newspaper. Sand won't pack well onto steep sidewalls, however, and it can be heavy to transport, and newspapers tend to deteriorate over time. (Even carpet padding deteriorates eventually.) So most water-garden suppliers offer a tough, flexible underlayment material; you can also buy liners with underlayment material bonded to the liner material.

If your soil is especially rocky, full of roots, or subject to excessive shifting during winter months, install both a layer of sand and of underlayment fabric.

PREFORMED POND SHELLS

Pond shells may be made of rigid or semirigid materials that are premolded to a specific shape and are easy to install yourself. Although they come in an array of sizes, shapes, and depths, they won't give you the design choices that a flexible liner does. They are generally more expensive for their size but are also more durable and puncture-proof. Shells can last from 5 to 50 years, depending on their composition, thickness, quality, and installation conditions. The thickest shells (¼ inch or more) can be installed aboveground with little support around the sides, provided the bottom rests on a firm and level base.

Your first choice should be rigid fiberglass, which is easy to repair and durable. It may discolor if exposed to sunlight but should last 10 to 30 years. Semirigid plastic shells are more difficult to repair, aren't sturdy enough to be used aboveground, and become brittle. Their life span is less than 10 years. Make sure whatever you buy is resistant to ultraviolet radiation.

Most manufacturers offer between 10 and 15 pond-shell designs. Depths range from 9 to 18 inches. (If you want to raise water lilies, the shell should be a minimum of 18 inches deep. Unless you live in a subtropical climate, shallower ponds are likely to freeze solid in winter, so you'll need to bring fish indoors.) Capacities range from about 30 to 500 gallons. Keep in mind that the shell will look larger when out of the ground than when installed. Decide the dimensions you want ahead of time, and don't change your mind if the shell looks too large in the store.

Many preformed shells have ledges partway down the sides for shallow-water (marginal) plants. Make sure these are at least 9 inches wide, though, or they won't be practical. A few shell models also have depressions around the perimeter for wetland plants. Some shells have integrated premolded waterfall lips; you can also buy separate premolded waterfall courses.

The perimeter of a preformed pond can be more difficult to disguise with edging and offers less "give" to heavy rocks, as well as less support. Burying a line of concrete blocks around the outside of the perimeter will help hold the rim vertical against the weight of rocks on top and the weight of water inside the pond. (See "Extra Support for Pond Foundations" in Chapter 4, page 78 for more on this technique.)

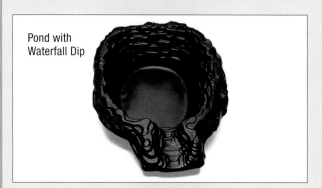

Pond with
Waterfall Dip

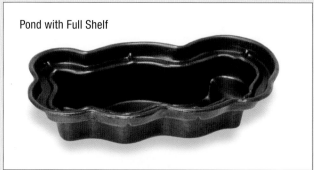

Pond with Full Shelf

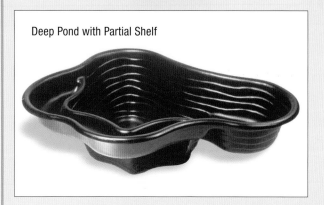

Deep Pond with Partial Shelf

Pond with
Stream

You can use separate overlapping pieces of flexible liner to create a stepped-down design.

The rocks positioned along the perimeter of this pond conceal the edge of the liners.

A GUIDE TO FOUNDATIONS

You need to decide between a flexible liner and a preformed shell. Each offers benefits and drawbacks. Whichever you choose, specify quality material for durability.

CHOOSING MATERIALS

MATERIAL	ADVANTAGES	DISADVANTAGES
Flexible Liner	■ Unlimited shapes, sizes ■ Less expensive than preformed shell ■ Inexpensive to ship ■ Folds small enough to transport in car ■ Easy to customize for wetland, marginal plants ■ Easier to conceal edges	■ Less durable ■ Punctures easily ■ Degrades in sunlight ■ Any exposed material must be covered
Preformed Shell	■ Lasts longer ■ Resists punctures ■ Small units easy to install ■ Relatively quick to install ■ Poses no design concerns ■ Easier to clean	■ Limited sizes, shapes ■ Hard to customize ■ More expensive than flexible liner ■ Hard to conceal edges ■ Needs to be perfectly level ■ Requires firm foundation to prevent buckling

OTHER OPTIONS

Concrete Ponds. Years ago, practically all garden ponds were made of poured concrete, concrete block, or a combination of the two. But the popularity of these materials waned with the advent of flexible pond liners and premolded pond shells, which are easier to install and can even be dug up and moved if you relocate. Not only does pouring a concrete pond require a great deal of skill and backbreaking work, it is also more expensive than other options, even if you do the work. A concrete pond can last a lifetime if properly installed but will crack and leak almost immediately if it is not. Once a crack opens, there's usually no way to permanently repair it. The best fix is to cover the concrete with a flexible pond liner. (See the discussion "Repairing a Pond Foundation" in Chapter 11, page 194.)

If you decide to use concrete, have the pond installed by a masonry contractor familiar with this sort of construction in your particular climate (and familiar with local building codes). In cold climates, the concrete shell must be at least 6 inches thick and adequately reinforced with ½-inch (No. 2) reinforcing bar ("rebar") or wire mesh to ensure that the pond will survive alternate freezing and thawing. In milder climates, the shell should still be 3 to 4 inches thick.

New concrete can leach lime into the pond water, so you must neutralize the lime with acidic chemicals—or seal the concrete with a coat of paint—before adding fish and plants to the pond. You can paint concrete with a rubber-based pool paint to create various effects: use earth tones for a natural look, white or blue for a more formal appearance, or dark colors for a "bottomless" look.

Clay and Bentonite. To create the most natural wildlife or farm ponds, where edging is minimal and punctures unheard of, it's possible to construct a clay-bottomed pond. For very large ponds, where handling a liner becomes unwieldy, this is often the preferred approach. Where the soil is already heavy clay, you can make the pond bottom watertight by stomping it, pounding it with a post, or renting a tamper to compact it. You can also make the soil more watertight by mixing in bentonite, a powdered clay made from volcanic ash. In addition, you can buy flexible liners made of bentonite granules sandwiched between layers of landscape fabric; you may be able to order them through your water-gardening supplier under the brand name Bentomat or Bentofix. The bentonite swells when it gets wet and forms a tight seal. The downside of a clay pond is that the

Unless the site's soil is fine-grained and rock-free, it's best to provide protection for the liner with an underlayment fabric and a layer of sand.

bottom and sides will crack if allowed to go dry, and it's easily damaged by roots or tunneling animals.

Pond Kits. Some manufacturers offer complete pond kits. These include a rigid shell or flexible liner with a matched pump, filter, and in some cases a fountainhead or self-contained waterfall, planting containers, and pond-treatment chemicals for the initial start-up. If you find a design you like, the kits are much easier to install than separate components. Such kits are usually limited to smaller ponds, however.

A pond with a rock bottom looks more natural than one with a liner—even a flexible one. But rocks tend to collect debris and may be difficult to maintain.

Edging

Pond edgings are typically rock, other masonry materials, or wood. The edging serves to hide the rim, visually define the pond perimeter, and keep surrounding soil from washing into the water. The material you choose can complement nearby landscape features; the edging for a formal pond might also be decorative in its own right. Or the edging can blend into the surroundings, as is the case with an informal pond edged with lawn or native stone. Plan for the edging (also called coping) to overhang the pond by a few inches so that it hides the liner.

At least one section of the edging should be wide and flat enough to allow easy access to the pond for maintenance tasks. (An overhang of a deck or patio could also serve this purpose.) Because stepping on edging could dis-

Irregularly cut stone provides an appropriately informal edging for this pond, opposite.

lodge it, be sure that the area intended for maintenance access is secure; you may wish to mortar at least a portion. Design the edging so that it rises slightly above the surrounding ground to direct runoff away from the pond.

Solid Edging. Formal pools usually have the same edging all the way around, typically poured concrete, brick, pavers, patio tiles, or cut stone. The most common edging for an informal pond is one line of natural stones, either boulders or flagstones. But you may stack flagstones in several vertical layers or arrange boulders and round stones several feet from the pond, decreasing in size as they get closer to the water. Or you can edge an informal pond with a mix of plantings and different types of stone.

Wood Edging. In the unlikely event that you use wood as an edging material, make sure it's labeled for marine or seawall use. Avoid pressure-treated wood because it is treated with chemicals that are toxic to fish and plants.

Lawn Edging

Lawn grass can make a handsome edging, but you'll have to trim it by hand, taking care not to drop grass clippings in the water. The high nitrogen content in grass will disturb the chemical balance of the pond. If you use lawn for edging, you can make a solid edge for it by embedding stones or bricks in mortar on a ledge along the edge of the pond and bringing sod to the edge on a thin layer of topsoil.

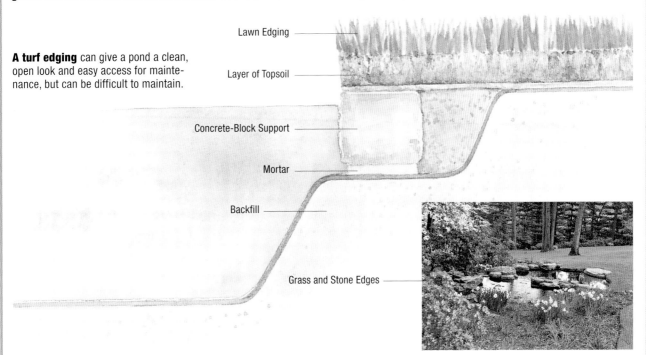

A turf edging can give a pond a clean, open look and easy access for maintenance, but can be difficult to maintain.

Lawn Edging

Layer of Topsoil

Concrete-Block Support

Mortar

Backfill

Grass and Stone Edges

Pebble Beach

For a wildlife pond, a pebble beach is a popular edging option because it allows birds and mammals to bathe or to wash their food in the shallow water. To create a beach, dig a gradual slope into your pond on one side, and surface it with pebbles. Unless you want pebbles on the bottom of your pond—which is not advisable because the plant debris that gets trapped between them makes the pond hard to clean—you need to create a lip, or stone stop 4 to 6 inches under the water surface to keep the pebbles from rolling into the pond. (Mortar is another option, but it will have to be neutralized with vinegar or acid. See Step 6 in Chapter 4, page 71.) The beach will look more natural if you gradually decrease the size of the pebbles as they get nearer the pond. Lay them down thickly enough so that the liner doesn't show through; some coarse sand may help fill the gaps. If your pond is small, keep the beach area small, or the high percentage of shallow water will cause excessive algal buildup.

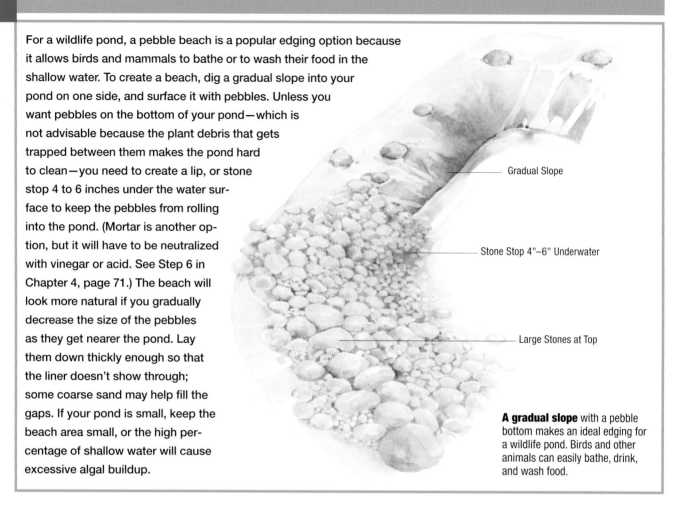

Gradual Slope

Stone Stop 4"–6" Underwater

Large Stones at Top

A gradual slope with a pebble bottom makes an ideal edging for a wildlife pond. Birds and other animals can easily bathe, drink, and wash food.

BUYING ROCKS FOR YOUR POND

Most stone dealers will sell natural stone for informal ponds as well as stones machine-cut in geometric shapes appropriate for edging a formal pool. If you can afford and handle them, large boulders will look better than small stones. Buy the largest stones you can manage easily, but also look for smaller stones of the same type to fill gaps and create a transition between them and the pond.

A landscape designer, a local nursery, or your water-garden dealer may be able to suggest a local quarry with a good selection and helpful service for do-it-yourselfers. A quarry will offer local stone, which will look more appropriate in your landscape than exotic imports. Ask for local stone if you visit a dealer rather than a quarry. If possible, visit a couple of quarries or dealers to get an idea of what's available. If you call first, you may get a sense of which ones will be most helpful. A visit to a good rock quarry can be a fun experience. You can find rocks with holes for waterfalls,

flat rocks perfect for the waterfall lip, rocks with natural depressions for a Japanese basin, and moss-covered rocks to give your pond an instant weathered look. Rock is usually described as either permeable (allowing water to penetrate) or impermeable. Permeable rock such as sandstone will weather quickly and develop a natural-looking roundness; it provides a good home for moss and comes in a variety of colors. Slate has a handsome sheen when wet. Avoid limestone, as it will turn the pond water too alkaline. Granite is an impermeable stone that, while handsome, is more suited to a formal pool. It is durable but hard to cut.

The dealer will probably deliver the rock to the pond site. It will be up to you to move it into place. A medium to large rock can weigh more than 250 pounds, so it's best to hire a contractor for the job or rent a small backhoe. Even if you're in good condition, enlist friends to help, and allow several days to complete the job to reduce the possibility of muscle strain.

Visit a few quarries to see which type of rock might be available for your project. The decorative rocks at right and below came from a local quarry.

Designing the Pond Configuration

A formal reflecting pool with no plants or fish needs to be only 12 inches deep. Other ponds should be at least 18 to 24 inches deep, considered the optimum for growing water lilies and other aquatic plants and sufficient for nearly all types of fish except koi. Ponds less than 18 inches deep heat up and cool off quicker than large, deep ones.

Except in very cold climates (Zone 3), a depth of 24 inches is sufficient to prevent the pond from freezing to the bottom and killing fish or damaging the pond shell. A pond for Japanese koi needs to be at least 3 feet deep, preferably 4 feet deep, so that these somewhat demanding fish get room to grow and can escape summer heat.

Shallow and Sloping Areas. You may want to build in some special shallow areas for marginal plants, which need water depths of a foot or less. You can design either separate planting beds or shelves around the pond perimeter. But many people find it easier to keep their pond a uniform depth and raise containerized plants to their recommended depths on bricks or blocks of some kind. Plastic milk crates are a popular option because they are lightweight and easy to handle. (For information on depth requirements for specific plants, see Chapter 12, page 196.)

Your pond will look best and hold more water if it has steeply sloping sides—about 20 degrees off vertical. Clay ponds should have a shallow bowl shape to make the edges less prone to cracking or crumbling if they dry out. Wildlife ponds often have one side that is a shallow pebble beach so that birds and other creatures have a place to wade.

And don't make your pond's bottom perfectly flat. Slope it slightly toward a sump hole, which will trap dirt and debris and ease cleaning. You can also use this sump area as a drain location or as a place for a submersible pump to improve water circulation. You need to elevate the pump on a brick (or by other means) to keep it above sediment in the sump bottom, so dig your hole deep enough to accommodate both pump and brick.

A shallow pond is more subject to excess algal growth, opposite, during the hot summer months. Also, extreme changes in temperature can harm fish.

The Pond Bottom

Before you begin digging your pond, think about the needs of its future inhabitants. Water lilies require a minimum depth of 18 inches. Koi and other large fish need ponds 3 feet deep. If you want to have marginal plants, such as grass, sedges, arrowhead, and pickerel weed, you will have to accommodate them in water depths ranging anywhere from an inch or two to a foot, either by building shelves or raising them on bricks or plastic baskets. Sloping the bottom toward the sump hole will make pond cleaning much easier.

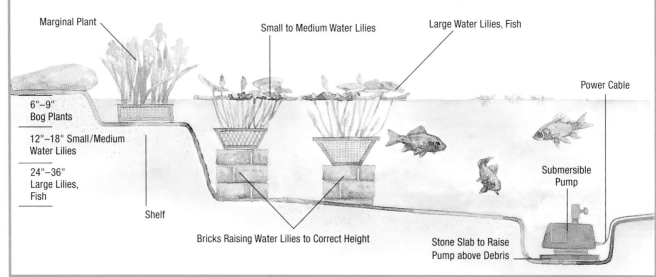

Marginal Plant

Small to Medium Water Lilies

Large Water Lilies, Fish

Power Cable

6"–9"
Bog Plants

12"–18" Small/Medium
Water Lilies

24"–36"
Large Lilies,
Fish

Shelf

Bricks Raising Water Lilies to Correct Height

Submersible
Pump

Stone Slab to Raise
Pump above Debris

how to

Make a Site Plan

If you've selected a site for your pond and you plan to leave the rest of the yard pretty much as it is, a site plan isn't necessary. Otherwise, it's a good idea to develop one. It's relatively easy and even fun to do, and it will help you (and others involved in the project) visualize how the pond fits into the overall scheme. The plan can also be submitted to your local building department for approval if that is required. Local building codes are likely to have requirements relating to setbacks and safety barriers to protect young children. Check before you begin.

Make copies for your records. Once you've finalized the design, make a neat tracing. Attach this final tracing-paper overlay to the base map, and make photocopies. Keep one copy for your files; give another one to building officials; and retain at least two more copies for reference during the project installation. The records will make any further revisions in the pond design easy to note.

Tools and Materials: graph paper (¼-inch grid); tracing paper, several sheets; 50-foot measuring tape; pencil; ruler; site survey map (plat), if available

When you are planning your pond, consider other elements in your landscape. Here, a dramatic garden gate is an integral part of the Asian-inspired design.

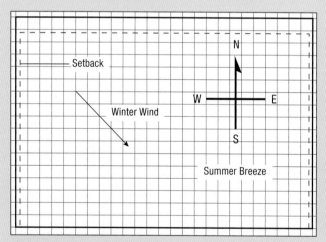

1 Mark the property lines. On the graph paper, mark your property lines (a scale of ¼ in. = 1 ft. is standard). If only a portion of the property will be affected (the backyard, for instance), you don't need to include the entire lot. Indicate north, south, east, and west. Also mark the directions of prevailing summer and winter winds. (Ask neighbors or your local Cooperative Extension Service if you're not sure.) Check with the building department to see how far the pond or any added structures must be set back from lot boundaries; mark these setbacks as dotted lines on your plan.

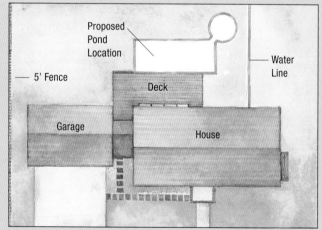

2 Locate existing structures. Starting from a front corner of the house, measure the house dimensions, and transfer them to the plan. Again, if only one yard (front, side, or back) will be affected, you need only show the part of the house that faces it. Include the locations of exterior doors and windows on the wall facing the pond site. Measure and mark the locations of your garage, storage shed, and any other detached buildings and permanent structures, including patios, decks, fences, and paved walks. Show any underground or overhead fixtures, such as utility lines and septic systems. Utility companies will mark these for you.

When your pond is part of a larger project, draw your site plan carefully, and then bring it to your local building department. You may need a permit, particularly if you will be adding or removing structures. There will probably also be safety issues that you'll have to address.

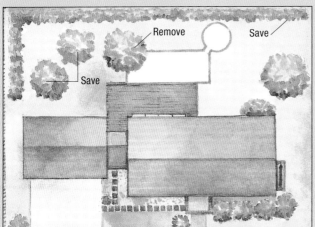

3 Locate plantings. Mark the locations of existing trees, shrubs, and other major plantings; specify which are to be kept and which need to be removed or relocated. If applicable, make notations on the shade cast by trees, tall shrubs, fences, or other structures near the pond site. Remember to factor in growth of any immature trees and large shrubs.

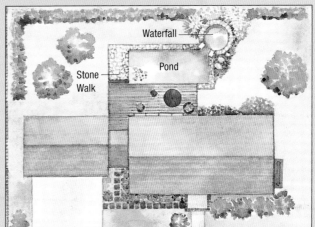

4 Locate the pond on overlays. On a tracing-paper overlay, draw in the exact size and location of the proposed pond. Include edging materials, a waterfall if you plan one, and other proposed pond features, such as walks, planting beds, and fountains. Show the path of new utility lines to the pond. Use as many overlay sheets as you need to design a suitable plan.

PART 2

Installing Your Pond

I f you're like most most people who water garden, you'll choose a flexible liner or a pre-formed shell for your pond. Installing this foundation is an important step in the process of creating your water feature because it marks the end of dreaming and planning and the beginning of years of enjoyment and pleasure. This section contains detailed instructions for how to do it correctly.

Start with a Pond Foundation

Most people choose a flat site on which to build a water feature. This is the simplest option for home gardeners building their first pond. The bottom of a slope is definitely not the best choice. Although nature places ponds in low-lying areas, the lowest place in your garden may be the worst spot for an artificial pond for several reasons: it will catch runoff that may be full of harmful pesticides and other toxins and will definitely contain soil and organic debris; it may be colder than the rest of your landscape; and it may be too close to the water table, greatly increasing the likelihood that groundwater could bubble up under a liner or heave a pond shell out of the ground.

A good foundation and careful planning will keep your water feature beautiful for years. Consider all of the aspects of the site. A flat location is the easiest for building a pond, although slopes offer dramatic possibilities.

Special Sites

Slopes. As previously noted under "Slopes and Runoff" on page 36, a hillside can lend itself to some creative possibilities for waterfalls and streams. On some properties, a slope may be the only choice. If that is the case with you, you'll need to build a retaining wall for the pond. You can do this with soil, using the "cut-and-fill" method. Use subsoil excavated from your pond to build a mound on the downhill side, cover it with topsoil you've removed from the area, and landscape it with plants and rocks.

You can also build a brick or concrete retaining wall on one or both sides of the pond. A wall on the uphill side can be designed so it's almost invisible aboveground. It will help prevent that slope from eroding, and its top edge can keep soil and other matter from washing into the pond. A wall on the downhill side will provide additional support for your liner or shell and the weight of the water it contains, but depending on your slope, it may be visible from below and may obstruct your view of the pond. If you build this wall of stone, you may be able to turn it into an attractive rock garden to complement an informal pond. For a formal pool you can use brick and turn it into a raised bed in which to grow annuals, flowering perennials, or ornamental grasses.

If your property has a high water table, your best solution is to plan on a raised or at least a semiraised pond. (You'll find instructions for a semiraised pond beginning on page 84.) You may be able to deal with seasonally poor drainage by installing gravel-filled trenches to divert water around the pond and into a dry well. It will be helpful on the uphill side of a slope to catch runoff before it reaches the level of the pond. A more attractive option is a wetland garden on the uphill side of the pond to catch runoff. (See pages 134-149 for information on creating wetland gardens.)

A sloped site offers creative possibilities such as incorporating a naturalistic waterfall.

how to

Install a Flexible Liner

DIFFICULTY LEVEL: MODERATE

Flexible pond liners of PVC plastic or rubber are by far the most popular options for pond foundations. They are both relatively inexpensive (compared to preformed shells) and easy to install, and they provide unlimited creative opportunities in pond size and shape. It's also easy to load a roll of flexible liner into your car's rear seat or trunk. Most flexible liners are black, which gives ponds the illusion of additional depth. You may occasionally see other colors. The liners come in a variety of stock sizes, with larger sizes available as special orders. Some garden suppliers carry large rolls of liner material in standard widths. You simply pull the length you need off the roll. If you don't have a well-stocked supplier within easy driving distance, consider ordering the liner by mail-order or online. Most mail-order suppliers and Web sites have knowledgeable, helpful staff.

ESTIMATING THE SIZE TO BUY

Quality liner material is not inexpensive. Nor will you enjoy calling in your helpers and digging the hole, only to find that you don't have enough liner to fill it. Water-garden expert and supplier Charles Thomas recommends that anyone installing a water garden for the first time should add a foot to the calculations in both directions. Check your math a couple of times, and then have someone recheck your figures.

Tools and Materials: rope and stake (for circular ponds); garden hose (for irregular ponds) or batter boards and string (for rectangular ponds); framing square (for square or rectangular ponds); sharpened stick (for circular ponds); flour, powdered gypsum, or nontoxic spray paint (for marking outlines); measuring tape and calculator

IRREGULAR

SQUARE

1 Outline the Shape. After clearing the site of plantings and other obstructions, outline the pond shape on the ground. For irregularly shaped ponds, use a rope or garden hose to mark the pond perimeter. For squares or rectangles, use batter boards, string, and a framing square to make sure all corners meet exactly at a 90-deg. angle. For circular ponds, make a simple "compass" with a stake, sturdy twine or rope, and a sharpened stick, screwdriver, or other pointed object. Drive the stake in the center of your pond area; attach a rope the length of its radius; and use the sharp stick or screwdriver tied to the other end to mark the pond's outside edge. Go over the marked line with flour, powdered gypsum, or nontoxic spray paint to make it more visible.

CIRCULAR

Plants such as hosta and pontederia (also known as "pickerel weed") create a soft border around this lily pond.

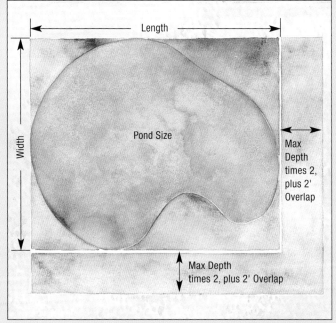

Formula for Liner Size

Liner Width =
Pond Width + 2x Depth + 2-foot overlap

Liner Length =
Pond Length + 2x Depth + 2-foot overlap

Example:
The pond is 24 inches deep and fits inside a 10 x 12-foot rectangle. To figure liner width, add 10 feet (the width), plus 4 feet (the depth, doubled), plus 2 feet (for overlap), for a total of 16 feet. To figure liner length, add 12 feet (the length), plus 4 feet (the depth, doubled), plus 2 feet (for overlap), for a total of 18 feet. You would therefore necd a 16 x 18-foot liner for a 10 x 12-foot pond.

2 Calculate Liner Size. Measure the overall width and length of the pond; then determine the smallest rectangle that would enclose the pond area. To allow for pond depth, decide on the maximum depth of the pond, double it, and add this figure to the width and length of the rectangle. To allow for overlap around the edges, add an additional 24 in. to the width and length of the liner. This will provide 12 in. of overlap around the pond rim once the liner is installed. It is obviously best to overestimate when calculating the liner size you'll need, particularly if the shape of the pond is quite irregular. (Refer to the example above, showing how to compute a 16 x 18-ft. liner for a 10 x 12-ft. pond.)

Note that for irregularly shaped ponds, you may need to trim excess liner material to provide an even overlap around the entire pond. If you are creating one or more wetland gardens alongside the pond, you may be able to use the excess for that purpose. Be sure to add extra liner to your calculations if it appears that you will not have enough for a desired wetland.

how to

Construct a Lined Inground Pond

DIFFICULTY LEVEL: MODERATE

Installing a flexible liner in the ground requires four basic steps: digging the hole, laying down the liner, filling the pond with water, and adding stones or other edging around the pond perimeter. Some sites and designs may require a few additional steps. If you plan to install statuary, read about footings on page 122 before you begin your pond.

Tools and Materials: measuring tape; spirit level; tamper; flexible liner; shovels (flat shovel works best for removing sod; rounded shovel works best for digging); wheelbarrow (for moving excavated soil); straight boards (for checking level); underlayment fabric or old newspapers, carpet, or damp sand; stones for temporary liner weights; heavy-duty scissors or utility knife.

1 Dig the Hole. Use a flat shovel to remove patches of sod within the pond outline and about 6 to 12 in. beyond the perimeter. Digging shallow shelves around the perimeter is optional; they are about 12 to 16 in. wide and 9 to 12 in. below the top edge of the excavation. After excavating the pond area to the depth of the shelf, compact the soil firmly in the shelf area using a tam-

per. The perimeter should be the depth of the shovel blade. Use a straight board and a spirit level to make sure the shelf is level. Then excavate the rest of the pond. Check the depth frequently by measuring from the bottom of the hole to the top of a long 2x4 or 2x6 placed across the pond. The sides should slope in about 20 deg. from vertical; 45 deg. in loose or sandy soil. Slope the bottom of the excavation about $\frac{1}{2}$ to 1 in. per foot toward the center or one end; at the lowest point, dig a shallow (6 to 8 in. deep) sump hole to facilitate draining the pond for future cleaning.

4 Position the Liner. Work shoeless so as not to damage the liner. To make it more flexible, unroll it and let it warm a few minutes in the sun. Heat will build up underneath it and kill a lawn, so spread it on sun-warmed pavement. Avoid dragging the liner across the ground. With a helper, drape the liner loosely into the excavation, leaving an even overlap on all sides. After it's centered, weight down the edges with concrete blocks, bricks, or stones. Then fill the pond with water.

5 Adjust the Liner. As the pond fills with water, adjust the liner to conform to the sides of the pond and smooth it out. Ease off the stone weights. When the pond is full, trim off excess lining using a scissors or a utility knife. Leave enough around the rim to extend underneath and a few inches behind the first course of stones. To keep the liner in place while you add edging, push large nails or spikes through the liner into the ground every foot or so around the pond rim.

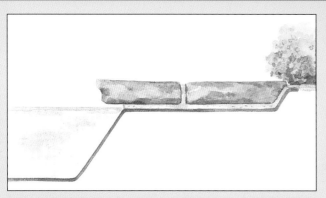

2 **Cut a Ledge for the Edging Materials.** Using a flat-blade shovel, cut a ledge that is about 12 to 15 in. wide and deep enough to accommodate the combined thickness of the edging and any underlayment. If you will be mortaring the stones, include an extra 2 to 3 in. The top of the edging should be at least 1 in. above the surrounding terrain and overhang the pond edge by a few inches to hide the liner and protect it from the sun. If you'll be installing a statuary fountain that weighs more than 100 lbs, install a 4-in.-thick concrete footing for it before you lay the liner.

3 **Make Sure the Pond Edges are Level.** Use the same board you used to measure hole depth. Place a level on top of it; then move the board to various points across the length and width of the pond while checking for level. Remove sharp stones or roots from the site. If your liner does not have a built-in underlayment, you need to give it additional protection with pond underlayment from your supplier, 2 to 3 in. of damp sand, old carpet, or a 1-in. layer of newspapers. Pack damp sand or soil into any voids in the sidewalls and bottom. If your soil is mostly sand and your liner is heavy, omit underlayment on the bottom only.

6 **Add Edging Materials.** A single line of natural stones is the simplest form of edging. Place large stones over an extra layer of liner. Or set stones in 2 to 3 in. of mortar reinforced with metal lath. Treat and allow the mortar to cure for a week. Then scrub the edging with a vinegar solution of 4 parts vinegar to 1 part water to neutralize the lime leaching from the mortar. Drain the pond, rinse the liner, and add fresh water; repeat until the water tests neutral. (See page 81.)

7 **Add Plants Around the Perimeter.** Tuck plants between rocks—either directly into the soil or in pots sunk into the ground—to soften the edges of the pond. (See the sidebar "A Moss Milkshake" on page 46 for information on how to encourage moss to grow between stones.)

Working with the Terrain

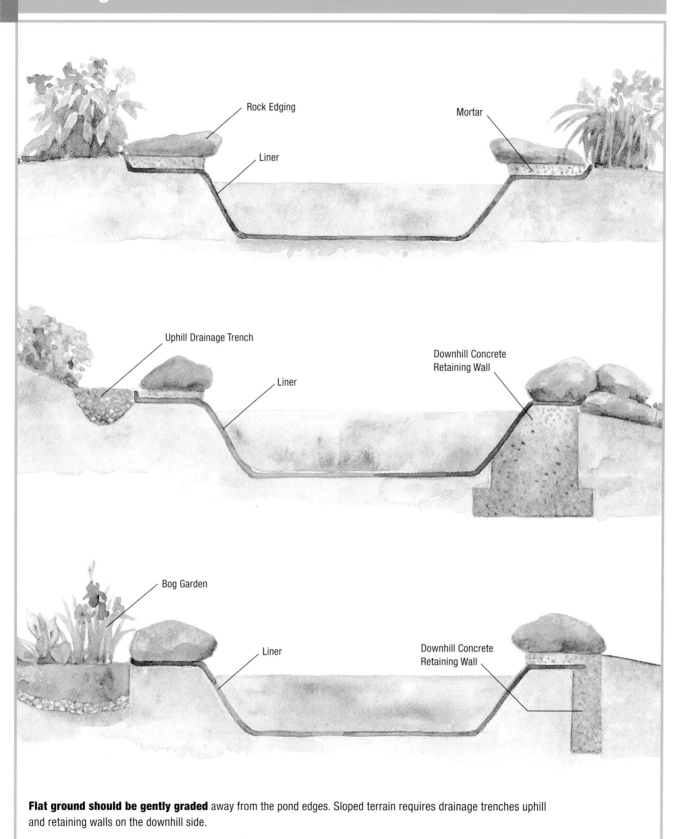

Rock Edging

Mortar

Liner

Uphill Drainage Trench

Downhill Concrete Retaining Wall

Liner

Bog Garden

Downhill Concrete Retaining Wall

Liner

Flat ground should be gently graded away from the pond edges. Sloped terrain requires drainage trenches uphill and retaining walls on the downhill side.

A small shallow pond and various plantings add interest and color to this hilly landscape.

A small deck and chairs overlooking a pond and surrounded by greenery is a perfect at-home getaway for relaxing and reflection.

Planting-Shelf Options

Although some pond designs have shelves all the way around the perimeter for containerized plants, these are optional. On a practical level, you will often discover that containers are too big or the wrong shape for such shelves. Many water gardeners find that raising their containerized plants on bricks or plastic milk crates allows them to be more flexible about the placement of their marginal (shallow-water) plants. Another option is to create permanent planting areas that allow you to grow your plants without containers but still keep them from spreading. To create planting areas for marginals, excavate a ledge wide enough to allow you to lay a stone or brick retaining wall along the outside edge on top of the liner. Mortar the stones or bricks only enough to keep them in place because it's no problem to have water seeping between them. Fill the area with good garden soil. After planting, top the soil with gravel to keep it from being dislodged. The shelf shouldn't be wider than about a foot, so you can easily reach plants for deadheading, dividing, and other chores.

Planting Beds. In formal pools, some people use bricks to create permanent planters for water lilies in the middle of the pond. In a deep koi pond, permanent planting beds with edges 12 inches below the surface and 24 inches across will hold the largest water lilies and protect them from the fish. (Koi are less likely to bother plants this close to the surface.) For marginal plants, build the planter walls so that the edges are 6 inches below the surface to accommodate a wide range of species. You can create deeper areas within the planter for species that need to grow 8 to 12 inches below the surface. Different plants grouped together look more natural in such beds, but obviously you can't rearrange them as easily as with containers. Such large planter beds are heavy; installing a concrete footing under your liner will help protect it.

You can build permanent shelves into the side of your pond. But many water gardeners find that raising container plants on bricks, plastic crates, or other platforms gives them more flexibility in plant placement.

Planting Pockets

Spaces between pondside stones allow for container plants or inground plantings. Give the latter good garden loam topped with gravel.

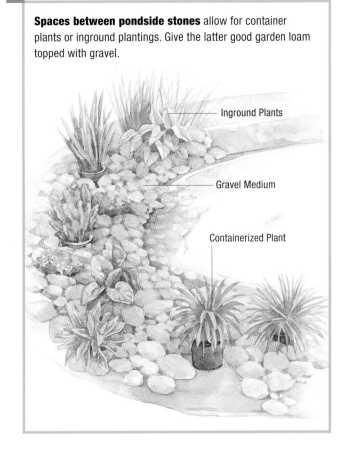

Inground Plants

Gravel Medium

Containerized Plant

Planting Options

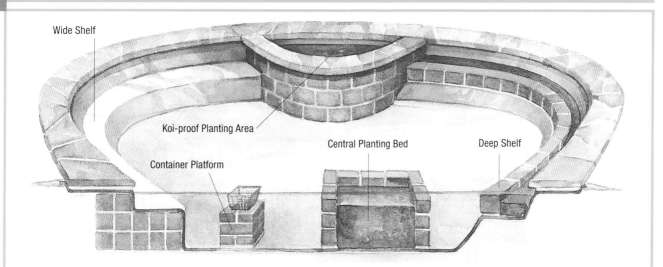

Although you wouldn't want to include all of these in one pond, this drawing illustrates the many possibilities for creating permanent planting areas within a water feature. Large central planting beds require a concrete footing if you're using a flexible liner.

Plant Island

Shape a flat-topped mound of earth lower than the water level, and cover it with the liner. Build a retaining wall of upside-down sod pieces around the perimeter, and fill the center with heavy garden soil. For a dry island, build a flat-topped mound 6 to 12 inches higher than the water level, and drape the liner over it. Cut a hole in the center of the liner. Dig organic matter into the soil before planting it with perennials or small shrubs. Upside-down sod can hide the liner around the edges.

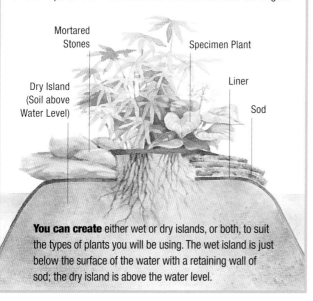

You can create either wet or dry islands, or both, to suit the types of plants you will be using. The wet island is just below the surface of the water with a retaining wall of sod; the dry island is above the water level.

Gravel and mulch add a natural look around the pond, and they provide a surface that you can walk on to deadhead or divide plantings.

Extra Support for Pond Foundations

In sandy or crumbly soil, or where you'll be using large boulders for edging, it's a good idea to create additional support for the pond edges. The easiest way to do this is by burying a line of concrete blocks along the edge of your pond site before excavating the pond. The blocks don't need to be touching, so it's possible to align them around an irregularly shaped pond. Buried blocks will also lend important additional support for plastic or fiberglass preformed pond shells; they'll help contain the substantial outward pressure exerted by water when a lined or preformed pond is filled. It will also be easier to lay stone edging without mortar on the resulting flat, solid surface. Use a spirit level to verify that all the blocks you install are level.

Bring the edge of your liner up and over the edges of the concrete blocks (or poured concrete). The installation of underlayment or heavy landscape fabric under the liner helps prevent punctures from the sharp edges of the blocks. The liner should extend at least a foot past the blocks, so the block material can be hidden. If you prefer to use poured concrete rather than blocks to strengthen the construction, bring in professional expertise. The foundation is far too important to cut corners.

Buried concrete blocks along the edge provide extra support for this pond's preformed liner.

Pond netting, which protects koi against heron attacks, should be supported above the water.

Optional Cement Overliner

A thin layer of cement-like material spread over the liner will protect it from the damaging effects of ultraviolet rays as well as from punctures caused by waders in the pond. Plastic cement is the material of choice for a liner mixture because it contains latex additives that make the mixture highly resistant to cracking. Most lumberyards and masonry suppliers carry this product; mix 1 part plastic cement to 4 parts sand to make a good liner mixture. If you like, you can add coloring agents to the cement and/or produce various surface textures by brooming or troweling before it dries.

After installing the flexible liner, cover it with a layer of chicken wire to provide reinforcement. Hand-pack a 1-inch layer of plastic cement into the chicken wire over the entire surface of the pond; wear heavy gloves for this procedure. Start packing cement at the base of each sidewall, building up to the top in 6-foot-long sections. After the sidewalls are

Pond Supports

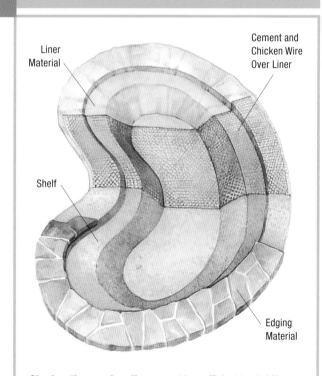

Sloping the pond walls may not be sufficient to stabilize them if the soil is very sandy or crumbly. Mortar may be needed to significantly strengthen the sides; a cement overliner with chicken wire adds stability to the entire pond area. It is applied to the pond sides and entire bottom.

Nonsupport versus Support

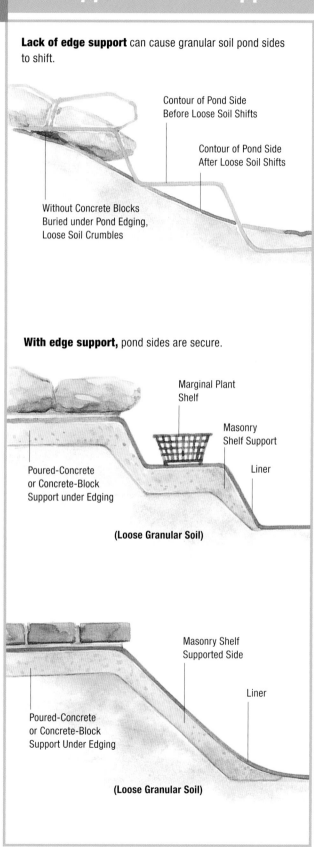

Lack of edge support can cause granular soil pond sides to shift.

With edge support, pond sides are secure.

covered, do the pond bottom. Brush or trowel the surface smooth; then allow the plastic cement to harden (about 10 to 12 hours, or overnight).

Once the cement has hardened, fill the pond with water. Add 1 gallon of distilled white vinegar per 100 gallons of water; allow this mixture to stand one week. (The vinegar serves to neutralize the lime leaching from the cement.) Drain the pond. (See page 192 for information on draining a pond.) Rinse the overliner thoroughly before refilling the pond with fresh water. Test the pH of the water before adding fish or plants. (For more on pH, see "What's In Your Water" on page 179.) If the water tests too alkaline, repeat the vinegar treatment and test again.

Installing a Preformed Shell

Rigid, preformed pond shells of molded plastic or fiberglass are quick to install and resist punctures better than flexible liners. You don't have to fret about creating the design, and if you move, you could conceivably take the pond with you.

These durable plastic or fiberglass foundations, above, come in many shapes and sizes, but minus the unlimited design options of flexible liners.

PREPARING THE GROUND

Although the conditions for a rigid shell aren't as exacting as for a liner, the ground where you install a preformed pond must be free of rocks, projecting roots, and other sharp objects and—above all—must be stable. The shell, which can weigh several tons when full of water, will need to be fully supported by firm, well-packed earth. Any air pockets or bumps can cause it to crack or buckle.

Groundwater (from a high water table) can erode loose or sandy soil around the shell. In cold climates, frost heaving can deform or buckle it. If you anticipate either of these conditions, make the excavation about 6 to 8 inches deeper and wider than the shell. Then backfill the hole with 3 to 4 inches of smooth pea gravel, top with 2 inches of sand or finely sifted soil, and tamp firmly. (If you plan to install a statuary fountain, stepping-stone boulders, or other heavy objects in the pond, read about footings in "In-Pond Statuary" on page 122 before you begin construction.)

The full weight of heavy rocks can damage the rim of a pond, and so they are artfully arranged slightly to the side here, right.

how to

Construct a Preformed Inground Pond

DIFFICULTY LEVEL: MODERATE

Once you dig the hole, you'll have to remove any rocks or other sharp objects. For added protection to the liner, cover the bottom of the hole with 2 to 3 inches of damp sand or finely sifted soil. (For thinner shells, you may also want to use an underlayment fabric; see "Flexible Pond Liners" on page 49.) Tamp all surfaces. Then use a spirit level to make sure the bottom of the excavation is perfectly level in all directions.

Tools and Materials: preformed shell; plumb bob or spirit level and stakes; rope, garden hose, or nontoxic spray paint (for marking outlines); shovel and tamper; damp sand or finely sifted soil; measuring tape; long, straight 2x4; spirit level; edging material; mortar and mixing equipment; vinegar or commercial concrete-curing agent (optional)

1 Mark the Shell Outline. Except for very small ponds, you will need help with installation because you will be lifting and moving the shell several times. Place the preformed shell upright in the desired location. Use a plumb bob or a spirit level and stakes to transfer the shape of the pond rim to the ground, and mark the outline with a rope, garden hose, or nontoxic spray paint. Use stakes (spaced about 12 in. apart) to keep the rope or hose in place.

The outline of the preformed pond liner is mostly visible, above, but it does not detract from the appeal of the water feature.
Small, not-too-heavy rocks can be arranged on top of the liner's edge if you wish to make the pond blend seamlessly into the landscape.

2 Dig and Prepare the Hole. Excavate the hole, allowing an extra 2 in. around the perimeter and 2 in. in the bottom of the hole to be backfilled with sand. If the shell has shallow-water shelves, dig the hole only to the depth of these shelves; then tamp the outside edges of the bottom firmly. Put the shell in the hole, and mark the outline of the bottom of the pond. Remove the shell, and dig out this lower portion to the distance between the bottom of the shelves and the bottom of the pond (plus 2 extra in.). Flatten the bottom with the edge of a board, and firmly tamp the soil. (Thinner shells must have firm support under the shelves as well as on the sides and bottom.)

3 Set the Shell. Place the pond shell into the excavation, and check the height of the rim. The rim should be about 1 in. above the surrounding ground to prevent runoff from entering the pond. Add or remove sand from the bottom of the hole (and soil from the shelf support) until you achieve the desired height.

4 Level the Shell. Place a long, straight 2x4 across the shell rim in several places, and check with a spirit level. If the shell isn't level, pull it out of the hole and relevel the excavation. The pond must be perfectly level before you add any water. Even a few inches of water in the pond bottom will make the shell virtually impossible to move.

Once the shell is level, start filling it with water slowly. As the water level rises, backfill the hole around the shell with sifted dirt or damp sand, tamping it gently with a shovel handle or the end of a 2x4. Make sure you fill any gaps or holes, especially around any shallow-water shelves. Check the rim for level frequently. Don't allow the water level inside the pond to rise above the backfilled earth outside the rim, or else the shell may bulge outward.

5 Add Edging. When the shell is filled with water, you can conceal the exposed rim with rocks, masonry materials, or overhanging plants. If you use flagstones or flat pavers, allow them to overhang the pond edges by 1 to 2 in. Don't allow the full weight of large rocks to rest on the pond rim, because the weight may deform or damage the pond walls. Instead, embed the rocks in a 3- to 4-in.-thick bed of mortar, raised slightly above the lip of the shell, or bury a line of concrete blocks along the rim of the shell. If you use mortar, neutralize the lime in it with distilled vinegar after the mortar has cured for about a week, as described under "Constructing a Lined Inground Pond," step 6 on page 71.

BUILDING A SEMIRAISED POND WITH A PREFORMED SHELL

It's possible to install some of the thickest preformed pond shells completely aboveground using a skirt of wood, brick, or masonry block to hide the sides and to hold up the rim. But it's difficult to give even the sturdiest shells enough support to keep them from buckling and shifting.

Do-it-yourselfers will have better luck with a partially raised pond, which involves sinking the lower part of the shell up to the shelf level and building a low wall to mask the raised portion. As with an inground pond, make the excavation 2 inches deeper and wider than the shell, line the bottom of the hole with 2 inches of sand, and set the shell in place. Then build a wall from the ground to the lip of the pond, backfilling behind the wall with soil (or concrete) as you go. If your wall is stone or other masonry, you'll need to have a concrete footing (foundation) installed to support the wall before you start constructing it. The footing should be at least twice the width of the wall and a minimum of 4 inches deep (even deeper in colder climates, with a layer of gravel underneath; check local codes). Use reinforcing bar (rebar) for stability. Place cap stones over the lip of the shell to hide it; secure the cap stones with mortar.

There are a variety of design treatments that can be attempted with a semiraised pond. Your local water-garden dealer is the place to start looking for ideas. He or she may be able to show you excellent examples of a semiraised pond or suggest a design.

Geometric Semiraised Ponds. These are the easiest shapes with which to work. You can support any straight-sided geometric shape (rectangle, square, L-shaped) with a fairly basic design of concrete block, which is fast, economical, and durable. Then you have an extensive choice of materials to decorate your wall, including easy-to-apply veneers that look like old brick or various types of natural stone. More-skilled do-it-yourselfers may choose to build the support of concrete, in which case they will first need to build supports of plywood and 2x4 stakes. Remember to make any provisions for wiring and electrical hookups for pumps and lighting before you begin erecting your support wall.

Semiraised Pond

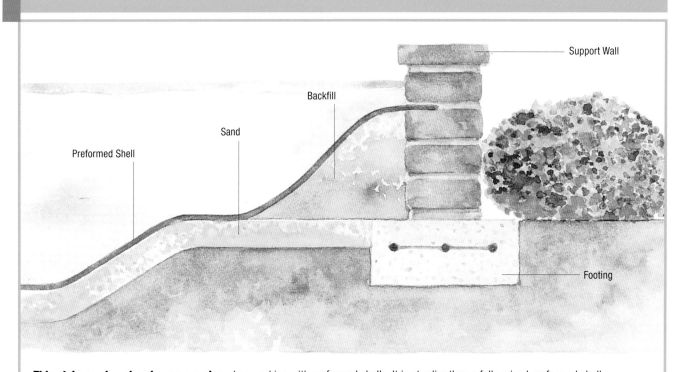

This style can be a handy compromise when working with preformed shells. It is sturdier than a fully raised preformed shell, yet the inital excavation will be easier than that of a sunken pond.

Free-Form Semiraised Ponds. A preformed pond shell with an irregular outline will be more challenging to enclose with a support wall than a shape with regular edges. Standard 16-inch concrete block may be too large to adapt to the curvature of your shell; brick may be a better choice for following a free-form path.

Using concrete would allow you to follow the pond edge more precisely, but you will need to find flexible materials with which to make your form. These might include flexible plywood or plastic sheet laminates.

This pond, above, is built from a preformed shell raised partway out of the ground. But a woodland setting creates a more informal impression than that of more geometric forms. Creating the same free-form design, right, as might appear in nature, would not be possible with a rigid shell.

Mortared brick, stone, or concrete are all excellent choices for supporting the walls of a raised pond, such as this one, left.

CHAPTER 5

Moving-Water Features

Adding movement and sound through a waterfall, stream, fountain, or some combination of these can increase the beauty and pleasure derived from a charming but simple reflective pond. These features also have practical benefits, such as aerating the water, providing oxygen for fish and other pond life.

Design Pointers

What moving features you add to your pond will depend on its overall style as well as on your terrain. If you have an informal pond, design your streams and falls to emulate those found in nature, and edge them with local rocks ranging in size from large boulders to small stones and pebbles. A crashing waterfall will look right on a steep natural slope. If you live in the flatlands, though, a waterfall more than 2 to 3 feet high will look artificial; consider a meandering stream instead. If you have a formal pool, possibilities include a straight-sided canal or water "stairs" that incorporate landscaping ties, poured-concrete slabs, precast concrete basins, masonry blocks or bricks, or even ceramic tiles.

In both formal pools and informal ponds, waterfalls and streams usually consist of a series of small pools or catch basins linked by low cascades. If space is limited, you can install a single raised basin above your pond, connected by one fall, or have a fall gush springlike from a fissure in a rock wall or ledge above the pond.

Building a successful watercourse is largely a matter of trial and error. To create the effect you want, you'll need to experiment with different sizes and shapes of rocks, as well as with their placement in and around the watercourse. Before starting, give a good deal of thought to just what effect you want to create. Look at photographs of creeks and waterfalls. Take hikes along local streams, noting the size, shape, and texture of the rocks and how the water moves over and around them. Study artificial streams and waterfalls in public gardens, in friends' gardens, and anywhere you can find them. Once you've gained access to these gardens, be sure to ask their owners about the hardware they used to get their effect, particularly the type and size of pump they installed. Just as genius is a mix of inspiration and perspiration, creating a successful watercourse is a mix of art and engineering.

SHAPING A WATERFALL

Keep a waterfall in scale with the pond. A small trickle in a large pond won't be very dramatic, nor will it be very effective at recirculating and oxygenating the water. And a large cascade gushing into a small pond will stir too much of the water surface, churning up sediment and making it nearly impossible to raise fish, water lilies, and other aquatic plants that prefer still water. If you want both a large, splashing fall and aquatic plants, you'll need to design the pond so plants can be placed well away from the wave action.

Resist the temptation to be too flamboyant. To maintain the main pond's water level, the surface of the fall or stream should be smaller than that of the pond. And a big, splashy water show can speed the loss of pond volume through evaporation. You can hold evaporation to a minimum by keeping the falls low and the watercourse relatively short. For the same reason, small, deep basins are preferable to larger, shallow ones. As you proceed, you must also minimize any possibility of leaks between rocks along the bank and behind the falls.

Creating a watercourse such as this, left, gives you an opportunity to combine artistic flair with engineering skill. But if this is your first such project, you may want to consult an expert.

Streams associated with formal ponds are similar to canals; they usually have straight sides and uniform edging.

The sound of moving water, even from a small stream such as this, is a delightful feature next to a patio.

Creating a realistic stream design requires deft placement of rocks and plants.

Waterfalls. These look best and are less prone to water loss when large, overhanging rocks are used for the lip of the falls. Use smooth, flat flagstones to produce a wide, thin curtain of water, or direct the water through a narrow gap between large boulders to produce a gushing effect. Creating a hollow space behind the falls will amplify and echo the sound of falling water. While the lips of informal falls are formed from naturalistic materials with irregular shapes, those of formal waterfalls can be brick, tile, flagstone, or landscaping ties. Some formal designs incorporate a sheet of clear acrylic plastic to create a wide, nearly transparent curtain of water. The plastic itself is all but invisible when the falls are in operation.

SHAPING A STREAM

For some people, a trickling rivulet is more picturesque than ocean waves. A winding stream is a particularly apt addition to a woodland or a rocky hillside; it's also at home on a prairie, where a waterfall would look contrived. Although you'll need a pond to feed your stream (unless you bury a water tank to take its place), you can make the stream the predominant feature by virtue of its length, placement, or elaborate planting and rock surrounds.

Stream Design. Nature usually arranges streams into a series of short, fairly flat sections separated by low falls or cascades. In a home water garden, streams need to be as level as possible so that they will retain some water when the pump is turned off. Alternating between wet and dry conditions can shorten the life of plastic or fiberglass foundation materials and crack mortar or concrete. And a stream that holds some water at all times also looks more realistic. A drop of 1 to 2 inches per 10 feet is all that's needed to make the stream flow downhill. At that point, changes in width can change stream speed.

Stream Speed. To increase the speed of a stream's current, bring its banks closer together; for a more leisurely current, move the banks farther apart. If you want to grow shallow-water plants along the edges, a deep, wide, slow-moving stream will be preferable to a fast, narrow one. But avoid large areas of slow-moving shallow water, which can quickly become clogged with thick mats of algae.

In either case, twists and turns in the course will make it look more realistic than will a straight channel. Vary the size of the rocks along the banks and the distance between the banks. Placing large rocks inside the watercourse will create rapids; placing smaller stones and pebbles will produce a rippling effect. Either approach will also make the stream look and sound more natural. Straight or parallel channels are appropriate only for formal designs.

Choosing and Buying a Liner

To prevent water loss between rocks or other edging, artificial waterfalls and streams are lined with the same types of materials that are used to line a pond. Most of the same purchasing, design, and installation considerations also apply. In addition to the liner, remember to purchase sufficient underlayment material to cover the entire watercourse. (See the discussion of underlayment under "Flexible Pond Liners" on pages 48-49.)

The stream must not be so large as to overwhelm the pond or so small that it's barely noticeable.

FLEXIBLE LINERS

The easiest and most versatile material to use is a flexible liner, which will adapt to both formal and informal waterfall designs. Ideally, you should use one large piece of liner for constructing both the main pond and the waterfall or stream to provide a continuous, seamless barrier. In practice, though, it's not always easy to align one large square or rectangular sheet of liner with the selected watercourse site without creating large amounts of waste material.

If the watercourse will be approximately the same width along its entire length, you can use one long strip of liner. However, if the watercourse consists of pools and cascades of different lengths and widths, or if you have designed several bends in a meandering stream, you may need two or more separate pieces of liner. You still may be able to save money by ordering one large sheet of it and then cutting one or more strips from it to line the watercourse. This may cost less than if you were to order separate sheets for the watercourse and pond. Tape or glue the sheets together where they overlap, using seam tape or adhesive available from the liner dealer.

Flexible Liner Watercourse

To determine the amount of liner you'll need for your watercourse, measure the width and length of the course, and then add twice the depth of the fall or stream plus 2 feet to allow a foot of overlap on each side. (See the sample calculations on page 69.) If you plan to create wetland areas on either side of your fall or stream, add in this additional width. If you'll be piecing the liner along its length, add at least 12 inches (for each junction) to allow sufficient overlap to prevent leakage at joints. When planning the main pond, make sure the liner for the main pond is large enough to extend upward into the first catch basin.

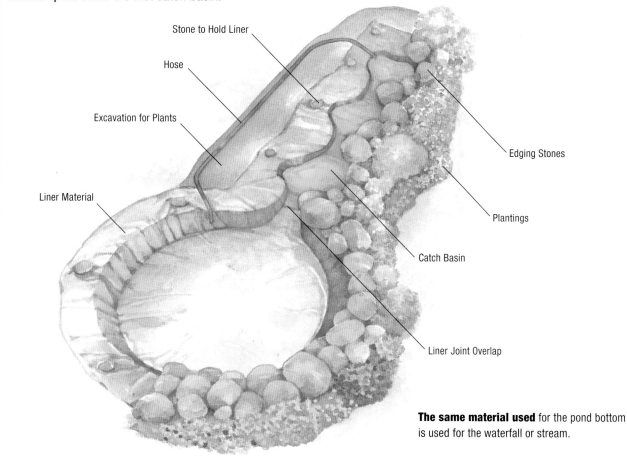

Stone to Hold Liner

Hose

Excavation for Plants

Liner Material

Edging Stones

Plantings

Catch Basin

Liner Joint Overlap

The same material used for the pond bottom is used for the waterfall or stream.

Moving Water

The water for your fall, stream, or fountain is recirculated from your pond by a small electric pump. Buy one that's big enough to operate your waterfall and any other water feature in your pond.

In general, a pump that recirculates one-half of the pond's total water volume per hour will provide the minimum flow for a pleasing proportion of moving water for the size of the pond. For example, if the pond holds 1,000 gallons of water, buy a pump that will deliver at least 500 gallons per hour at the top of the falls. For a larger, bolder cascade, select a pump that will turn over the full 1,000 gallons in one hour. It's better to err on the side of a too-large pump than have one that's too small.

You can also calculate the amount of water required for cascades of various sizes. First measure the width of the spillway over which the water will flow. Then decide how deep you want the water where it flows over the lip. For a light sheet of water (¼ inch deep), you'll need a pump that produces 50 gallons per hour for each inch of lip width. For a heavy flow (1 inch deep), look for a pump that produces 150 gallons per hour for each inch of lip width. For example, if the falls will be 6 inches wide, you'll need a pump that can deliver 300 gallons per hour for a ¼-inch-deep flow or one that delivers 900 gallons per hour for a 1-inch-deep flow.

The right size pump, which will recirculate the pond's water efficiently, will provide a suitably streaming cascade.

PREFORMED WATERFALLS

Most companies that make preformed fiberglass or plastic ponds also offer preformed waterfall runs or courses of the same material. These are installed much like a preformed rigid pond shell. (See "Installing a Preformed Shell" on page 81.) The units consist of one or more small basins with built-in cascades and a lower lip that empties into the pond. You can combine two or more short watercourses to produce a longer watercourse, with each unit emptying into the one below it.

Styles. Informal preformed watercourses are shaped (and sometimes colored) to simulate natural rock, although most look fake unless the edges are disguised with overhanging stones or other materials. Formal preformed waterfalls are usually smaller versions of square or rectangular preformed ponds, with the addition of a built-in lip or spillway.

Materials. Fiberglass and plastic watercourses are lightweight and inexpensive. But as with preformed ponds, the sizes and designs are limited. In fact, preformed watercourses are often designed for use with a specific pump size. On the other hand, you may find it an advantage that your design has been worked out in advance because you can skip some planning and measuring. Preformed watercourses made of cement or reconstituted stone are also available. Although these are more substantial and natural-looking than plastic or fiberglass units, they are much heavier. As a result, the practical size of these units is limited to only a few square feet.

A smooth, flat overhanging stone provides a perfect lip for a wide, thin curtain of water. Hollow space behind the waterfall creates a pleasing echo of falling water.

Determining Pond Capacity

In order to buy the right size pump, you need to figure your pond's capacity in gallons of water. (You'll also need this information for choosing a filter and determining correct dosages of plant fertilizers, fish medications, algaecides, and other chemical treatments.) The most accurate way to determine pond capacity is to attach a flow meter to your faucet or water-supply line and record the number of gallons used when you fill the pond.

Here's a less accurate but easier and less expensive method: turn on the garden hose at a steady flow rate, and time how long it takes to fill a 5-gallon bucket (say, 10 seconds). Then time how many minutes it takes to fill the pond at the same flow rate (say, 20 minutes). Now figure out the flow rate of the hose in gallons per minute (5 gallons in 10 seconds x 6 = 30 gallons per minute). Next, multiply the gallons per minute by the number of minutes it took to fill the pond (30 gallons x 20 minutes = 600 gallons).

If it isn't practical to fill (or refill) the pond with water, calculate capacity in gallons using one of the following formulas. Each assumes that the pond sides are straight (or steeply sloped) and that the bottom is flat.

■ **Rectilinear ponds:** If the pond is roughly square or rectangular, measure its average depth, width, and length. Then multiply the three figures to determine cubic feet. Multiply the cubic feet by 7.5 to get capacity in gallons.

■ **Circular ponds:** Multiply the diameter by the diameter (diameter squared) times the depth times 5.9.

■ **Oval ponds:** Multiply the depth by the width by the length by 6.7.

■ **Free-form ponds:** It's tough to calculate the volume of an irregularly shaped pond accurately. For the closest estimate, determine the average depth, width, and length, and then use the equation for oval ponds.

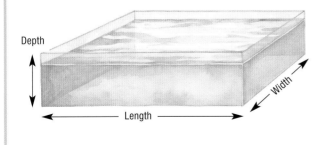

Depth

Width

Length

Other Considerations. Placing the recirculating pump or pump inlet close to the falls increases the pump's efficiency because the pump then needs to push the water a shorter distance. (You'll also need less tubing or pipe between the pump and the head of the falls.) As a rule, every 10 feet of horizontal pipe or tubing is equal to 1 foot of vertical rise in reducing the performance of the pump. Thus, theoretically, you could power a 30-foot stream with the same pump you would need for a 3-foot waterfall. (That's only theoretical because the stream will have a modest incline, and the fall will have at least a short horizontal run.)

Buy a pump that is slightly more powerful than you think you'll need. You can always restrict the flow if necessary. Some pumps have valves that let you adjust the flow. If yours doesn't, you can restrict the flow by installing a separate valve on the outlet, or discharge, side of the pump or by using a special restriction clamp that attaches to the outlet tubing. (Never restrict the flow on the outlet side by more than 25 percent, however, or you'll burn out the motor.) Before buying the pump, find out if the dealer will allow you to exchange it for a larger size if it turns out to be too small to operate the waterfall to your satisfaction.

Pump Performance

Pump Head (Lift). When shopping for a pump, check the performance charts that come with the product. Most pumps are rated in gallons per hour at various heights above the water surface. This height is referred to as *head* or *lift.* The higher you place the discharge for the waterfall above the pond, the lower the pump output (because the higher your waterfall, the harder the pump has to push to deliver water to the top). For example, a pump that delivers 300 gallons at a 1-foot head may deliver only 120 gallons at a 4-foot head.

In pump-performance charts, manufacturers also provide a maximum head figure, which is the theoretical maximum height to which the pump can lift water. For best pump performance, purchase a pump whose maximum head height is well above the total height of the falls. You can buy moderately priced pumps offering a maximum head height of more than 20 feet.

If you intend to incorporate a fountain in addition to your waterfall, you need to add to your overall figure the gallons per hour required to operate the fountain. If you're adding fish, you'll need a separate mechanical or biological filter, which will further restrict flow and thus necessitate a bigger pump. (Your choice of filters will be limited with certain types of pumps; other pumps are more versatile. See "Filtration" on page 180 for more on filters.) Your pump supplier can help you work out details for these more complicated setups.

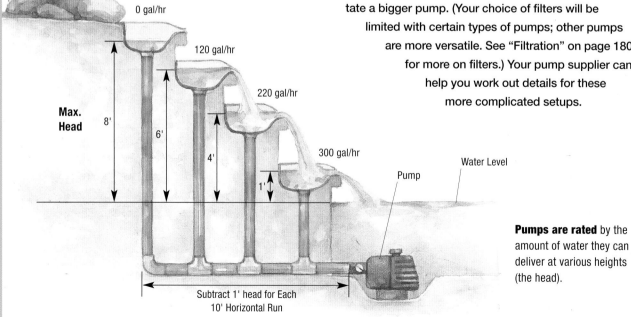

0 gal/hr

120 gal/hr

220 gal/hr

300 gal/hr

Max. Head 8'

6'

4'

1'

Pump

Water Level

Pumps are rated by the amount of water they can deliver at various heights (the head).

Subtract 1' head for Each 10' Horizontal Run

Large overhanging rocks, such as flat flagstones, can be used to form an informal, natural-looking waterfall.

SUBMERSIBLE OR EXTERNAL PUMP?

Submersible pumps, as the name implies, are submerged in the water and are removed only periodically to allow cleaning of the built-in filter or strainer that keeps them from getting clogged with leaves and other debris. Submersible pumps are used in most garden ponds for a number of good reasons. They run cooler and more quietly than external pumps and are generally less expensive. In most cases, they're more economical to install and to operate because they require less plumbing. Reasonably priced models range in capacity from 180 to 1,200 gallons per hour; high-capacity models will handle up to 3,400 gallons per hour.

If a submersible pump doesn't work with your pond design, you can buy a pump designed to operate either in open air or submerged. Compact in size, these devices are a good compromise in situations where a submersible pump would pose safety hazards or be prone to damage and where a typical external pump would be too big for the pond. Their capacities are similar to those of submersible pumps. For external operation, these pumps usually need to be placed in a dry sump below the water level of the pond. Dig a hole deep enough to accommodate the pump but above the water table; provide a cover for the hole that's easy to camouflage and to remove for inspection or maintenance.

External pumps are those that sit outside the water, like those used for swimming pools. They're usually appropriate only for very large waterfalls and fountains or in situations where a submersible pump would be dangerous or impractical—such as in a pond that doubles as a wading pool. With capacities ranging from 2,400 to more than 8,000 gallons per hour and a maximum head of up to 80 feet, external pumps are overkill for most backyard ponds, and the noise they make can distract from the pleasant sounds of your water feature. They also require their own housing to

protect them (which is difficult to camouflage). If you're installing a swimming pool, though, you might consider plumbing the pump and filtration system to operate a pond and waterfall also.

1,200-gph Submersible Pump with Prefilter

Adjustable Flow Submersible Pump

500-gph Submersible Pump

Pump Kit with Fountainhead

DETERMINING QUALITY

When selecting a pump, buy the best you can afford—even if it's a small one. The least expensive (and least durable) pumps have a shorter life span. Suitable only for relatively small water features, they also tend to clog more easily.

Moderate-Quality Pumps. Most moderately priced pumps have aluminum or cast-iron housings with a corrosion-resistant epoxy finish. They tend to be tougher and more impact-resistant than plastic pumps and come in a wide range of capacities. Aluminum-housed pumps are the less expensive of these two types and will corrode more quickly in salt water, chlorinated water, or water frequently treated with pond chemicals.

High-Quality Pumps. The most long-lasting (and most expensive) pumps are a combination of brass, bronze, and stainless-steel components and housings. These pumps will withstand a variety of water conditions—including salty and chlorinated water—and can handle continuous operation.

As a rule, they come only in larger sizes (capacities of 800 gallons per hour or higher). If you expect the pond to be a permanent feature in your yard, these pumps are well worth the extra initial cost.

Efficiency. Compare the pump's amp rating (or wattage, if it's given) to its output in gallons per hour. If two pumps have the same output, the one with the lower amp rating is more energy efficient. Many pumps come with a 6-foot cord, which won't work if local codes require the electrical outlet to be 6 or more feet away from the pond edge. You can usually order longer cords from the pump manufacturer as an option. Use only cords and plugs designed for use with the pump. Don't use extension cords unless they have a built-in ground-fault circuit interrupter (GFCI).

It's a good idea to order all the required fittings, valves, and pipes needed to operate your waterfall at the same time you order your pump, as well as other features such as a separate filter or fountain.

ELECTRICAL REQUIREMENTS

Your pond will require an underground electrical cable from your home's power source, not only for a pump but also for any underwater or perimeter lighting. In many municipalities, a licensed electrician must do the wiring. In all cases, check local codes for outdoor electrical requirements before you start.

For Outdoor Components. Make sure all outlets, wiring, and connections are designed for outdoor use. The National Electrical Code (NEC) does not, but local codes may, require that you put the cable in conduit. When a circuit is protected by GFCI as that for any pond must be, the NEC requires only that the cable be 12 inches deep. But consider burying the cable at least 18 inches deep to prevent it from being disturbed by spades, rototillers, or other gardening equipment.

For Pumps. Most small submersible pumps come with a waterproof cord that you simply plug into a three-prong electrical outlet near the pond site. You must protect this receptacle with GFCI in a weatherproof outlet box with a watertight-while-in-use lid. With some larger pumps (both submersible and external), you hard-wire the cord directly into a circuit, en-

closing the connection in a weatherproof junction box near the pond. The latter requires a GFCI breaker wired into the circuit, either in the main electrical panel or in a subpanel. In either case, you should wire a switch into the circuit so that you can control the pump and lights from inside the house. If possible, locate the outlet or junction box in an inconspicuous and protected area, such as under a deck or against the side of a building. It's best to put the pump and pond lights on a separate circuit, with their own breaker at the main service panel. If you tap into an existing branch circuit, make sure it can handle the additional load of the pump and any outdoor lighting.

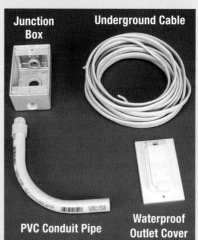

Every electrical component must be rated for either underground or outdoor (exterior) use.

Plumbing Your Moving-Water Feature

Plumbing for most pumps is relatively simple. Complexity will vary depending on the pump model, the length of the pipe between pump and outlet, and the number of water features the pump will operate.

Locate the pump as close as possible to your moving water feature. For submersible types, this usually means placing it at the base of the falls (or statue). Remember to raise submersible pumps a few inches off the pond bottom with a brick or a stone to prevent silt and other sediment from clogging the pump intake. For nonsubmersible types, you'll have to use your creativity to find a spot that's relatively close to the pond yet as unobtrusive as possible.

Tubing. Some pumps are sold with a length of inexpensive clear plastic tubing, which is a larger-diameter version of the type used for aquarium pumps. Although such tubing is adequate for short runs, it has several drawbacks. First, the thin walls of the tubing are easily crushed or kinked, so you can't bury it underground or make it conform to sharp bends. Conversely, if the tubing is exposed to sunlight, algae will build up on the inner walls, restricting flow. Because exposure to sunlight will eventually make the tubing brittle, it must be replaced periodically.

One solution is to run a short piece of flexible tubing from the pump to the edge of the pond, connecting it to a rigid PVC pipe that runs from there to the top catch basin at the head of the falls. Alternatively, you can use a higher-grade flexible tubing for the entire run, either a reinforced type or a special black-vinyl tubing sold by pump suppliers. Make sure the diameter of the tubing meets or exceeds the size recommended for your pump model because a smaller diameter will restrict water flow.

Plumbing Waterfalls. When plumbing the waterfall, keep sharp bends and right-angle pipe junctions to a minimum, as these tend to restrict flow. Lay the outlet tube along the ground as close as possible to the edge of the watercourse. Camouflage the outlet tube where it runs between the pond and the top of the watercourse with rocks, plants, or mulch. It's best not to mortar it permanently behind your landscape rocks because you'll need easy access to deal with any future maintenance problems.

Water Pressure. When you run the end of the outlet hose or pipe into the top of the watercourse, you may find that the water pressure produces a strong jet, causing water to splash outside the catch basin. If this happens, either run the hose under a small pile of rocks in the catch basin, or fit a short section of larger perforated pipe or hose over the end of the outlet to break the force.

You can camouflage plumbing and electrical outlets with small rocks around your pond.

Fittings

Pump suppliers offer a wide range of fittings and adapters to connect pumps to various water features. Use nontoxic plastic valves and fittings wherever possible; brass and other metal fittings can corrode with time and may be toxic to fish. Most fittings for flexible plastic tubing are a barbed, push-fit type; when using these fittings, install hose clamps at all connections to prevent leaks. Fittings and connections for rigid PVC pipe are either screwed on or welded on using PVC cement. Some pumps require brass fittings on the pump discharge, which may or may not include a flow-control valve. Depending on the pump design, you may need to install an adapter fitting so that you can attach flexible tubing or rigid PVC pipe.

If you add a T-fitting with a diverter valve to your pump discharge, as shown in the drawing below, you will be able to operate two water features, such as a fountain and a waterfall, at the same time. However, you can accomplish the same result by installing a plain T-fitting plus an in-line flow-control valve in the shorter of the two pipe runs. Both types of fittings will allow you to regulate the amount of water that is supplied to each feature.

If you don't install a diverter or flow-control valve, the pumped water will take the path of least resistance (i.e., the shorter pipe run). The result will be either too little flow to operate one feature or too much flow to the other, or both. The pump should have enough capacity to operate all attached features.

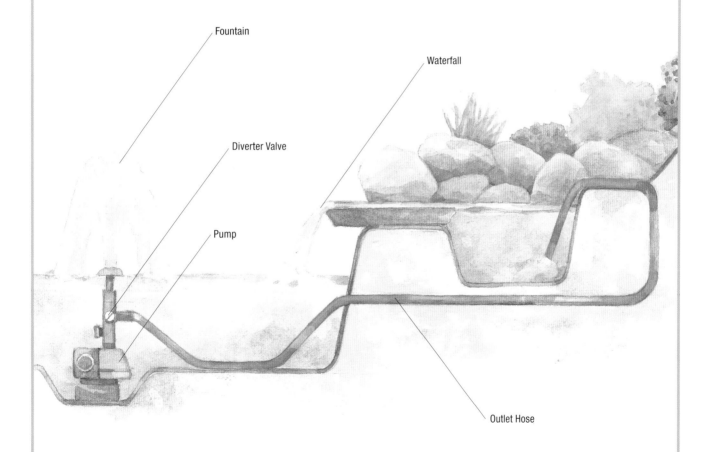

The right fittings and valves, in this case a T-fitting and a diverter valve, let you run several water features simultaneously.

Purchase a pump for your waterfall that is a bit more powerful than you think you'll need. You can always restrict the flow.

Good Planning. As with all aspects of your pond design, careful planning is paramount. If you buy a pump with the intent of operating only one water feature and decide later that you would like to add more, you will face the choice of either buying a new, larger-capacity pump to run all the features simultaneously, or buying a second pump. The latter choice would allow you to power them independently (so that you can run your waterfall but not your fountain and vice versa), but may require additional electrical work or the use of an outlet that was originally planned for lighting. Water garden suppliers report that return customers inevitably want larger ponds with additional features. Thus your best bet may be to think big in the beginning and plan for all future contingencies.

Maintain Pond Levels Automatically with a Float Valve

Because ponds and fountains recirculate water, you don't need to run a water line directly into the pond or fountain. Just make sure there's an outdoor faucet nearby so you can add water to the pond from a garden hose. Small ponds in particular may require topping off every week or so during the hottest months of the year. To eliminate this chore, install a float valve. This device floats on the water. When the water level drops, the float lowers, opening a valve that allows more water to be fed into the pond through a pipe or tubing connected to a nearby faucet. These inexpensive setups are available through water-gardening catalog suppliers and nurseries that carry water-garden accessories.

Simple ball-cock valves, such as those used in toilet tanks, will also work. These are larger than float valves, however, and therefore harder to disguise.

An inexpensive float valve can be clamped to a short steel rod mortared between stones just below the waterline. The valve is connected to the main water supply with a ¼-inch-diameter copper or plastic tube. When installing such a system, make sure there's no chance of pond water siphoning back into the water supply and contaminating your drinking water with fish waste and other toxic substances. Most building codes require some form of backflow preventer (also called anti-siphon device).

Inexpensive types screw onto a faucet (just be careful to install it facing the right direction). For added protection, install a check valve (almost as inexpensive) on the faucet before you install the backflow preventer.

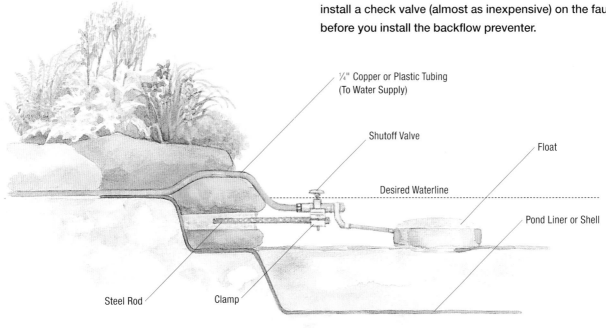

¼" Copper or Plastic Tubing (To Water Supply)

Shutoff Valve

Float

Desired Waterline

Pond Liner or Shell

Steel Rod

Clamp

Installing a diverter valve will allow you to create separate effects such as the small waterfalls shown here.

Installing a Submersible Pump

DIFFICULTY LEVEL: EASY

Submersible pumps add movement and sound to a water garden. They're very easy to install and relatively uncomplicated to maintain. If the pump will be used only for filtration, place the submersible pump/filter in your sump or in the deepest part of the pond. Run the outlet tube to the far end of the pond for better circulation. If the pump will be feeding water to a falls or fountain, locate the pump as close as possible to the foot of the falls or the fountain. Plumbing connections at the outlet hose (or pipe) must be high quality and the necessary electrical connections must meet required electrical codes. Raise the pump several inches off the pond bottom to prevent frequent filter clogging.

Tools and Materials: submersible pump/filter kit; outlet hose & fittings (sufficient length from pump to top pool of falls); electrical outlet accessibility; platform material (to raise pump off pond floor); material (stone, gravel) to hide lines and cables

Basic Installation Tips

- Place pump on a brick at the bottom of the pond.
- Keep bends and right angles in tubing to a minimum to maintain a steady, even flow.
- Disguise all hoses and electrical lines under mulch or rocks.

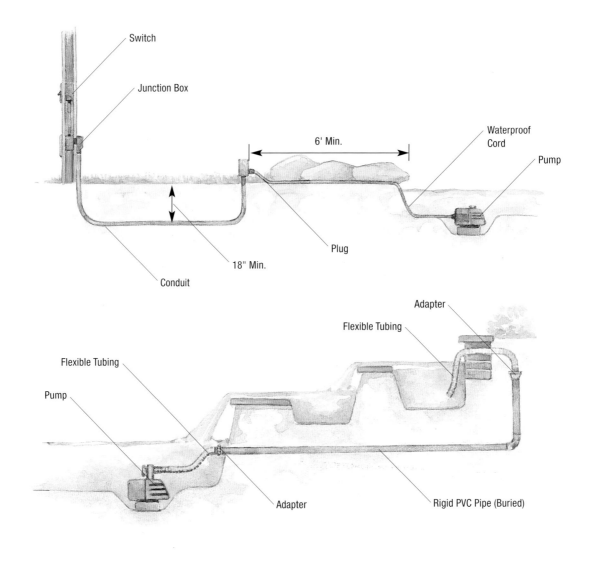

A narrow stream splashes over a stone ornament, creating a spray as it empties into this pond.

how to

Install a Lined Watercourse

DIFFICULTY LEVEL: CHALLENGING

If you're using a flexible plastic or rubber liner for your pond, it's easiest to excavate for the watercourse and install its liner at the same time. You can, however, also add a lined watercourse to an existing pond with any material at a later time.

Tools and Materials: Flour, nontoxic spray paint, or stakes and string (for marking outlines); shovel; tamper for compacting soil (or a scrap of 2x6 nailed to the end of a long 2x4); spirit level; long, straight 2x4 (for check-ing level of large areas); concrete blocks (optional, to provide increased support for outer edges and/or waterfall lip); pump, tubing, and connecting fixtures; adhesive or tape for liner joints (optional); heavy-duty scissors or utility knife for cutting liner and underlayment; underlayment; liner; 3-inch or longer nails (to hold liner in position); edging material such as rocks; mortar (optional, for securing stones along edges); landscaping materials (rocks, plants); watering can or hose

1 Grade the Site. If you're working on flat ground, you may want to rough out the shape, left, of your watercourse before you begin changing the grade. Then build up a berm of compacted soil next to the pond at your waterfall location (this is a good way to make use of the soil excavated from the pond). Make the berm wide enough to accommodate the watercourse, with sufficient space around the perimeter for rocks, plants, and other landscaping materials. Tamp the soil firmly to compact it. Slope the sides gently away from the proposed excavation to prevent rain from washing dirt into the watercourse. Avoid steeply sloped mounds, which not only look unnatural but will be more prone to soil erosion. If you are working on a naturally sloping site, especially one that is very rocky, it will dictate the shape of your watercourse to a great extent. Now working on your slope—natural or otherwise—cut a series of level terraces to create what looks like a staircase. Each terrace will serve as a catch basin for your waterfall or stream. For a stream, you will have long steps with short risers; for a steep waterfall, you will have shorter steps with taller risers. Make each step large enough to accommodate rocks or other edging material or concrete supporting blocks if you are using them, right.

2 Creating Catch Basins. You want each one of your stair steps to hold water even when the pump is turned off. Things will always look natural as a result. There are several ways you can accomplish this. If you are using concrete block supports, which is essential when you are working with either sandy or flinty soil, they will form the sides of your catch basin. (They will look straight and artificial, but you will make them look natural later by artful placement of rocks on top of and around them). Dig your terrace and shape it so that it slopes backward slightly, away from the pond.

If you are working with clay soil that packs solidly you may not need concrete blocks. Instead, you can excavate a catch basin in the middle of each stair, leaving a ledge of earth on which to place your edging stones. (Even if you have clay soil, however, the concrete blocks are a good idea if you are edging your stream with large, heavy boulders.) If the basin is large enough, you may want to cut another ledge around the perimeter in which to set partially submerged boulders. But remember that the finished watercourse will look smaller than the excavated holes once the rocks or other edging materials are in place along the sides.

The catch basins are mini versions of the main pond, so follow the procedures outlined in steps 1 through 7 on pages 70–71 to dig and level the basins. As with your pond, your stream should be level across its width. To make sure that it is, use a spirit level placed on top of a 2x4.

Now on the leading edge (the edge that is the closest to the pond) of your terrace or catch basin, you need to provide a stable base for the waterfall lip. Do this by creating a berm that is at least 12 in. wide. You can use well-compacted soil, but again, when you are dealing with loose or sandy soil, use concrete blocks or poured concrete for a firmer base.

3 Install the Tubing and Pump. Position your pump at the foot of the lowest falls. (Elevate it on a brick or a flat stone; raising it a few inches off the bottom will keep sediment from clogging the pump intake.) If your pump isn't a submersible type, put it close to the base of the falls. Run the pipe or tubing, left, from the pump alongside the watercourse from the point where it exits the pond to the top catch basin or head of the falls. (For more information about choosing and installing pumps, see pages 90–102.) All fittings must go together securely so that no leaks occur, right.

Continued on next page.

Install a Lined Watercourse (cont'd)

4 **Position the Liners.** If you're using underlayment, position it first, right. If you're using a single liner for the pond and watercourse, drape the liner over the entire excavation and over the supporting concrete blocks if you have used them, opposite top. Then slowly fill the pond with water to hold the liner in place, allowing the liner to settle before filling the watercourse.

If you're using separate pieces of liner, start by fitting the liner for the main pond, allowing enough overlap at the waterfall end to extend up and over the first waterfall lip. Cut and fit the next piece of liner in the lowest catch basin, providing at least 12 in. of overlap with the main-pond liner. Overlap the liners for additional catch basins in the same manner.

For additional protection against leaks, you

5 **Position the Edging Stones.** Position the overhanging rocks or other edging materials, left, across the waterfall lip, inset, and on either side of it. For a more natural effect, place stones behind the waterfall beneath the lip to hide the liner. The top surface of the lip stones should be just slightly below the water level of the stream or basin, above left, so that water will flow from one basin to the next without overflowing the banks. The last major stone to be laid is the one on the exit spillway, above right. The type of stone and its positioning will determine the pattern of the waterfall entering the pond.

can join adjacent liner sections with a special liner adhesive or tape available from your supplier, although with sufficient overlap this is not necessary.

Next, it's important to check for level. Use a hose to fill the catch basin(s) with water to settle the liner in place, as you did for the pond.

Check for leaks, and note the water level around the rim of each basin. If you see any high or low spots, remove or add soil beneath the liner to level the basin.

Then, to keep the liner in place while you add edging material around the water feature, push large nails through the liner into the ground every foot or so around the overlapping edges. (Note: you do not have to remove the nails later.)

Alternately, you can use several large stones to keep the liner positioned until you have installed all your edging.

6 **Fine-tune the Waterfall.** Now install your pump. (See "Installing a Submersible Pump" on page 102.) Turn on the pump and notice how water flows over the lip; adjust the height and angle of the stones, if necessary, to provide a pleasing cascade. When you're satisfied with the results, place your remaining stones along the edge of each basin, on top of your concrete blocks or along the ledge you've shaped around the perimeter of each basin or along the stream banks. Hide the liner edges with the edging rocks, or bury it with soil. Mortaring the rocks in place prevents them from slipping into the watercourse. You can place more stones in the watercourse to alter the flow pattern, but avoid using gravel in the streambed because it will become clogged with algae and silt.

Last, add landscaping. If you're building a natural-looking watercourse, arrange additional rocks on and around the mound for the waterfall and near the stream. Use boulders, medium-size rocks, and small pebbles to avoid making the waterfall area look like a pile of rocks. Make planting pockets between stones for installing low shrubs, grasses, ground covers, and other plants.

Install a Preformed Watercourse

DIFFICULTY LEVEL: MODERATE

Just as with a lined watercourse, you can install a preformed watercourse at the same time as your pond or you can add it later. If you're planning to install more than one unit, see the instructions in step 5 before beginning your project.

Tools & Materials:
preformed watercourse; pump, tubing, and connecting fixtures; flour, nontoxic spray paint, or stakes; landscaping materials (rocks, plants); concrete blocks (optional), mortar (optional); shovel, fine sand, ruler (to measure sand depth); tamper for compacting soil; cement and mixing equipment (only for precast stone and cement units); spirit level and long, straight 2x4

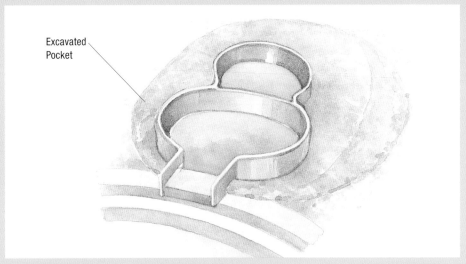

Excavated Pocket

1 Grade the Site. If you're working with a natural slope above the pond, excavate a pocket in which to place the watercourse. On flat ground, build up a berm of firm soil to support the shell at the appropriate height above the pond. The sides of the berm should slope gently away from the watercourse and be wide enough to accommodate rocks or other materials used to disguise the edges. Firmly tamp the built-up soil. Test soil firmness to see that the watercourse won't sink unevenly into it. Next, set the preformed watercourse in position on top of the mound and mark its outline on the ground with flour, nontoxic spray paint, or a series of short stakes.

Plantings will blend the watercourse into the landscape.

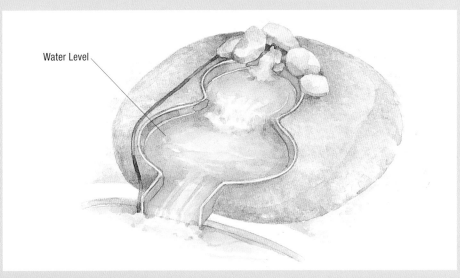

Water Level

4 Test the Watercourse. Fill the unit with water and check the water level around the rim to make sure the unit remained level during the backfilling. If you haven't already done so, install the pump; attach the outlet tubing to it; and fill the main pond. Then pump water down the course. The water should flow evenly over the lip and any built-in cascades at a level of about 1 in. below the rim. Adjust the pump flow rate if necessary.

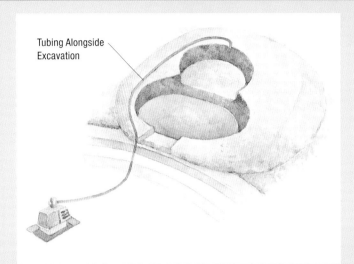

Tubing Alongside
Excavation

2 **Dig the Hole.** Dig a hole to match the size and shape of your preformed watercourse unit. Tamp the soil firmly to keep the sides and bottom from bending and warping when filled with water. If your soil is loose or sandy, create extra support with an encircling collar of concrete blocks. (See "Extra Support for Pond Foundations" on page 78.) Lay the unit in place to see if it fits. If not, lift it out and either add or remove soil as necessary.

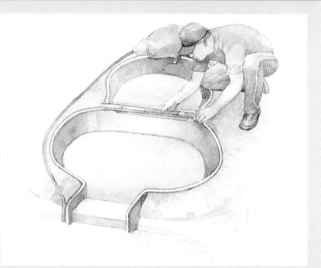

3 **Place the Watercourse.** Position the lip over the pond edge. Use a spirit level to make sure basins are level in all directions. Backfill around the edges (and between concrete blocks if you used them) with fine sand to a height of 1 to 2 in. below the outside edge of the shell, or as recommended by the manufacturer. Run the pipe-outlet tubing into the top basin. Secure it at the top with rocks, or as specified by the manufacturer.

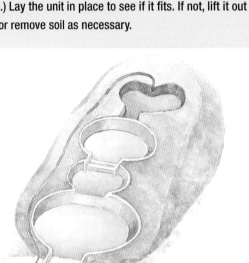

5 **Place any Additional Units.** If you'll be installing additional sections of watercourse, follow steps 1 through 3. Then, after installing and leveling each one, you'll need to test them by filling all of them with water and allowing the water to run down the rest of the course (step 4). Make any needed adjustments at this time to the height and position of the unit. Make sure each unit is firmly positioned before installing the one above it.

6 **Add Landscaping.** Install edging material above ground level. If water runoff is heavy, mortar stones for a better seal. Dense planting will help prevent erosion and deter water pollution. Turn on the pump. Position the pump outlet pipe or tubing at the top of the watercourse and disguise it with rocks or plants. Run the watercourse continuously for 48 hours; then recheck it for settling and readjust the flow or the position of the hose if necessary.

CHAPTER 6

Fountains & Light

The soothing sound and delightful vision of water in motion is an excellent reason for incorporating a fountain into your garden. Added to a pond, it breaks water's reflected light into shimmering patterns. If you plan your fountain as you design your pond, you can best take advantage of your garden's exposure to capture sunlight in the spraying water. As a practical benefit, a fountain will enhance the life within your pond by adding oxygen to the water.

So Many Choices

You can find a fountain that's right for just about every type of garden design. To decide which type is best for you, consider not only sound, style, and size, but also the relationship to other landscape elements. If the fountain will be in your pond, you'll also need to keep in mind its effect on your plants and fish.

Sound is one of the greatest benefits of a fountain, adding music to your landscape and masking traffic and other noises. The effect can range from the creeklike burble of a low geyser to the high musical tinkle of a fine spray to the deeper, rainy-day resonance of a tall water column. Think about which type of sound will bring you the most enjoyment. Even on the smallest patio or in the tiniest yard, you can enjoy the soothing sounds of a fountain by installing a self-contained unit, a wall fountain that spills into a small basin, or a cobblestone reservoir.

SPRAY OR STATUARY FOUNTAINS?

Choose a style that suits your landscape. Fountains of all styles come in two basic types: spray fountains (essentially just water nozzles, or jets, that spray water in different patterns) and statuary fountains, which spray water from a sculpture or figure of some type. Save the more elaborate spray patterns, and certainly fountains that incorporate classical statuary, for a formal design. In a pond that's informal but not meant to mimic nature, a simple spout or geyser will look the most appropriate. As a rule, fountains will look out of place in a wildlife pond, unless you choose a simple model that bubbles up from the surface like a natural spring.

A fountain should suit the style of your garden and your house. This one with its classical motifs, such as the acanthus leaves, blends well with the formal style of the home's architecture.

A geyser, spouting from the center, adds interest to a water feature.

Almost any spray-type fountain works with a modern-style home and pond; for statuary, look for a contemporary sculpture. For a bungalow or a farmhouse, an old water pump is the perfect accessory for a small pond or basin.

ENVIRONMENTAL CONSIDERATIONS

Also consider the overall shape of your pond. With a square or circular pond, fountains typically look best in the middle. If your pool is rectangular, you may want to install a line of pipes down the center spraying to the sides.

Look around and notice the shape of existing landscape elements, or envision shrubs or other large features you plan to add. You can complement the shape of nearby plants or garden furniture by choosing fountains that have vertical or rounded spray shapes, for example.

A modest-size statuary fountain graces a small pond which, together with flowering plantings, softens a garden's stone wall.

Wind Strength. Wind is also a factor that will affect the style of fountain that will work best in your garden. If you have a windy site, fountains that create a fine spray of droplets, or those that produce a thin film of water, such as a bell fountain, are unsuitable, as their pattern or symmetry will often be disturbed. If this is your situation, look for a geyser style that shoots up a heavy column of water.

Water Disturbance. If you want to grow floating or marginal plants, keep in mind how much the fountain will disturb the water surface of your pond. Water lilies and many other pond flora can't tolerate splashing or moving water; they'll need to be kept to the edge of the pond if you choose a tall, exuberant style of fountain. A low water column or the semispherical bell pattern will disturb the surface less than other designs would. If fish are more important to you than plants, however, choose a splashier fountain for more aeration.

Pond Size. The size of your pond will limit the size of your fountain. In a totally sheltered, windless garden, a fountain jet could be as high as the pond is wide, but this is a rare condition. The more usual guideline is to make the height of your fountain no more than half the width or diameter of your pond to avoid drenching pondside benches, light fixtures, decks or patios, or you and your guests. Also, if the spray is too large for the size of the pond, the resulting water evaporation will lower the pond's water level.

Spray-Fountain Patterns

Geyser and Tulip

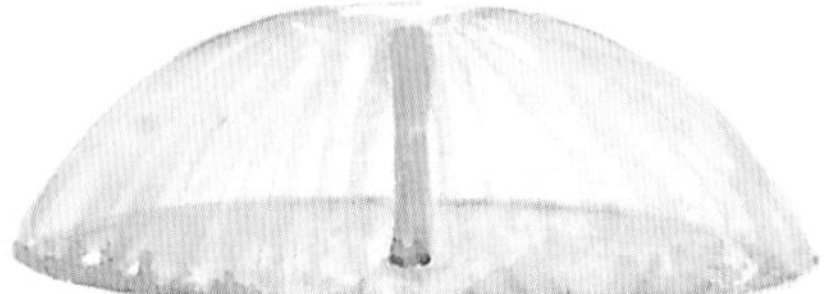

Bell

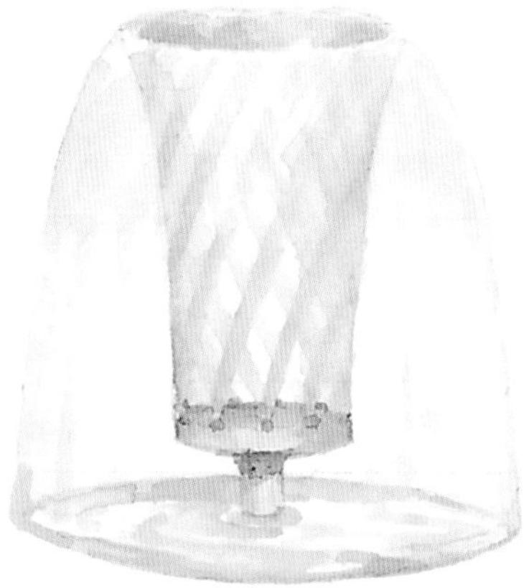

Inverted Cone

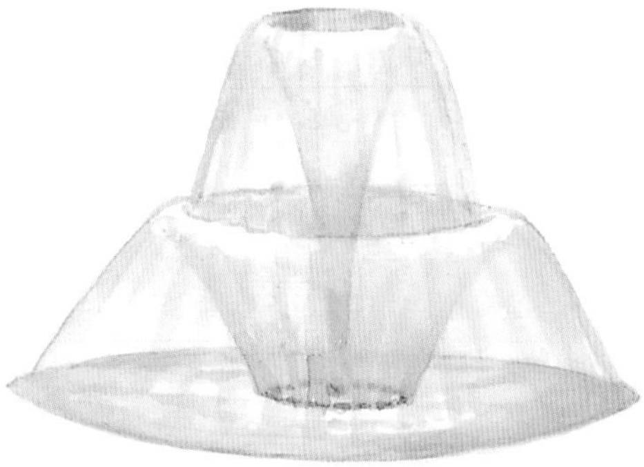

Double-Tier

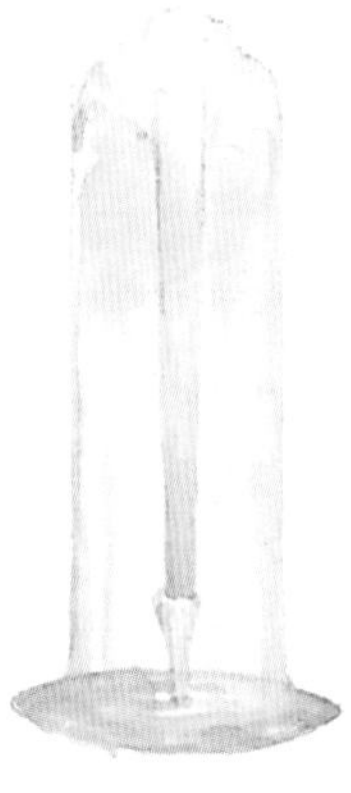

Geyser

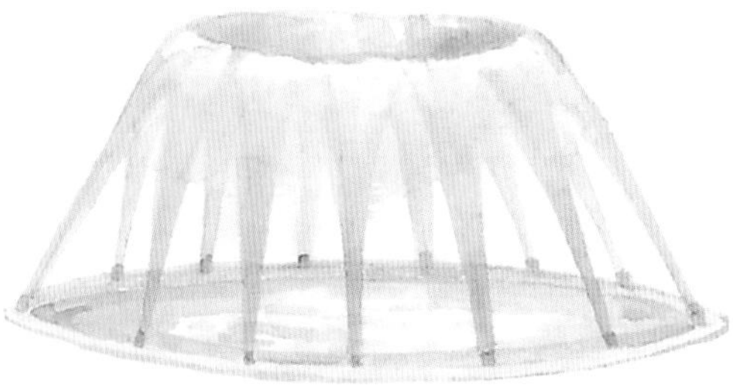

Ring

In this large naturalistic pond, two spray fountains look like natural geysers between the rocks.

Spray Fountains

A spray fountain consists of a nozzle or ring attached to the outlet pipe of a pump at or above the pond's water level. The simplest style is a length of vertical pipe, run to a level just under the water surface, which provides a natural-looking geyser effect. Adding a narrow nozzle to the pipe will give you a taller, more dramatic geyser. Because geysers introduce air bubbles into the spray, they are especially good for aerating the water. (But size and place them carefully to avoid stirring up silt and sediment in the pond, producing cloudy water.) To be visually effective, high, showy geysers require powerful, large-capacity pumps.

Most spray fountains come as complete kits. Such kits include a molded plastic nozzle, the right-size pump, various fittings for installation, and a flow-control valve which allows you to adjust spray height. Some kits contain several spray heads to change patterns. Others come with a tee fitting and diverter, which you'll need to attach a second feature, such as a waterfall or filter. Before you assemble any of the kit components or other features, be sure that your pump has the power for these add-ons.

You can also purchase a floating fountain that is very

FAR EAST FOUNTAINS

In a Japanese-style garden, you can create a simple bamboo spill fountain or the more complicated *shishi odoshi* (stag scarer). The simple bamboo fountain can be displayed in concert with a *tsukubai*, a basinlike stone used for washing one's hands and face in preparation for the Japanese tea ceremony. Set the stone basin on rocks so that water spills into it from the pipe and then spills over the edge onto the rocks before being recirculated. Instead of drawing its water from a reservoir, a shishi odoshi could substitute for a waterfall in a small stream; this device was originally used as a noisemaker to keep deer and other animals out of the garden. You can buy these deer chaser features ready-made.

Instead of hooking your pump to a pipe and nozzle, attach the pump outlet to rubber tubing, and run the tubing through a bamboo pole. Be sure to hollow out all the bamboo "joints" so that the tubing will pass through. (You may have to split the cane and glue it back together.) To join this vertical bamboo pipe and your spout at a slightly downward-facing angle, make an elbow joint with a block of wood or a short section of bamboo. Working from both sides, use a drill to create the angle.

To make the rocking stag-scarer fountain, hollow out a second length of bamboo. Cut one end at an angle, and plug the other end solidly so that the bamboo will hold water. Mount this on a horizontal arm below the first water outlet, either through a hole in your first vertical delivery pipe or on its own support in front of the upper pipe. Your goal is for the upper pipe to slowly feed into the lip of the lower pipe. When the upper half of the moving pipe fills, it will tip down, spilling out the water; once empty, it will bounce back to its original position. Adjust the water flow so that the rocking pipe fills and empties rhythmically. To get the noise-making effect, position a stone under the closed end of the bamboo; the pipe will strike it when it returns to its original position.

This stag scarer fountain sends water through two bamboo pipes from an underground reservoir.

suitable for short-term or periodic use. These relatively inexpensive spray fountains are designed with a built-in nozzle that attaches to an existing pump without plumbing (if your pump has an unused discharge valve).

Higher-quality nozzles can be disassembled to make cleaning the jet holes easier; lesser-quality nozzles are more difficult to clean. Brass nozzles are generally used for larger water displays, but they're more expensive than plastic. Keep in mind that nozzles with small holes clog easily and will require frequent cleaning. (Cleaning isn't a big production—just disassemble the nozzle, and hose it off or brush it with an old toothbrush.) Your nozzle will be less likely to clog if your pond also has a mechanical filter.

Connecting a Spray Fountain

DIFFICULTY LEVEL: EASY

Installation is relatively simple but varies depending on the type of fountain, pump, and fittings. The easiest route to a spray fountain is to buy a complete kit and follow the instructions given for its components. The fittings either push or screw together, so the fountain can be easily assembled in just a few minutes.

Tools and Materials: Saw (to cut PVC pipe); adjustable wrench; necessary adapters; PVC pipe (cut to length); elbow fitting (for side discharge pumps); prefilter or filter screen (if necessary); bricks or prop material.

Installation. On most submersible pumps designed for fountains, the water outlet is on top. This conveniently allows you to attach the rigid vertical PVC discharge pipe directly to the outlet. (You may need an adapter fitting on some units.) Cut the pipe to extend the required distance above the water level (typically 4 to 6 inches), and then simply attach the spray nozzle.

For pumps with a side discharge, you'll need to install an elbow fitting. To prevent the nozzle from clogging, buy a special prefilter or filter screen that attaches to the pump inlet. Some units combine the pump and filter in a single housing. The filter should be easily accessible for routine cleaning.

Once you've attached the fittings and spray nozzle according to the manufacturer's instructions, place the pump in the pond on a flat, level surface such as a short stack of bricks. (Raising the pump off the bottom lessens the chances that it will get clogged with debris.) Both pump and discharge pipe must be firmly supported, so the pipe remains perfectly vertical.

If the unit has a tendency to tip or to move out of position once it's running, place a few bricks along the sides of the pump to hold it in place. (If it still tips, try a brick on top for more weight.) Follow the guidelines given in "Electrical Requirements" on page 95 to provide the appropriate electrical connection for the pump.

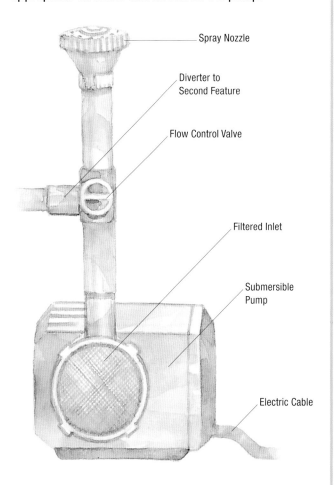

Spray Nozzle

Diverter to Second Feature

Flow Control Valve

Filtered Inlet

Submersible Pump

Electric Cable

Many are sold as kits. When buying a pump separately, be sure it's powerful enough for the job.

Water cascades over the sides of this ceramic pot and into a small pond filled with cobblestones and grass.

How to Build a Cobblestone Reservoir

Here is a natural water feature that installs easily and requires no pond. It can be placed almost anywhere.

Tools and Materials: Shovel; scissors; spirit level; large plastic bucket, tub, or garbage pail reservoir; galvanized wire mesh (at least 5 inches larger than the diameter of the reservoir); submersible pump; foaming gusher or bubbler spray-fountain kit; flexible pond liner (polyethylene is sturdy enough); small, smooth pebbles or river rock (approx. 2 to 4 inches in diameter, or larger than the wire mesh)

Installation. This simple water feature gives the illusion of a natural spring or geyser welling up from the earth and returning to it. It's a good stand-alone fountain if you don't want the hassle of maintaining a large pond. Even better, it makes a safe water feature for families with toddlers and small children.

The reservoir can go in a lawn or a flower bed or be sunk in a flagstone terrace. It can be as small as a dinner plate or a garden centerpiece 4 feet or more across; the vertical gusher fountains or bubblers usually used with these features can be adjusted to shoot water from 3 to 24 inches or higher, depending on the size pump you attach to them. Seek the advice of your water-garden supplier if you have any questions about buying the pump and fountain to match the desired size of your reservoir. As with any fountain, you need to have easy access to electrical power with a ground-fault circuit interrupter, or GFCI. (See page 95.)

Begin the installation by digging a hole in which to place the fountain assembly. You'll need a hole slightly larger than your plastic bucket or tub. Lower the bucket into the hole, and use a carpenter's level to make sure it is straight. Backfill the hole with soil, and create a bowl shape around it, sloping up.

Next, place the liner over the reservoir, and push the material down slightly into the bucket. Using scissors, cut a hole that's big enough to allow you to lower the pump to the bottom of the reservoir. Make sure the edges of the liner slope down toward the bucket; the liner needs to collect water from your fountain and return it to the bucket. Center the wire mesh over the lined reservoir, cutting a hole in the mesh large enough for the vertical pipe that connects to your fountain. Trim the pipe if needed so that it will be hidden by your stones.

To test the assembly, fill the bucket with water. Arrange stones around the fountain. A fountain kit with a flow adjuster will allow you to experiment with higher and lower geyser settings. When you are satisfied with the effect, arrange stones out to the edge of your liner, trimming off its corners.

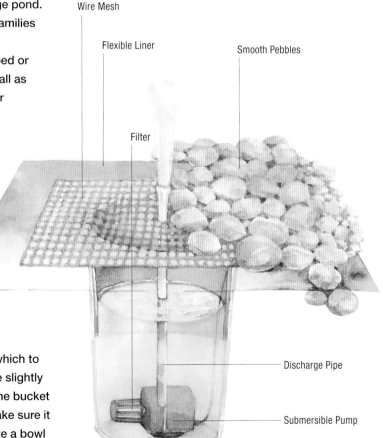

Wire Mesh

Flexible Liner

Smooth Pebbles

Filter

Discharge Pipe

Submersible Pump

This cobblestone reservoir is easy to assemble. It requires no pond and can be placed practically anywhere. Select smooth, matched stones bigger than the holes in the wire mesh.

A pair of "lotus" fountains offers a low burble of water that bubbles up from the center of each "flower" in this pond.

Statuary Fountains

Statuary fountains run the gamut of designs from classical Greek figures and wall-mounted gargoyles to sleek modern art forms and whimsical spouting frogs or fish. Most of those sold at garden and patio suppliers are precast concrete and have a variety of surface finishes to simulate other materials, such as stone, alabaster, or bronze. Some suppliers also carry modern sculpture fountains of copper, brass, or bronze; most dealers can expand their offerings by ordering what you want from wholesale catalogs. In the past, fountain statuary was often made of lead. If you find one of these relics, be warned that lead can be toxic to fish and other aquatic creatures.

Statuary fountains are commonly sold as separate units, designed to be installed in the pond or next to it. You need to buy a pump to install with them, and a precast pedestal of the appropriate height on which to mount them. Other statuary fountains are complete, self-contained units with precast reservoir bowls and integrated, preplumbed pump/filter systems. These are designed to be stand-alone water features. (Some are small enough to fit on a tabletop.)

INSTALLING A STATUARY FOUNTAIN

Most statuary fountains come with installation instructions. Use these in combination with the guidelines that follow to install the unit you've chosen. As with any moving water feature, you'll appreciate being able to turn the fountain on and off from indoors, so plug it into an outlet with an indoor switch. (See page 95 for guidelines on electrical installations.)

Self-Contained Fountains. This type of fountain includes a pump, a power cord, and all fittings. Typically, a small submersible pump sits in the statue pedestal, which sits in a reservoir bowl. Water spills from the fountain into the reservoir bowl, where it gets pumped back to the top. Units such as these can be placed anywhere within reach of a power supply. The pump cord runs from an overflow area inside the pedestal, down through a tube in the hollow base. Make sure the design of the unit you buy provides some way to gain access to the pump for cleaning and maintenance.

To install the fountain, simply set it on a sturdy, level base; fill it with water; and plug it in. Check the water level frequently and refill the reservoir when needed; water can evaporate quickly from these shallow reservoirs. Follow the manufacturer's recommendations for regular care.

Designs can be based on animals, characters from mythology, abstract sculpture, and the like.

Wall Fountains

A wall fountain usually spills water through statuary—such as a mask or a decorative plaque—into a basin that hides a small pump. The statuary can be terra-cotta, plastic, fiberglass, cast concrete (often designed to mimic terra-cotta or stone), or metal. A stone water feature will be more expensive than one made of these other materials. Stone and cast-concrete wall fountains require a wall strong enough to support their weight, as well as sturdy, well-secured mounting hardware.

Wall fountains look best if the return pipe doesn't show. Thus the best place for these fountains is a freestanding wall that allows you to run the plumbing behind it. However, this is rarely practical for many of the situations where these small features work best, such as on a townhouse patio. Alternatives include hiding the tubing with vines or chiseling a vertical niche down the wall in which to run the tubing and then mortaring over it.

A more satisfactory option is to build out the wall using similar material—a new line of bricks, for instance, or an enclosure covered with clapboards to match your home's siding. Mount the fountain on the new surface, and run the pipe behind it.

If the fountain doesn't come with its own basin, homemade options range from building an elaborate brick or concrete reservoir to recycling a half barrel or an old sink or trough. Don't make the catch basin too small or rapid evaporation will necessitate frequent topping off. To keep splashing to a minimum, mount the fountain no higher above the catch basin than the diameter of the basin.

These focal points may or may not include ponds and can be classical or contemporary in style.

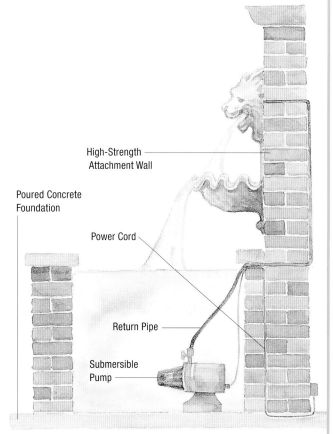

High-Strength
Attachment Wall

Poured Concrete
Foundation

Power Cord

Return Pipe

Submersible
Pump

Mount the fountain no higher above the catch basin than the diameter of the basin.

In-Pond Statuary

The mechanics of installing fountain statuary in the pond are relatively straightforward. The hardest task is dealing with the weight of the statue. If it and its pedestal weigh more than 100 pounds, a concrete footing is needed to support them before installing a flexible liner or preformed pond. On top of the liner or shell, mount the statue on a hollow in-pond pedestal. Or build your own pedestal with mortared bricks, stones, or other masonry. Then use flexible tubing to connect the pump to a supply pipe that projects from the statue's base.

The footing under the pond shell or liner should be a 4-inch-thick concrete subbase, a few inches wider and longer than the statue base or pedestal. If you forego a footing, the statue's weight may crack the rigid pond shell or tear the flexible pond liner. The footing must be smooth and level to give stable support; unless you have experience pouring concrete, hire a good contractor. For lighter statues, all you

need to do is compact the soil firmly under the statue location with a tamper before installing the shell or liner. If you are unsure how firmly compacted the soil is, rent a powered compactor or a roller for this purpose. Once the shell or liner is installed, you're ready for the next step. (See pages 64-85 for installing shells and liners.)

Protect flexible liners with a small piece of liner underlayment under your pedestal. If you've purchased a pedestal, place it in the pond. If you haven't, build a pedestal by mortaring bricks or stones. Leave an opening near the bottom of the pedestal through which to run tubing from the pump to the statue. Use a spirit level to check your work as you build up the height of the pedestal, as the top needs to be absolutely level.

(If you doubt your handiwork or are installing a valuable statue, hire an experienced contractor.) To facilitate cleaning and other maintenance chores, leave the pump outside the pedestal. Situate it as close to the pedestal as possible, and then run flexible tubing from the pump up through the pedestal into the statue. Be sure that you allow enough tubing at the top to connect easily to the statue.

With a helper, move the statue into position on the pedestal. While your helper tilts the statue slightly, reach underneath to make the connection between the pump outlet tubing and the pipe projecting from the statue's base. (You may need an adapter fitting. Check before you have the statue in place.) Secure the connection with a hose clamp, and then rest the statue in its final position. Don't mortar or otherwise attach the statue to the pedestal—you may need to replace the outlet tubing later.

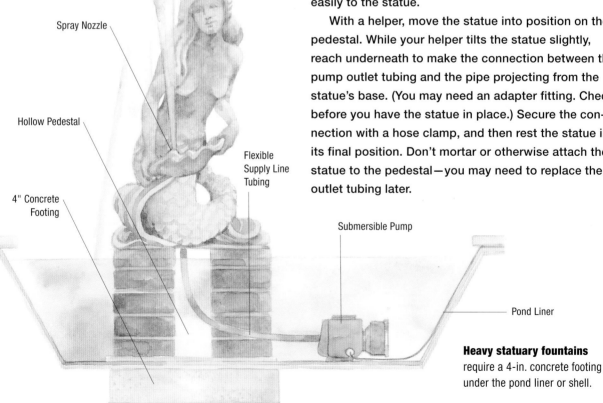

Fountain Statuary

Spray Nozzle

Hollow Pedestal

4" Concrete Footing

Flexible Supply Line Tubing

Submersible Pump

Pond Liner

Heavy statuary fountains require a 4-in. concrete footing under the pond liner or shell.

Heavy statues and pedestals—those 100 pounds and over—require a concrete footing for support.

Lighting

When you consider ways to illuminate your pond at night, underwater lights may seem like the obvious choice, and some fountain systems come equipped with them. When well placed in clear water, underwater lights can highlight water lilies, waterfalls, and other features. But poorly placed underwater lights create glare. They also eliminate pond reflections of the moon or of garden features you highlight with aboveground lights.

A few lights well positioned in the landscape around a water feature are generally more effective than underwater lights. You can create dramatic nighttime reflections by directing hidden, ground-level spotlights up toward surrounding trees or tall shrubs. Waterfalls or fountains will sparkle when you direct lights toward them from the pond edges. Keep it simple: generally, a few well-placed spotlights or accent lights will produce a more desirable effect than strong floodlights that light up the entire yard. Spend time moving the light fixtures around from one location to another until you are satisfied.

Consider using lighting for safety reasons, like illuminating walkways or steps to the pond. Low-level, ornamental downlighting fixtures placed knee-high at intervals along the borders of a walk or attached to step railings provide enough illumination to define walkways without over-lighting.

Carefully selecting sites for aboveground light fixtures lets you highlight rocks, waterfalls, trees, and pondside planting areas to create extra excitement.

Fixture Kit

Clear or Colored Lens Choices

Position Fixture to Highlight a Specific Pond Feature

Specially Sealed Underwater Fixture

A number of lighting suppliers now offer fixture kits. If you select a low-voltage (12-volt) system, you will have a lighting arrangement that is less expensive to buy and easier to install than a standard 120-volt system.

Lighting the way to your pond invites strolls at any time and helps ensure the safety of visitors.

FIXTURE TYPES

You can choose from two basic systems for your lighting fixtures: standard 120-volt systems and low-voltage (12-volt) systems. Standard-voltage systems run directly on household current; 12-volt systems require a transformer (to reduce the voltage), which is connected to a 120-volt power source. As a rule, 12-volt systems are much safer and easier to install than standard systems. The 12-volt fixtures and bulbs are also much less expensive; most use standard automotive-type bulbs. You can even buy these fixtures as do-it-yourself kits, although these offer a limited number of lights and effects. Because low-voltage lamps don't produce as much light as standard systems do, they're best for lighting pathways or providing subtle lighting around ponds. They aren't as effective in illuminating large areas as 120-volt floodlights are. No matter which system you choose, make sure the fixtures, bulbs, connectors, and junction boxes are designed for outdoor use. Because outdoor lighting will be exposed to the weather, the circuit should be protected by a GFCI. Check local codes for additional requirements.

Bulbs for outdoor lighting vary in both intensity and color. For standard and low-voltage systems, ordinary tungsten bulbs are the cheapest and most readily available. They come in a variety of wattages, giving you a choice of intensity. The type most commonly used has thickened lenses and built-in reflectors. They come in the form of spotlights, narrow floodlights, and broad floodlights in both high and low voltages. More-expensive high-intensity halogen bulbs are becoming popular for outdoor lighting because they produce more light per watt than tungsten bulbs and have a longer life span. They produce incandescent light that's a bright, clear white yet still natural-looking.

Other high-intensity bulbs include mercury vapor (bluish white), sodium (amber yellow), and metal halide (intense, harsh white). In general, the light they produce is too bright and artificial to be appealing around a pond; they're best for lighting up streets and large parking lots.

For underwater lighting, you need special bulbs and watertight housings. You can buy colored lenses for underwater and general lighting. If you plan to highlight plants and trees, choose colored lenses carefully to avoid giving foliage an unnatural appearance.

Underwater Lighting

Fountain Kit
with Integral
Underwater Lights

Lights Swivel
for Effects with
Fountain

This can be dramatic and eye-catching, but easily overdone. So go slowly and start simply. Low-voltage systems are the safest and easiest to install.

FIXTURE PLACEMENT

To highlight fish or submerged plants, position lights around the edge of your pond. Point one up toward a waterfall or tuck one in behind it and aim the light up toward the fall. Angle two at the foot of a fountain to allow its spray to sparkle.

Avoid situating aboveground fixtures where they will create glare off the water surface or shine in the eyes of viewers. To get a sense for placement, it may help to experiment first with one or more bright flashlights.

Hide Lights from View. Fixtures with a black or dark green finish will be the least obtrusive. Hide fixtures among plantings, beneath a deck overhang, behind a tree, or within its canopy. Or recess fixtures below ground in light wells. Prefabricated units consist of a bulb and reflector encased in a watertight housing with a metal grille or clear plastic cover. If you're installing other types of fixtures belowground, be sure they are waterproof.

Wires and conduit can be buried underground. Conceal low-voltage systems under a layer of mulch. Install junction boxes and transformers for low-voltage systems aboveground. You can make them less visible with judicious placement of plant containers, small shrubs, or ornamental grasses.

CHAPTER 7

Bridges & Stones

B ridges and stepping-stones can be pleasing additions to your pond. Besides providing a way to cross over water, they give you another viewpoint from which to enjoy your pond. For the best results, plan them while you are designing your pond rather than trying to add them later. You may need a permit to install a bridge. Play it safe and ask your local building inspector about codes before you begin.

Wooden Bridges

Wooden bridges can be as simple as a weathered plank across a stream or as ornate as a lacquered Japanese "camelback." They add architectural interest and direct the flow of traffic in the garden. A bridge just plunked down across the water detracts from the charm of your pond. Give viewers a reason to get to the other side, such as a bench, a garden ornament, or interesting plants.

Size the bridge so that it is in proportion with the pond or stream in length, width, and height. Make the bridge wide enough to cross easily and safely; 2 feet is the narrowest you should consider. For a very narrow stream or a small natural pond, a couple of wide, sturdy planks laid from one bank to the other may suffice. Bridges more than 12 to 18 inches above the water surface will need handrails, both for safety and for aesthetics. Be sure to provide a sturdy foundation for the support posts when you build a bridge of any size. If you plan to build a bridge with a span longer than 8 feet, you may want to consult a building contractor, because bridges of this size will require larger beams, additional supports, or both.

In buying material to build your bridge (or working with a contractor), specify the use of pressure-treated lumber, as well as rust-resistant hardware and fasteners. Lumber that is used at or near the ground should be rated for ground or

In a true Zen garden, above, a red bridge represents a transformation from worldliness to wisdom.

Building a bridge such as this one, opposite, requires using treated lumber that is rated for marine or seawall use.

soil contact. Any wood that will be in regular contact with water, such as the mid-span support for a bridge longer than 8 feet, you will need to use treated lumber that is rated for marine or seawall use. However, you should avoid using wood treated with creosote or penta-chlorophenol, both of which are toxic to fish and plants. (If you have any treated lumber left over from your project, remember that it is not safe for burning in the fireplace. Check with your lumber supplier or your county sanitation department for specific guidance on how to properly dispose of it.)

If you've decided that a bridge is appropriate for your pond but aren't sure how to go about designing one, you will find the plans to build one described on the next few pages.

You can build a simple footbridge across your pond with doubled 2x8s for support beams, 2x6s for decking and handrails, and 4x4s for the posts. Use pressure-treated lumber and galvanized carriage bolts and nails. The following instructions are for a 5-foot-wide bridge that can span a pond or stream up to 6 feet across.

how to

Add a Footbridge

DIFFICULTY LEVEL: CHALLENGING

Tools and Materials: Measuring tape; circular saw; hammer; mortar hoe; wheelbarrow or mortar pan; spirit level; drill, $\frac{5}{8}$-in. spade bit, $\frac{1}{2}$-in. spade bit (for optional handrail); wrench; portable saber saw; power sander; six 8-ft. 2x8s; six 4x4s (length depends on depth of postholes and handrail); nine 10-ft. 2x6s; two 8-ft. 2x6s (for optional handrail); 1 cu. ft. gravel; concrete (amount depends on depth of postholes); six 20d common nails; 3 lbs. 10d galvanized common nails; 1 lb. 8d galvanized common nails; twelve $\frac{1}{2}$ x $7\frac{1}{2}$-in. carriage bolts, nuts, washers; eight $\frac{3}{8}$ x 6-in. carriage bolts, nuts, washers (for optional handrail)

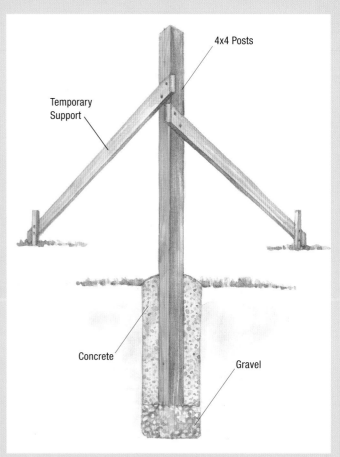

4x4 Posts

Temporary Support

Concrete

Gravel

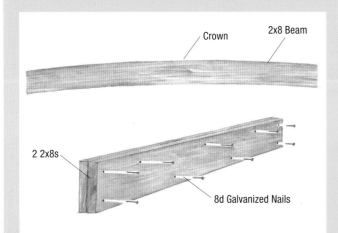

Crown

2x8 Beam

2 2x8s

8d Galvanized Nails

1 **Make the Support Beams.** Each of the three beams is made with two 2x8s nailed together. Most long boards have a slight *crown*, as shown in the illustration. You can best determine which edge is crowned by looking down the length of each board. Attach and install the boards with the crowns facing up.

Make sure that the boards are all the same length; trim if necessary. Stack two 2x8s on top of each other; align the edges; and fasten with 8d nails, about 10 on each side, spaced and staggered as shown.

2 **Position the Posts.** Place three 4x4 posts on each side of the pond, stream, or depression. Extend the posts 1 ft. above grade. For a bridge with a railing, extend the four corner posts at least 4 ft. above grade. (See "Install a Handrail," on the next page.) Center the two sets of posts no more than 7 ft. apart. Measuring from the center of the middle post on each side, set one corner post 2 ft. on center and the other 2 ft. 6½ in. on center.

Measure and stake the locations of the posts. Then dig 8-in.-diameter postholes at least 6 in. below the frost line. If frost is not a problem in your area, dig the holes at least 30 in. deep. Add 6 in. of gravel. Tamp the gravel.

Install the posts. Center the 4x4 posts in each hole. Brace the posts so that they are plumb. Mix and pour concrete an inch or so above grade at the support posts. Tamp the concrete with a piece of wood so that it completely surrounds each post. Slope the concrete away from the posts for good drainage. Let the concrete set undisturbed for at least a day.

3 Install the Beams and Decking. Set the beams against the posts. Study the illustration for proper beam placement. The two outside beams should be installed on the insides of the corner posts. Align the beams so that they overhang the posts equally on both sides of the bridge. Check the beams for level in both directions using a spirit level. For temporary support, attach the beams with one 20d nail into each post. With the beams leveled and temporarily attached to the posts, trim the posts flush with the tops of the beams. (Do not, however, trim the corner posts if you are installing a handrail.)

Secure the beams. At each post, drill two ⅝-in. holes through the posts and beams. Secure the beams to the posts permanently with ½-in.-diameter, 7½-in.-long carriage bolts, nuts, and washers.

Cut the 10-ft.-long 2x6s in half. Fasten the decking across the tops of the beams with 10d nails. The decking should overlap the outside beams by about 4½ in. on each side. Keep the decking square by starting at one end, installing the first 2x6 flush with the ends of the beams. Leave a ¼-in. gap between each board (a ¼-in. diameter bolt makes a handy spacer). If nailing causes the boards to split, first predrill a hole slightly smaller than the diameter of the nails.

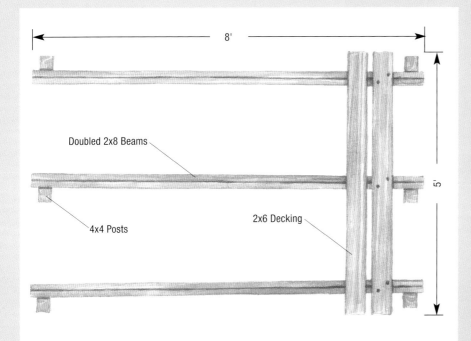

8'

Doubled 2x8 Beams

4x4 Posts

2x6 Decking

5'

4 Install a Handrail. If building codes require, you'll need to install a handrail. A single or double handrail provides an extra measure of safety for bridge crossers and also provides a feeling of security. (The local building code may require one and specify how it is to be constructed.)

For a handrail, extend the 4x4 corner posts 3 ft. above the decking surface or to the height required by local codes. Attach a 2x6 handrail, 3 ft. high or to the height specified by the local code, narrow edge up. Handrails should be bolted with a minimum of two ⅜-in.-diameter 6-in.-long carriage bolts at each post. Affix the bolts securely with washers and nuts. Note: you may add one more board (a 1x3), turned on its side, to the very top of the handrail. This will provide a wider surface area.

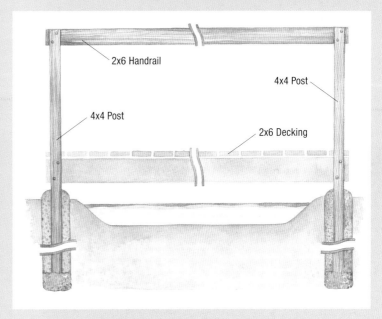

2x6 Handrail

4x4 Post

4x4 Post

2x6 Decking

A short bridge over a shallow watercourse adds charm and directs traffic to another part of the garden.

Stepping-stones

If you want to provide a means for crossing your pond but don't want to block the view of the other side, stepping-stones can be both a practical and an attractive solution. They can lead either all the way across the pond or simply a few feet out into it for observing or feeding fish. For formal pools, use square or rectangular cast-concrete slabs, large quarry tiles, cut stone, or similar geometric shapes. For informal ponds, use irregularly shaped flat rocks or flagstones. No matter the style, stepping-stones usually look best in a zigzag or random pattern rather than in a straight line.

If the pond is shallow enough, you may be able to use large rocks or stone slabs set directly in the pond. If these aren't perfectly flat on the bottom, however, they can shift dangerously; you may need to embed them in a nest of concrete. In a deeper pond, build up a layer of mortared flat rocks, or construct piers of poured concrete, brick, or block to support the stones. Cardboard tubes sold for making concrete piers are easy for amateurs to use as molds.

If you've installed a flexible liner or preformed shell, you'll need to provide a suitable concrete footing to support the stones and piers if you've used them. Stepping-stones need a firm foundation under a liner or shell, especially if the combined weight of the stone and its support is more than 100 pounds.

Concrete stepping-stones need a strong foundation under the pond liner or shell.

Stepping-stones

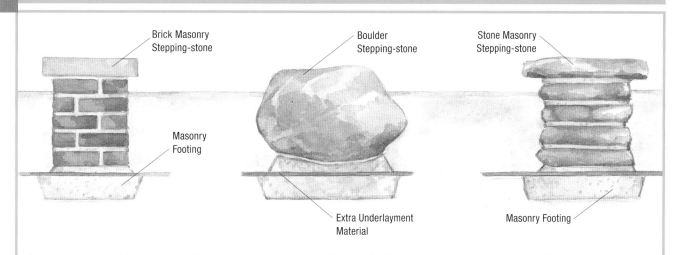

Brick Masonry
Stepping-stone

Masonry
Footing

Boulder
Stepping-stone

Extra Underlayment
Material

Stone Masonry
Stepping-stone

Masonry Footing

A variety of materials may be used for pond stepping-stones: brick, large flat boulders, flat stones, quarry tiles, and concrete slabs. A stable footing should be placed under each one.

The best solution is a poured-concrete footing as large or slightly larger than your supporting pier. Protect the liner or shell by sandwiching it between layers of pond-liner underlayment—one between footing and liner and another between liner and support pier or stepping-stone.

You can risk adding stepping-stones later without the footing if you are sure the soil under your liner is firm. Protect the liner with an extra piece of liner between it and the stepping-stones, and use the lightest stones possible. Make sure each stone is large enough to provide a stable footing, and place the stones close enough together so that people can walk across the pond without hopping. (A gap of 12 to 15 inches between stones is comfortable for most people.) The surface of the stones should be high enough above the water so that they stay dry; wet rocks are often slippery, and if they're constantly wet, they can develop algae or moss that makes them even more dangerous. For that reason, avoid placing your stepping-stones near a waterfall or fountain, where they are likely to have water splashing on them continuously. Porous rocks such as sandstone are more prone to develop moss than nonporous rocks such as granite. Check your rocks regularly for any slick buildup, and scrub it off with a stiff brush. Walking across the stepping-stones from both directions on a regular basis will alert you to any looseness or stone movement that could contribute to someone's fall.

Massive stone slabs make ideal stepping-stones or a bridge. If you can handle their sheer weight and bulk, you can build this style of bridge quickly.

PART 3

Wetland Gardens

Bordering your pond with plantings that grow in damp areas is one way to make your water feature look as though Mother Nature had created it herself. At one time, wetland gardens might have been raised or drained because they were worthless for sustaining a lawn. Now we appreciate them as places to grow unusual varieties of flowers, grasses, ferns, and shrubs.

CHAPTER 8

Creating a Wetland

Your wetland can be a narrow strip or a sprawling bed, a simple edging of a few sedges and cattails or an elaborate planting with rare wetland species. Even if you don't have a naturally wet area, consider creating one to broaden the type of plants you can grow.

If your goal is a natural-looking pond, you need to have wetland areas around it to make it look realistic. Wetland plants include some of the flowers most attractive to hummingbirds and butterflies, such as bright-red cardinal flowers and towering Joe-Pye weed.

In nature, ponds are surrounded by wet meadows or marshes (where soft-stemmed plants grow) or swamps (which may be home to shrubs and trees). These wetlands act as filters for ponds and streams by absorbing silt and pollutants. In addition, in your home garden, wetlands can absorb water that overruns your pond due to a heavy rain.

In this chapter, the term wetland garden refers to a manmade marsh or swamp in which the soil never dries out; the plants are not, however, growing in standing water. Appropriate plants include moisture-loving perennials and many grasses, ferns, and shrubs.

Although some gardeners and water-garden suppliers may refer to these specialized gardens as "bog gardens," a true bog is a more specialized habitat where the soil is highly acidic and low in oxygen and nutrients. If you mimic the conditions of a true bog, you can grow fascinating carnivorous plants such as pitcher plants, Venus flytraps, and sundews, as well as terrestrial orchids.

Plants that thrive in the shallow-water areas between a natural pond and a marsh or swamp are called "marginals." (You'll find marginal plants beginning on page 223.) In garden ponds, these plants are grown inside the liner or the pond shell in containers.

If you have an area in your yard where the soil is saturated with water, consider using it as a site for an informal wetland garden. Lacking that, you can create a natural-looking bog garden using a flexible liner.

A low spot or a depression in the land-scape is the natural choice for locating a spontaneous-looking wetland, or bog, garden, right. If you re-create the conditions of a true bog, you will be able to grow carnivorous plants, such as the Venus flytrap.

A Pondside Wetland or Bog Garden

If you want to have a natural-looking pond, you'll need to create a wetland garden along one or more sides of it to establish a smooth transition into the rest of your landscape. If you plan the wetland (or bog) garden before you build your pond, it will be easy to create both at the same time.

Visit natural ponds in local parks or gardens to study the way that plants are grouped. Try to resist amassing a collection of individual specimens. Instead, concentrate on several representatives of a few species that occur together naturally. A trip to a native-plant nursery in your region or a good book on regional plants (known as a "flora") can help you (Creative Homeowner's Regional Home Landscaping Series, for example).

You must make the wetland watertight. You can do this either by extending your pond liner or by using a piece of liner cut from an unused corner. If you use a scrap, seal the gap between it and the pond liner with liner tape to minimize leakage from your wetland.

To keep soil from washing from the wetland garden into the pond, you must create a division between them. This can be a solid division, in which case you'll need an independent source of water to keep the garden area wet.

An attached wetland with a "leaky" division allows the pond to provide water for the wetland. If you don't have time to check and water the wetland frequently, this second option is probably better. Keep in mind, though, that a large wetland or bog garden connected to a pond can lower the pond's water level if water is allowed to seep out too readily. Most experts advise against the connected option for a true bog garden because it might allow chemicals or nutrient-rich fish wastes in the pond water to upset the bog's chemistry.

Independent Wetland Garden

To create an independent bog or wetland, simply leave a mound or berm of soil along one edge of your pond higher than the planned water level (usually the same level as the rest of the edge). Run the pond liner over the mound and into the wetland area. Ensure good drainage for the top few inches by puncturing holes around the sides, about halfway down from the top. Follow the directions under "Creating the Wetland Environment," on page 142, for installing perforated pipe to maintain soil moisture. Camouflage the liner with whatever you use as edging material or with large stones.

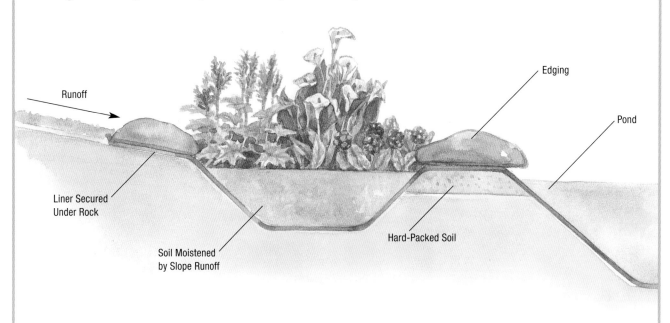

Soil cannot infiltrate the pond when there is a solid barrier. Wetland garden soil is moistened from slope runoff.

Attached Wetland Garden

To create a connected wetland, make the berm between your pond and garden a little lower than the expected water level. Then, on top of the solid berm, create a semipermeable barrier that extends a little above the eventual water level. There are several different ways you can go about creating this barrier, which will serve as an automatic-watering device for your wetland. You may find that one of the following options allows better control of water flow for your particular design or is more aesthetically pleasing than the others.

▦ Stones are a popular option. Some people find that they get enough control of the water flow by stacking stones on the mound and letting pond water seep between and under them.

▦ Mortar some of the stones together to reduce the gaps for seepage if too much water flows through.

Or combine stones with the sod option, described next. This is very easy to put in place.

▦ Sod, stacked in layers, is another popular material for the semipermeable barrier. Top the mound with pieces of sod turned upside down; hold them securely in place; and hide them with large stones or other edging.

▦ Stones with two or three pieces of perforated pipe run between them and into the soil in the wetland area is a more involved option. Mortar the rest of the stones together so that water flows only through the pipe.

Now you're ready to add your planting medium. (See "Filling Your Wetland Garden," on page 143.) For attached wetlands, add the soil mix gradually, saturating it as you go and testing the amount of water that's running between pond and wetland. Wait to plant until you're satisfied that you have the right amount of water seepage.

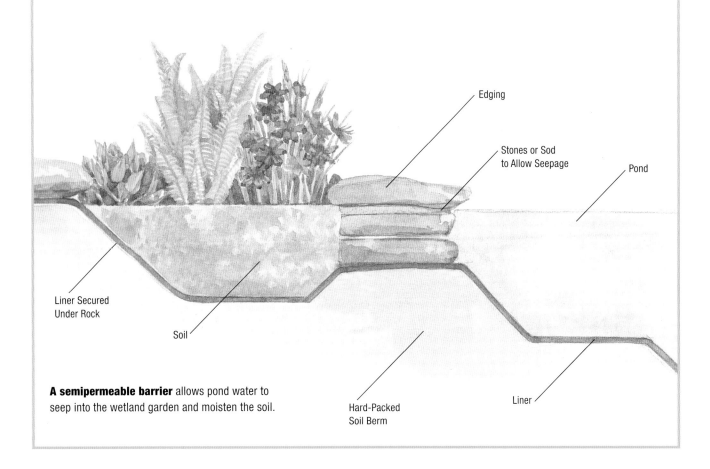

A semipermeable barrier allows pond water to seep into the wetland garden and moisten the soil.

Edging

Stones or Sod to Allow Seepage

Pond

Liner Secured Under Rock

Soil

Hard-Packed Soil Berm

Liner

A Freestanding Wetland Garden

Although many people place wetland gardens next to their ponds, you don't need a pond to create a wetland. If your yard already has an area that's always soggy, stop trying to grow grass there and instead transform it into a home for a whole array of wonderful plants that thrive in constant moisture.

If you're starting from scratch, design the wetland or bog so that it will blend in with its surroundings. If it's not next to a pond, situate it next to an area of dense, informal planting. If you want to locate it next to a woodland or much taller plants, be sure to put it on the south side so that it will get enough sun.

Try to visually tie it in with an existing dense planting. If that's not possible, try to echo the shape of another bed in your garden that you've filled with typical dryland perennials or shrubs. Any of these options will help make the wetland garden appear as though it belongs rather than looking like an afterthought.

Access to water is crucial so that the wetland will never dry out. Many people locate wetland gardens where the plantings can capture runoff from rooftops. This is helpful if you are trying to mimic a true bog, in which case you want to avoid the chemicals and alkaline minerals often present in tap water. (The quality that makes rainwater soft is its acidity. Tap water that's hard is too alkaline for bog plants; commercial water softeners fix the alkalinity but make the water too saline for bog plants.)

Keep in mind the sun requirement of the plants you want. A number of moisture-loving perennials thrive in partial shade, and shade will reduce the need to water the wetland garden. But carnivorous plants and many other wetland species require full sun to flower and grow well.

Freestanding Wetland Garden

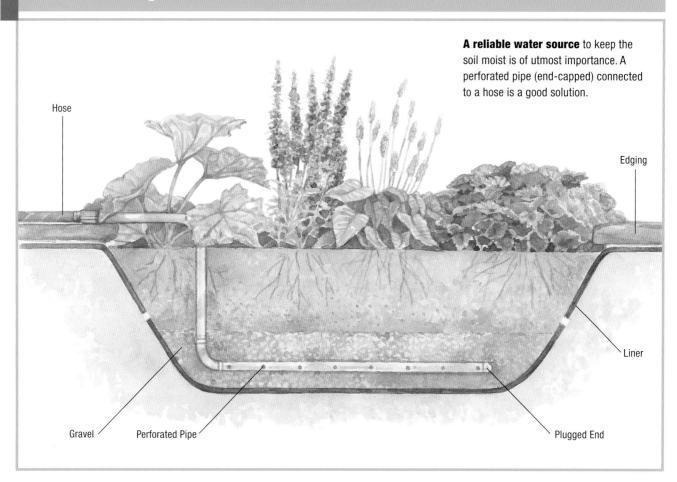

Hose

A reliable water source to keep the soil moist is of utmost importance. A perforated pipe (end-capped) connected to a hose is a good solution.

Edging

Liner

Gravel   Perforated Pipe

Plugged End

A half barrel is a good choice for containing a freestanding wetland garden.

CREATING A WETLAND ENVIRONMENT

Wherever you place the freestanding wetland garden, the basic mechanics are similar. Your goal is to keep the soil at the bottom of your excavated area from ever drying out, while at the same time keeping water away from the crowns of the plants (the point where the stems or leaves meet the roots) so that they don't rot.

Building a wetland or bog garden in the ground is similar to building a pond—you dig a hole and make it watertight with a pond liner, but then you fill it with soil instead of water. Just as a large pond requires less maintenence than a small one, a large wetland or bog garden won't need watering as often as a small one. Dig the hole at least 2 feet deep; 3 feet is even better. You can make the sides of the wetland hole much less steeply vertical than those of your pond; the gradual slope will help keep them from caving in.

Calculate the size of your liner in the same way that you would for a pond. (See the example on page 69.) Liners for wetland gardens don't need to be completely watertight, so there's no need to buy the same high-grade PVC or rubber you bought for your pond. Look for a sheet of heavy-duty polyethylene large enough to cover the bottom and sides in one piece.

After you've centered the plastic sheet and let it settle into your excavation, ensure good drainage for the crowns of your plants by puncturing drainage holes around the sides, about halfway down from the top.

At this point most wetland gardeners install perforated pipe to help keep the soil evenly moist. Here are several options that will help you deliver water throughout the planting area during a drought.

▥ **Run one or more perforated pipes vertically** down the side of your wetland or bog, stopping a couple of inches above the bottom of the excavation and leaving 1 to 2 inches of the pipe above the soil surface. Block the bottom end of the pipe to ensure that the water seeps out slowly and to keep the drainage holes from getting clogged with dirt. You can camouflage exposed piping with plants.

WETLAND OR BOG GARDENS IN CONTAINERS

Y ou can create a small wetland or bog garden in a watertight container such as a half barrel, a trough, or even an old bathtub or child's wading pool. A wooden or plastic container is best, especially if you live in a cold climate because other materials will crack when they freeze in winter. Fill it with the same growing medium described in "Filling Your Wetland Garden," opposite: half compost, half garden loam for wetland plants; half peat moss, half sand for specialized bog plants.

You might want to install an automatic watering system to irrigate the container garden if you'll be away on vacation. A simple homemade device is a plastic gallon jug with a nailhole punched in the bottom; when filled with water, this will drip slowly until the jug is empty. A more elaborate option is to connect a line running from an automatic drip-irrigation system to your container.

As with any water garden, wetland and bog gardens in containers need special care in the winter. If you're growing plants at the northern edge of their hardiness range, sink the container into the ground in winter before mulching, or move the container to a protected place such as a garage. Check moisture levels periodically to make sure the soil doesn't dry out.

■ **Use one pipe inside another** for even more gradual seepage. Garden writer C. Colston Burrell suggests using two perforated pipes, one larger than the other (the larger at least 10 inches in diameter), inserting the smaller into the larger, and filling the space between with gravel. When you need to water, place the end of a hose or the spout of a watering can into the inside pipe; the water will slowly seep through the gravel into the soil. Again, camouflage exposed piping with plants.

■ **Run a length of rigid perforated pipe horizontally** across the bottom of the wetland. Join it to a vertical length of solid (not perforated) PVC pipe with an elbow connector. If you choose this option, lay 3 to 4 inches of gravel around and on top of the horizontal pipe to help keep soil out of the drainage holes. Again, remember to block the end of the pipe, and disguise the exposed inch or two with plants.

■ **Purchase flexible leaky hose**, or *soaker hose*. Intended for subsurface irrigation, flexible leaky hose is less likely to plug up with soil than regular leaky hose. Drape the hose around the bottom of your wetland so it forms almost a complete loop. Cap or plug the far end and attach the other to a hose at the surface.

Filling Your Wetland Garden

Once you've excavated and lined the bed (or chosen your container), you're ready to fill your wetland with soil—or, more accurately, growing medium.

For most moisture-loving perennials, use a mix of compost and good garden loam. The goal is to create a growing medium that retains moisture; if the topsoil you use is sandy or low in moisture-holding organic matter, you can add more compost to help compensate.

Compost and garden soil won't work for true bog plants, however, as both are too rich in nutrients. True bog plants require what is usually described as a "sterile" mix of half peat moss and half sand. (Here "sterile" describes a mix that is almost completely lacking in nutrients and therefore unable to support ordinary plants and soil organisms.) Some growers use as much as five parts peat to one part sand, so don't skimp.

Once your wetland or bog is filled to its rim with growing medium and thoroughly damp but not wringing wet, you're ready to plant. Plant densely to reduce the amount of soil surface exposed to evaporation. This will also reduce weeds, although you may find that they are less of a problem in a wetland garden. Even though wetland plants need to have their roots moist at all times, they will rot and die if their crowns don't have adequate aeration. Therefore you need to set your plants so that their crowns are at or just below the soil line. A winter mulch of leaves or pine needles and a summer top-dressing of compost will help protect the plants and keep the soil moist.

While planning your water feature, consider a wetland garden adjacent to it. It makes a smoother transition to the rest of the landscape.

A wetland garden on one or more sides of your pond is a natural-looking enhancement.

SPECIALIZED PLANTS FOR BOGS

Growing true bog plants takes a special commitment. Not only must you make sure that their soil never dries out, but you also need to water them with distilled water or rainwater. Tap water can make the soil too alkaline or introduce chemicals bog plants can't tolerate. Nor is the bog garden flexible about sunlight. You'll need to find a location with at least six hours of sun each day throughout the growing season.

Once your bog garden is established, it can only host a limited range of plants. A true bog lacks in soil nutrients and is too highly acidic for most moisture-loving perennials and shrubs that would grow in other gardens. Nevertheless, the array of fascinating and beautiful plants that grow in bogs has made this type of gardening an obsession for many, with its own international plant society and numerous Web sites and specialized nurseries.

Bog plants don't send their roots deep, so an excavation of 12 to 18 inches is enough in this case. After you add your peat/sand mix, wait three to four weeks for the pH to adjust and the medium to settle.

Remember that a bog is a nutrient-poor environment. Never fertilize it. And your carnivorous plants don't need any artificial food for their traps, either. *Little Shop of Horrors* and other popular images to the contrary, these species didn't evolve eating hamburger. Passing insects will suit them just fine. It's another matter if there is limited insect life in your area. Provide some bugs only if absolutely necessary.

In winter, carnivorous plants go dormant and don't need insects. But they do need protection from fluctuating temperatures; give bog plants a loose, acidic mulch of insulating pine needles or a mixture of oak leaves.

POPULAR CARNIVOROUS PLANTS

Carnivorous plants are not particularly hard to grow as long as they have three things: a good six hours of sun a day, a very acidic growing medium high in organic matter, and constant moisture. Carnivorous plants fail to grow as houseplants both because they don't get enough sun and because they aren't allowed to go dormant in winter.

American Pitcher Plants (*Sarracenia* species). There are eight species of native pitcher plants, some of which can reach 3 feet tall. They get their common name from modified leaves that form trumpetlike hooded "pitchers." These showy pitchers, often speckled and veined in different colors, trap insects attracted to the plant's nectar. They open shop after the unusual, droopy dogs-ear flowers (either yellow or red) finish their two-week bloom in spring. Most pitcher-plant species (some endangered) are native to the southeast United States and are cold hardy to Zone 7. An exception is the common or purple pitcher plant, *S. purpurea*, native as far north as Canada. It holds its pitchers low to the ground, growing only 6 inches tall. It traps insects by drowning them in rainwater collected in its leaves. There are many natural hybrids and several easy-to-grow named varieties.

Venus Flytrap (*Dionaea muscipula*). The only species in its genus, this carnivore can grow to 18 inches tall. Its insect-trapping mechanism looks like a clam with spikes along the edge of each "shell." Pink inside, it has three tiny hairs that serve as triggers: when an insect brushes against them, they cause the plant to slam the two halves shut. The Venus flytrap is native to parts of the Carolinas and is cold hardy to Zone 8, although some strands have been established in New Jersey.

Sundews (*Drosera* species). There are some 130 species of these fascinating plants, found from Alaska and Siberia to New Zealand and South America. Hairlike tentacles on a sundew's leaves are brightly colored. At their tips, a drop of gluelike nectar sparkles in the sun like dew, luring various unsuspecting gnats and similar tiny bugs. The insect's thrashing causes the sundew's tentacles to curl further inward, trapping its victim ever more securely. Sundew

American Pitcher Plant. The modified leaves, left, often colorful with speckles and veins, trap insects seeking nectar.

flowers vary widely in arrangement, although most are round and flat with five pink or white petals. Love-nest sundew (*D. intermedia*) has maroon foliage and white flowers and is hardy in Zones 6–9. D. limearis, which also has white flowers, does best in Zones 3–6. Both grow to approximately 6 inches tall.

Bladderworts (*Utricularia* species). There are more than 200 species of this highly advanced, somewhat bizarre perennial. Hobbyists grow them for their orchidlike flower. Harder to see are the bladderlike traps, some no bigger than a pinhead on their stems or roots. They can capture tiny organisms in 10 thousandths of a second. The easiest aquatic bladderwort to grow is *U. gibba*, which has ½-inch yellow flowers with a hood, curving spur, and tongue with red veins. It's not cold hardy, so you'll need to keep it in a container.

Butterworts (*Pinguicula* species). This genus of about 70 species from throughout the Northern hemisphere gets its name from its greasy leaves with glands that trap insects such as gnats and fruitflies; their struggles stimulate other glands to secrete digestive juices. From rosettes a few inches across, temperate species produce cone-shaped, two-lipped flowers with long spurs and beards, most often purple, violet, or white. Some you might find in cultivation are *P. caerula* (violet with a yellow beard, Zone 8) and *P. grandiflora* (deep blue violet, Zone 3), and *P. vulgaris* (violet with a white throat, Zone 6).

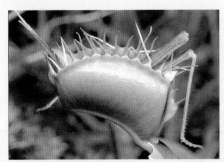

Venus Flytrap. Insects are trapped, left, by the plant's hairlike triggers.

Sundew. The plant's tips are covered in glue that snares insects, below.

BOG ORCHIDS

Most people think of orchids as exotic plants that grow only in rainforests. But North America is home to more than 200 species, many of which make their homes in bogs. They include the fringed orchids (*Platanthera* species), with frilly flowers in magenta, orange, and yellow. But because orchids are difficult to propagate, few nurseries sell them. Many species are threatened by development and should never be collected in the wild. They rarely survive transplanting to home gardens because they depend on the presence of particular fungi in the soil.

'Chadds Ford' (*Spiranthes odorata*). A native orchid that is both widely available and fairly easy to grow is a selecion of the fragrant ladies'-tresses orchid. Fragrant little waxy, white flowers spiral around its stems, which can grow to 18 inches tall. Ladies'-tresses aren't as particular about their growing conditions as most of the carnivorous plants, as long as they are grown in well-drained soil that remains constantly moist. They are hardy in Zones 5–8.

'Chadds Ford'. This fragrant ladies'-tresses orchid, above, is available from nurseries and is relatively easy to grow.

This garden offers an array of plantings that are suitable to grow in and around water.

RESPECTING NATIVE BOG PLANTS

In recent years, nongardening catalogs and even hardware stores have offered the Venus flytrap, a carnivorous bog species, as a novelty: a plant that behaves like a pet by eating insects. But there are two things wrong with this scenario. First, carnivorous bog plants demand special conditions and quickly die when they are treated as ordinary houseplants. Second, this and many other bog species are being collected from the wild, further depleting the populations of those that have managed to survive the draining of wetlands for development, agriculture, and other uses.

Fortunately, some nurseries are making an effort to propagate, or breed, their own carnivorous plants rather than buying their inventory from people who collect from the wild. Two North Carolina horticulturists, Larry Mellichamp and Rob Gardner, went a step further and developed two new pitcher-plant hybrids, 'Ladies in Waiting' and 'Dixie Lace', for home gardeners. "We thought that man-made hybrids that do especially well in cultivation might offer more enticement to grow them, and ease some of the pressure to collect them," says Mellichamp. Because these two pitcher plants don't grow in the wild, you can be assured that they've been propagated by a nursery, wherever you buy them.

'Ladies in Waiting' grows up to 16 inches tall. Its color is deep maroon with white spots; its hood has a scalloped edge. 'Dixie Lace' is smaller and has dark red veins on a light yellow background; the edge of its hood is wavy. Mellichamp believes that the new hybrids will grow to Zone 5 with some winter protection.

'Ladies in Waiting' hybrid

'Dixie Lace' hybrid

CHAPTER 9

Pond Critters

Fish, frogs, birds, and other animals bring a whole new level of vibrancy to a garden pond. Even if you don't buy creatures for your pond, they will come. Here are some of the visitors you can purchase or attract and tips on how to make them feel at home or—in other cases—encourage them to seek room and board elsewhere.

Fish

Doctors, dentists, and psychologists often have aquariums in their waiting rooms. They know that the sight of fish swimming to and fro is almost hypnotic, making us feel relaxed and peaceful. Fish have the same calming effect in an outdoor pond, whether they're 2-foot-long rare koi or a school of common minnows. Add to that the fun of seeing them race to gobble a handful of food or chase each other as frenetically as Harpo Marx during their annual mating ritual, and fish seem as indispensable to a pond as water lilies. In addition to being captivating, fish will help control bugs, provide nutrients for plants, and keep plants from spreading too fast. They can be an integral part of the pond as a thriving ecosystem.

Keep in mind, though, that adding fish to your pond also adds new challenges. Fish can eat prized plants, add waste that clouds the water, and break your heart by becoming dinner for any number of potential predators. You need to decide before you build your pond whether you want large fish such as koi, which need both ample room to swim around and extra depth for hiding and for surviving winter. Other fish likewise benefit from a deeper pond area, which will stay cooler and retain more oxygen in hot weather. Unlike water lilies, many fish will be better off in a shady pond. If your pond isn't in partial shade, you will need to create shade by introducing enough floating or floating-leaved plants, such as water lilies, to cover roughly half the pond's surface.

Predators can find your fish even if you have a formal pool on an urban patio; you'll need to create hiding places for fish with overhangs along the edge, terra-cotta drainage tiles, or black plastic drainpipes weighted down on the

Marsh wrens can typically be found hiding in the reeds or amid other tall plantings in a natural wetland.

This "turtle" is a harmless addition to a pond filled with koi.

pond bottom. You can create additional hideaways by the way you arrange your plants: fish can take refuge among the stems of oxygenators and marginals or under floating leaves.

Without water plants, you'll have additional concerns besides creating hiding places. You will need to feed your fish more often and invest in a good artificial filter to remove fish waste.

You'll minimize catastrophes and maximize enjoyment if you study this chapter and learn the needs of fish before you buy them. Fish, like other pets and like plants, can get sick and even die without proper care. While you don't have to take fish for walks, remember that they are outdoor pets in an environment that will never be completely natural. Plan ahead to make that environment as healthy for them as possible.

Fish and other creatures bring new dimensions of movement and color to your water garden.

Choosing Your Fish

If you have an existing pond, you will have to select the species and number of fish appropriate to those conditions. If you're still in the planning stages, check the entries in this section to see whether the fish you want need deep or shallow water, and make the pond large enough to accommodate them. A common rule for stocking your pond is that 1 square foot of well-balanced pond water can support 2 inches of fish. Thus in an area of 6 square feet, you could have four 3-inch fish or two 6-inch fish. (Koi are an exception to this rule; they need 25 square feet each.) In addition to the size of your pond, there are several other factors to consider when choosing among available fish species. Tropical fish species will need to be removed from the pond each fall and kept in an indoor aquarium, which can become a demanding chore if the fish become numerous. Other species are quite sensitive to high temperatures and will get sluggish or even die during hot summers. Some feed at the surface, skimming insects off the water and even jumping out to gulp them. This is entertaining but can make the fish more obvious to predators. Bottom feeders can hide better, but they have an annoying habit of churning up bottom muck and may be harder to see from the surface.

Overstocking a pond is a sure route to failure. Avoid buying more fish (or larger fish) than your pond will support. Fish often take care of overstocking themselves, by eating their own spawn or not spawning at all. If you hope to increase your stock for yourself or friends, choose fish that breed easily in a pond situation, and take measures to remove the fry. (See "Spawning" on page 160.)

If you want to create a wildlife pond, you may want to focus on native fish. Expect a natural pond to attract nature—

A healthy environment that includes well-balanced water and adequate space is essential for fish.

which means fish-eating raccoons and birds—and native fish are usually quite a bit less expensive to replace. In addition, some exotic fish have caused problems after escaping to natural waterways. (Refer to "Keep Pond Creatures in Their Place," below.)

When you start out, buy small fish of less expensive breeds. This will allow you to get comfortable with the routine of fish care, to observe any problems with your water supply or potential predators, and to see how your fish adjust to their new home. The following pages show some of the most popular and readily available fish for home ponds.

KEEP POND CREATURES IN THEIR PLACE

Never dispose of your fish, snails, or other pond life in nearby waterways or sewers. Animals outside their natural environments, just like non-native plants, can upset the healthy balance of waterways. (See "Beware of Invasive Plants" on page 202.) Water creatures that have caused the most trouble have been introduced by commerce: zebra mussel in ships' ballasts, tilapia to raise for food markets, trout for sport. The bullfrog has been taken beyond its native range in the eastern and central United States by connoisseurs of frog legs, and in their new homes these amphibians are wiping out small native frogs. These animals don't just dominate native species by eating them or their food but can also spread diseases for which native animals have no resistance. The common carp—a relative of koi—carries some 130 different parasites.

GOLDFISH (*Carassius auratus*)

This group of fish, which originated in China, is a favorite for either aquariums or ponds. Members of the carp family, they're colorful and tough, and they feed at all levels, so you'll have no trouble seeing them. All goldfish breed easily, although if you have more than one kind, they'll interbreed, and their distinguishing characteristics can be lost.

Common Goldfish. This popular fish, most often reddish orange, usually grows to about 6 inches long but can get bigger in a large pond. Goldfish can tolerate shallow, somewhat stagnant water and survive water temperatures up to 95°F for brief periods. They can overwinter outdoors where pond water won't freeze solid, and they can learn to recognize their feeder.

Comets. These specially bred goldfish have long, deeply forked caudal fins (tails) that can be as long as their bodies. Gold comets can grow more than a foot long. While they need a depth of 30 inches or so for wintering over, they can take even more extreme temperatures than their common cousin, down to almost freezing and up to 104°F. Sarasa comets, which have red-and-white markings on a silver base, do best in water that remains cooler than 70°F.

Fantail. Goldfish in this group have wider, more transparent fins and tails. This makes them slower swimmers and more vulnerable to predators, and their ballroom finery can soon look like Cinderella's rags. Only about half as long as the common goldfish, they have roly-poly bodies and are considerably less flexible about extreme temperatures. The Japanese strain is reddish orange, and the calico strain is mottled.

Shubunkin. This goldfish, developed in Japan, also grows to a robust 12 inches or longer with a long, flowing tail that is almost plumelike. Its most unusual multicolored body distinguishes the shubunkin, which is available in blue, purple, black, red, and brown. It prefers temperatures over 45°F and lower than 70°F.

Moor. This is a special type of fantail, easily recognized by its extremely dramatic black color, although the shadowy garb makes it especially difficult to observe in a pond. Slightly larger than other fantails, at 4 to 5 inches long, it also has a double caudal fin and may have comical *pop eyes.*

Common goldfish. These are highly recommended for beginners.

Comet. This fancy type of goldfish is very popular.

Fantail. Their hardiness makes maintenance fairly easy.

Shubunkin. "Calico" colors and black spots distinguish this fish.

Moor. These fish must overwinter indoors.

KOI (*Cyprinus carpio*)

Like goldfish, koi are members of the carp family. But while goldfish are easy, koi and most other carp relatives are more demanding and often unsuitable for smaller ponds. These big fellows aren't as tolerant of temperature extremes as goldfish are. They become listless if the water temperature approaches 70°F, although they can overwinter where the bottom of the pond remains unfrozen. The common carp, from which koi were first bred, really needs a lake to dart around in because it stirs up mud in which to hide from enemies. Most carp also have a tendency to nibble or uproot pond plants.

Of the carp sometimes mentioned in water-garden books, only koi are widely available and worth trying to include in a home pond. These fish, with a natural life span of several decades, are so revered in Japan that their image appears on flags and windsocks on Boys' Day, May 5, as a symbol of strength and loyalty. Little "whiskers" (barbels) lend personality to their faces, and they will eat out of your hand or even learn to jump through hoops. Those that have been carefully bred for specific color patterns can cost into three figures, but a small common koi can cost as little as $5. All can grow 2 to 3 feet long and have hearty appetites that will include your prized water lilies. That means you'll need to protect underwater plants with mesh; raise other plants high in the water, where koi rarely trespass.

Koi need water at least 3 feet deep, and each needs 25 square feet of pond to call its own. Their preferred temperature range is 39° to 68°F. Because of their hearty appetites, they also create a lot of waste, and so you'll probably need a pond filter to keep them happy and healthy. Butterfly koi, available from mail-order suppliers, are smaller and have longer fins and tails. They are costlier than common koi (although less expensive than collector koi) and hardier as well.

Koi. Members of the carp family, Koi need room—25 square feet per fish. Some of the elaborately patterned specimens are costly.

Butterfly koi. If you don't have a big enough pond for other koi, try this small type called "Butterfly," which is surprisingly hardy.

OTHER FISH

In addition to various types of goldfish and koi, there are other fish that you may want to consider for your pond. Here are some examples.

Orfe (*Leuciscus idus*). This slender fish is a good choice if your pond is well oxygenated, not subject to runoff that contains any toxins, and at least 40 square feet. Not only is the orfe large (18 inches in length), it's also a schooling fish that needs friends to bring out its natural friskiness—a half dozen is ideal. (A 40-square-foot pond will accommodate the school of six.) The orfe will reward you by nibbling on floating insects and sometimes jumping out of the water for airborne ones. It needs a gravel area in which to spawn. (The depth of this area isn't critical.)

Rudd (*Scardinius erythrophthal-mus*). This surface-feeding fish with reddish fins can be gold or silver. Although no more than 10 inches long, the rudd nevertheless needs some space in which to frolic as well as a generous amount of underwater foliage where it can hide and lay eggs. Native to Europe, the rudd can handle a wide range of temperatures, including a maximum of 102°F. The golden rudd (*S. e.* var. *aurata*) is bronze colored.

Tench (*Tinca tinca*). Once called the *doctor fish* because it was thought to cure pondmates of disease, the tench spends most of its time cleaning waste matter from the bottom of the pond. Look for the golden tench, which is bright enough for you to see it even when it's on the bottom. It usually grows about 18 inches long and is relatively tolerant of both temperature swings and occasional dips in oxygen. Its adaptability makes it a good choice for many different parts of the United States.

Orfe. Orfe, a frisky schooling fish, will entertain you by leaping from the pond for insects. It can grow 18 inches long.

Rudd. Although it is a compact species, the rudd needs a spacious pond as well as a lot of submerged plants to encourage breeding.

Tench. A school of tench is like having a professional sanitation crew at work. They're always cleaning the bottom of the pond.

FISH FOR WILDLIFE PONDS

If you're creating a wildlife pond, you are probably doing so out of respect for the natural environment, with a goal of balancing the plants and animals so that they'll need relatively little care. Native fish, like native plants, will do better than imported species—if you've taken care to create a habitat that's as much like their natural one as possible. They'll be able to get much of their food from the plants you've chosen, and they'll survive winter in the pond. They'll even look more appropriate in your pond.

Your wildlife pond is bound to attract predators that will eat some of your fish; if you buy native fish such as minnows, it will be less financially painful to lose some of them.

Minnow (*Pimephales promelas* or *Cyprinodon variegatus*). The common name *minnow* is used for several different small fish. These fish can grow to 6 inches long but are usually half that. Minnows like water that is shallow but also clear and well oxygenated. They need other minnows because they are schooling fish; they also need an area of clean sand or fine gravel in which to lay eggs.

Mosquito Fish (*Gambusia affinis*). If you live in a semitropical area, this fish can be a good investment because it has a prodigious appetite for the larvae of mosquitoes and midges. It is native to roughly the southeastern portion of the United States. Silvery blue-gray, mosquito fish grow to 2½ inches and breed quickly.

Three-Spined Stickleback (*Gasterosteus aculeatus*). The 2- to 3-inch stickleback is unusual not only for the triad of spines for which it's named but also for its fascinating behavior in spawning season: the fry are housed in a volcano-shaped underwater nest, to which the red-flushed male will return them by mouth when they wander. Sticklebacks can live for three years. The three-spined stickleback is a northern species, native as far south as New Jersey. A related four-spined stickleback (*Apeltes quadracus*) is native farther south, into Virginia.

Minnow. Several species of small fish go by the common name Minnow. Because all of them are schooling fish, you'll want to buy several.

Mosquito fish. Even the smallest pond can use a population of Mosquito Fish to gobble the larvae of mosquitos and midges.

Three-spined stickleback. A northern fish, the three-spined stickleback has a 4-spined cousin that is available for those south of New Jersey.

Koi swimming around lotus can add interest to your pond. But native fish are best for a wildlife pond.

WATER QUALITY

To keep fish healthy, pond water needs to stay within certain parameters. These include moderate temperatures, a sufficient oxygen content, a relatively neutral pH (a measure of the water's acidity/alkalinity), the absence of chlorine compounds, and minimal amounts of nitrites and ammonia (which come from both fish waste and fertilizer runoff).

Some chemicals used to purify water are toxic to fish. If your water comes from municipal or county sources, you'll need to check with local authorities to determine what chemicals are used to purify the water supply. If your water contains only ordinary chlorine, uncompounded with other chemicals, the chlorine will dissipate within 24 to 48 hours after you fill the pond. If your water supply contains chloramine (a compound of chlorine and ammonia) or chlorine dioxide, you'll need to treat the water with a dechlorinating agent, available from water-garden suppliers. Even if your water is free of these substances, it's a good idea to hold off introducing fish until the plants have had a couple weeks to become established, algae has cleared, and the pond's normal population of beneficial microscopic creatures has built up.

To monitor the water-quality parameters most important for fish, you will probably want the following items.

■ **A thermometer.** This is not so important for goldfish, which tolerate a broad range of temperatures, but it is crucial for some other fish that can't survive water temperatures above 70°F.

■ **A kit for testing pH.** Fish need a pH level near neutral, between 6.6 and 7.5. You should test your water supply to see whether it falls within this range; test the pond again after it's filled with plants and animals. You should also retest the water periodically to make sure the pH stays within the recommended range, especially after adding more than 20 percent new water or after introducing new fish and plants to your pond.

Water from some wells is naturally alkaline; if your water is hard, it will probably be alkaline too. (Both calcium and magnesium, often the cause of hard water, also cause alkalinity.) If you use a water softener or a water conditioner, don't use the treated water for your fish (or plants). If you don't already have a direct line for outdoor or garden use, install an outdoor faucet that connects directly to the water supply and bypasses the water conditioner or softener. Water can become alkaline if your pool is concrete, from contact with mortared edges, or if you use concrete blocks to raise water plants. Algae can sometimes change the pH level. You may also want to have on products for adjusting pH on hand.

A healthy environment. Just because your pond water is clear doesn't necessarily mean it's healthy for fish. Regular monitoring of water quality will prevent problems.

■ **A kit for testing ammonia and/or nitrites.** Some water-testing kits will also test for ammonia and nitrites, which can build up from fish waste when a pond is overpopulated. If your test kit doesn't, you'll need to buy a separate testing kit. (See "What's in Your Water," Chapter 10 on page 179 for how to correct excess ammonia and/or nitrites.)

■ **Dechlorinating formula.** This is essential if your water supply contains chloramine or chlorine dioxide. You'll need it especially during the summer, when it's important to keep ponds topped off with water. You can safely add up to 5 percent of pond volume once or twice a week without using a dechlorinator; if you add more, you'll need to retreat the water. Adding water with a spray or sprinkler will help dissipate ordinary chlorine as well as add some oxygen.

■ **Rock salt or pond salt.** Fish have a coating of mucus that protects them from disease but that can be lost when they are stressed. Periodic treatment of the pond with rock salt (not iodized table salt) at the rate of 2 pounds per 100 gallons will restore this protection. Salt corrects the electrolyte balance of the fish and helps prevent the loss of fluids. Salt manufactured especially for ponds includes beneficial trace elements. It's not good for plants, though, so it should be added to the pond as far away from plants as possible. If you prefer not to add salt to the pond water, you can give fish a salt bath. (See the aquarium discussion, above right.)

■ **A parasite treatment or preventive.** Use this when you add new fish—especially if they haven't been treated by the dealer—or when you spot the symptoms of parasites. (See "Common Fish Diseases," on page 163 for a discussion of various parasites.)

■ **An aeration kit.** The oxygen content of your pond can decrease rapidly in thunderstorms or during a sudden change in air temperature. (Warm water doesn't hold oxygen as well as cooler water does.) This kit may be needed to restore the oxygen level for your fish. Also, fish may suffer from an oxygen deficit at night, when plants release carbon dioxide, so it's usually a good idea to leave your waterfall, fountain, or other aeration device operating all night. (You can also help aerate the pond by splashing water in with a hose or even by stirring it.)

■ **One or more plastic buckets for transporting fish.** For medium-size fish, a 5-gallon bucket is a good size; for large fish, get a short, wide bucket.

■ **A soft net (on a pole) for guiding fish into the bucket.** Lifting fish out of the water in a net is stressful to them, so you should use the net only to steer them into the bucket.

■ **An aquarium.** You'll need to use an aquarium as a "hospital tank" for treating sick fish, as a holding tank to inspect new fish before adding them to your pond, or as a winter home for the fish if you live in a cold climate. Consult an aquarium dealer about what size to buy. Obviously, size isn't as important if one or two fish will be in the tank for a few hours as it will be if you bring all your pond residents indoors for several months.

The aquarium should be filled with water from the pond, unless you have reason to believe something is wrong with the water quality. It should be connected to an aeration device of some kind, as sick fish will be additionally stressed by a lack of oxygen. Medications in the water also increase the need for aeration. Where you put the tank is a matter of practicality, as long as it's kept out of the sun so that the water doesn't heat up; indoors is best, because some treatments might take as long as two weeks.

If you don't want to add rock salt to your pond as discussed above, use the aquarium for a salt bath and then return the treated fish to your pond.

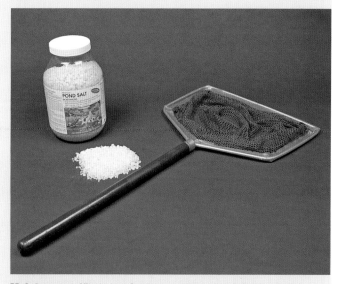

Maintenance. Kits to test for oxygen, ammonia, nitrites, and other substances are necessary to help keep fish healthy. Pond salt and a transfer net are two of the tools you will find useful.

Bringing Fish Home

Don't buy your fish until the water temperature in your pond consistently stays at least 50°F, which is the temperature at which most species become active in spring. If you have a reputable pond supplier in your area, it's worth driving out of your way to buy fish there. The salespeople will be more knowledgeable; they will probably offer a guarantee; and when they slip your new fish in a plastic bag for the ride home, they will inject the bag with oxygen.

Certain mail-order water-garden suppliers ship fish over long distances, although spending a day or two in the belly of a plane at a variety of different temperatures will stress out even the most well-packaged creature.

Fish from a pet store may have a harder time making the transition from indoors to out. But if buying fish this way seems your only option, study the list of fish diseases on pages 163 so that you can identify a sickly fish. Ask the store staff whether they guarantee the fish's health for a length of time, and if they can treat the fish for parasites before you take them home. On the ride home, keep the fish in a cool, dark place. A picnic cooler with a lid is a handy way to trans-port them. Don't put them in the trunk or keep them in a closed car while you run other errands.

Lower the bag into the pond, and add some of the pond water. Doing this over a period of 10 to 15 minutes will ease the transition to a different temperature and different water quality. It's best not to add the water from the bag to the pond, on the chance that it contains parasites. Instead, ease the fish out with your hand or, less desirably, a net.

Watch the fish for an hour. Fish are apt to try to jump out of a new pond. If they continue to jump out or gasp, check the water. Move them to an aquarium to fix the problem. Feed the fish sparingly for the next couple of days.

SPAWNING

Fish play their mating game in late spring and early summer, usually when the water has warmed to between 54° and 60°F. Males get tiny white bumps on their gills, and some become brighter colored. Females take on a slightly pregnant look because their ovaries are bulging with thousands of eggs.

A frantic morning chase around the pond convinces the female to lay her eggs, usually on an underwater plant, after which the male fertilizes them with his sperm, or milt. Babies, known as fry, hatch about a week later and spend the first day clinging to the plant or the side of the pond or hanging vertically in the water, absorbing their egg sacs for nutrition.

Fish fry are vulnerable not only to pond insects and other predators too small to bother adult fish but also to other fish species and even to their own parents. If you want to save as many fry as possible, buy a spawning mat (not unlike a crude welcome mat) to put on the pond bottom. Remove it to an aquarium when you see eggs on its surface. The young fry need a high-protein diet of flakes, brine shrimp, or daphnia.

FISH DISEASES

Even a novice can spot many of the changes in behavior or appearance that mean a fish is ill. A sick fish may act lethargic or huddle against the edge of the pond, gasp for air, swim frantically and bump the pond edge, or be bullied by other fish. It might clamp its fins against its body or develop red veins or fins, or its dorsal (spine) fin may be droopy.

If you see unusual symptoms, check the water temperature, pH, and levels of ammonia and nitrites to determine whether any of these is stressing the fish. Correct any water-quality problems, and see whether your fish improve.

When bringing new fish home or when moving them around, handle with care. They are easily stressed and do better with a gradual transition.

FEEDING YOUR FISH

In a well-balanced pond, fish theoretically do not need to be fed at all. But supplemental feeding is usually necessary. You'll enjoy watching them scurry after their food and hurry to the water's edge to greet you.

Fish need supplemental food in spring and fall. They become active as soon as the water has reached 50°F in spring, but this early in the season not many plants will have leafed out yet, nor will there be many insects and other little creatures for them to feast on. At this time, don't feed your fish protein. Instead, choose wheat germ or other similar high-carbohydrate foods, which are easy for fish to digest. Once the water has warmed another 10°F or so and their activity level rises dramatically, they need more protein in the form of chopped worms, daphnia (also called water fleas), or some frozen or freeze-dried fish foods. (Daphnia can be seen as pale pink clouds in the water and will help keep the pond clean by eating free floating algae.) Most fish-food products on the market contain around 40 percent protein, which should be adequate in a balanced pond.

These supplements come in sticks, pellets, or flakes. All of these forms float, which allows you to net out un-eaten food and keep the pond clean. A granular form, although often less expensive, will sink; you'll save money, but you can't be sure how much is turning into waste at the bottom of your pond. This waste is a potential cause of disease, so avoid overfeeding your fish.

The water temperature should be above 70°F for young koi to properly digest and metabolize their food. (Note the net to keep predators away from the fish.)

Always select reputable name-brand commercial fish food. The floating type lets you easily remove any leftovers.

Feeding Schedule. Feed your fish once or twice each day when spring first arrives; then gradually decrease your feedings to every other day or so. They should survive quite well without feeding if you take a short vacation. Never feed them more food than they can eat in five minutes, and use a net to remove any food that remains. Avoid feeding them late in the day. Their metabolism goes up after they eat, so they then need more oxygen. Because plants give off carbon dioxide at night, less oxygen will be available to the fish then. Cut back gradually on food as temperatures drop in autumn and fish become less active. Stop feeding for the winter once water temperatures fall below 50°F. Your fish will survive the winter by living off the fat they have stored. They will use these resources slowly because their metabolism has slowed.

Sometimes diseased fish will benefit from a change of diet; try a different brand of fish food, and see if your fish improve. Members of the carp family will also eat worms as well as vegetables, such as lettuce scraps and peas.

When fish become ill remove them from the pond using a net. Nurse them back to health in the aquarium water.

COMMON FISH DISEASES

If fish are clearly ill, it's often best to remove them to an aquarium, where you can treat them with a medicine or salt bath and keep the disease from spreading to the rest of the pond inhabitants. Handle the fish as little as possible to minimize additional stress. Net each fish underwater, guide it into an underwater bowl or bucket, and then lift out the bowl and lower into the aquarium water.

Some of the more common fish diseases are described below. Consult your supplier or a veterinarian for more specific treatments.

Anchor Worm. This isn't a disease but a tubelike parasite, about ¾ inch long, which attaches under the fish's gill with its hooked head while it produces two eggs at its nether end. The main symptom is a swelling where the parasite is attached. Catch the fish, and remove each anchor worm with tweezers; then treat the spot with an antiseptic such as merbromin or iodine (from a drugstore).

Dropsy. This ailment, most often caused by bacteria, has such a telltale symptom that it's sometimes called the pinecone disease: the fish swells, and its scales bristle away from its sides, making it look like a pinecone. Fish will also get bug-eyed. Dropsy is hard to cure, although a salt-bath treatment may help.

Finrot, or Bodyrot. The fish—often a fantail or a shubunkin—develops a white line on its caudal area (where the body joins the tail), and this area becomes inflamed. The tissue disintegrates and needs to be gently removed with a sharp knife; then the fish is put on treatment with a special antibiotic. Antibiotics can be administered in fish food, in water in an aquarium, or on the affected area directly. It's always an excellent idea to consult a veterinarian before you administer antibiotics, just to make certain that you're using the correct medication and dosage.

Flukes. There are both gill and skin flukes; in either case they are microscopic, parasitic flatworms. When they prey on fish, you'll see excess mucus plus irritated puffy patches or loss of color, and the fish will act irritated, banging against objects, twitching their fins, and opening and closing their mouths rapidly. A salt bath may help.

Fungus. When fish are stressed and their protective mucous layer breaks down, they become susceptible to fungi normally present in pond water. Instead of tolerating these fungi, the fish sprout cottony growths. Most fish suppliers sell fungicides that can treat the problem.

Lice. These flat, gelatinous creatures are only ¼ inch long but have clearly visible legs and eyespots. The tissue damage they cause by attaching themselves to the fish, often on the fins and gills, can eventually prove fatal to the victim. Remove lice deftly with tweezers, and treat the fish with an antiseptic such as iodine.

Tuberculosis. This is a highly contagious bacterial disease that can cause rapid weight loss, as the human version does. Fish may lose color and develop raw swollen patches, and fins may waste away. It is almost always fatal. To prevent the spread of this disease, remove any fish from the pond as soon as you suspect it is tubercular.

Ulcers. Bacteria common to pond water will cause stressed fish to develop ulcers, popped eyes, bloody patches, and ragged-looking fins. Treat with an antibiotic for fish, and test the water to determine what's stressing the fish.

White Spot. Fish with this disease (technically, ichthyophthiriasis, or "ich" for short) will have spots like grains of salt, similar to those that males develop on their gills during the mating season. But these will be all over the fish's body, and because they itch, the fish may bump against the sides of the pond. White spot is caused by the parasitic protozoan *Ichthyophthirius multifilis*, hence the disease's tongue-twisting technical name; consult your dealer or veterinarian about a cure.

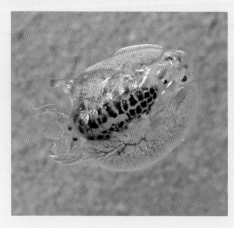

Fish tick or lice is a tropical-fish parasite that can be removed with tweezers.

Keeping Fish Healthy

- Test water quality regularly. If you have a lot of fish, be particularly vigilant about ammonia and nitrite levels.
- Be prepared to remove fish quickly. Have an aquarium or other hospital tank available should they display any signs of distress or illness.
- Be aware of predators. Install protective netting or fencing if you see birds or animals lurking around your pond.
- Find a reliable expert. Have a contact number handy for a trusted supplier or veterinarian whom you can call for advice.

WINTER CARE OF FISH

If you've made your pond at least 18 inches deep (2 feet deep in cold climates), goldfish and other hardy fish should survive winter there because the water in your pond won't freeze all the way to the bottom. But it's also crucial to keep the surface of your pond from freezing solid. If that happens, the normal exchange of oxygen and carbon dioxide can no longer occur, and poisonous methane released by any decaying organic matter will be trapped in the water. You can't just bang a hole in the ice, however, because the shock waves will carry through the water and can injure or kill the fish. An electric pond heater is the most reliable way to keep a hole open in the ice, but you can also use a pan of boiling water. Some northern gardeners erect greenhouses over their ponds to keep them from freezing. (See "Winter," on page 189 of Chapter 11, for more details and other ideas for protecting and maintaining your pond.)

FISH PREDATORS

Even if you live in a city, don't assume that your fishpond is safe from natural predators. In the heart of Washington, D.C., the owner of a rooftop pond has seen blue herons swooping overhead (although she hasn't caught them landing) and had to have a raccoon removed by animal-control officials. Because effective ways to protect fish from predators can be unsightly, you may have to forgo either finny friends or aesthetics.

BIRDS AND BEASTS

You can discourage or slow down terrestrial predators such as raccoons with dense plantings of grasses around the pond edge. Don't fret too much about cats, which love to watch fish but are rarely able to catch them (and hate to risk taking a swim). Retrievers and other water-loving dogs don't harm fish, but they make themselves a nuisance by knocking over planters and puncturing liners with their sharp nails.

Herons. These entertaining birds, which goose-step with backward-jointed knees, are plentiful along the coast as well as inland waterways. The great blue heron can grow 6 feet tall; the green heron and related egret are smaller but equally skilled fishers. Because they walk to the water, rather than swooping down like seagulls, they can be discouraged with fishing line strung around the pond about 6 inches off the ground. Statues of herons may deter them—these birds like to dine alone—but usually not for long.

Heron. Although herons are great fun to watch, they need to be kept away from your pond. Trip them up with a "fence" of fishing line.

Kingfisher. Belted Kingfisher go after prey by taking a vertical plunge. Remove any high perch from which they can dive.

Gull. Because gulls are divers, defeat them by to installing netting over the pond. This will make them move on to easier foraging.

Belted Kingfisher. This is another great bird to watch—for its spiky punk hairdo, distinctive loud crick call, and ability to plunge after fish in a vertical dive. Kingfishers kill fish by beating them against their perch, tossing them in the air, and swallowing them headfirst. Since you don't want this happening to your fish, avoid any kind of tall perch located conveniently near your pond.

Gulls. Compared to herons, gulls rarely fish in ponds. They're happier hunting around larger bodies of water or scavenging garbage dumpsters. If diving birds become a problem, the only solution is to suspend a fine net just above the pond.

Raccoon. Of all pond predators, raccoons are the most feared. But while they love water, always washing their food fastidiously, they like to enter the water at their own pace and won't appreciate a sheer drop off the side of a pond. In short, they're looking for the most graceful entrance possible. Where raccoons are common, design fishponds with steeply vertical sides and no shallow plant ledges. In addition, plant the perimeter thickly with grasses and other dense marginal plants. This type of barrier will put a real dent in their fishing efforts. If problems with raccoons become overwhelming, don't give up on keeping fish. Instead, call your local animal control agency or your state's fish and

Raccoon. Considered Pond Enemy Number 1, raccoons will often be deterred by a pond with steep sides.

game department for savvy ideas or assistance. Avoid direct contact with raccoons, which can be fierce fighters when cornered. If you see one out during the day, this may mean it has rabies.

TROUBLESOME INSECTS

There are a number of insects that you should be on the alert for if you see them in or around your pond. Some are fascinating to watch while others can be nuisances, preying on your fish. Following are some examples of troublesome bugs you may see hanging in or around your pond.

Diving Beetles (*Dytiscus* species and *Acilius* species). These dark brown or green oval beetles are native throughout North American waters and can range from $\frac{1}{16}$ to more than $1\frac{1}{2}$ inches long. Although they usually live on water insects, mites, and larvae, they will also attack small fish, frogs, and tadpoles. The great diving beetle, which is dark brown with golden trim, is especially fierce; it will attack fish and suck their body fluids.

Water Boatmen and Backswimmers (*Corixa* and *Notonecta* species). Somewhat elongated, these beetles are dark gray-brown, often with darker bellies marked with triangles. You can see the bellies of some species because they are swiming upside down, using their legs like oars. They are only capable of wounding larger fish but can claim their fair share of newborn fry.

Giant Water Bug (*Lethocerus americanus*). Sometimes more than 2 inches long and 1 inch wide, this brown bomber skulks around in bottom vegetation. The bug uses hooked front legs to grab its prey, injects fluids that paralyze it and dissolve its innards, then sucks it dry. Victims of giant water bugs include other insects, tadpoles, and small fish.

Dragonflies (*Order Odonata*). Who doesn't love to watch dragonflies and damselflies flitting colorfully and hovering among the water plants? During their aquatic nymph stage, though, some species will eat small fish.

Water Scorpions (*Nepa* species). These 1-inch-long insects lie in wait among submerged plants and, like the giant water bug, grasp their prey with their feet before biting it and sucking it dry. They will wound, although not kill, fairly large fish.

Whirligig Beetles (*Dineutus* species and *Gyrinus* species). These black oval beetles, less than ¼-inch long, are endless fun to watch because of the way they spin around on the water surface. They need air to breathe and can blow themselves a submarine bubble for diving underwater. They usually eat other aquatic insects but will sometimes eat fish fry. You can net them off the surface if you want to protect your fry.

Diving Beetle. These oval beetles are well-equipped predators that usually live on insects but have been known to snack on fish, frogs, and tadpoles.

Water Boatman. Entertaining swimmers, water boatman beetles will do the backstroke across your water surface and will keep down your fry population.

Giant Water Bug. This 2-in. water bug would be easy to spot if it didn't hide in bottom vegetation. It paralyzes and sucks dry its prey.

Dragonfly. Much like helicopters, dragonflies dart around on their gossamer wings to the delight of on-lookers. In their nymph stage, they may eat small fish.

Water Scorpion. A ferocious predator that can wound large fish and kill smaller ones, the water scorpion lies in wait, then pounces, grasping prey with its feet and sucking out the victim's innards.

Whirligig Beetle. Usually more amusing than harmful, a whirligig beetle spins like a top on the pond surface. It sometimes supplements its diet of other aquatic insects by eating fish fry.

OTHER WATER-LOVING CREATURES

In addition to fish and some members of the insect community, there are other creatures who enjoy the water. Here are some to consider.

Frogs (*Rana* species) and Toads (*Bufo* species). Toads are land dwellers but, like frogs, lay their eggs in water and spend the first part of their lives as tadpoles. Tadpoles are beneficial for ponds, acting as scavengers and cleaning up algae and spent vegetation. Toads will eventually hop away from water to live on land and will help keep your garden free from slugs and bugs. Frogs remain in and near water; they eat primarily insects, although bullfrogs (which can grow to 6 inches long) are capable of eating good-size fish. In winter, frogs hibernate in mud near the pond; in spring, they may move away from your pond to find a new mate at another one. Wildlife experts advise not buying bullfrog tadpoles, which have voracious appetites, but instead waiting for smaller, sometimes endangered, native frogs to colonize your pond.

Mussels and Clams. You may want to introduce these bivalves into your pond as natural filters—unless you have koi, which will eat them. They'll need a shallow tray of coarse sand to burrow in. Avoid the zebra mussel (*Dreissena polymorpha*), which has become a serious problem in our country's waterways. Look for the brown swan mussel (*Anodonta cygnea*), which requires a large pond, or the freshwater clam (*Elliptio crassidens*). Be sure to remove any dead mussels immediately, as they decompose with a strong unpleasant odor and can pollute your pond.

Newts (*Notophthalmus* species). These lizardlike reptiles spend the first few months of their lives as aquatic larvae. Most then spend a couple of years on land hunting insects, crustaceans, and worms; unlike salamanders, adult newts eventually return to water and again become aquatic. Males develop showy crests during the spring mating season.

Snails. Water-garden suppliers often sell snails to help keep ponds clear of algae, decaying vegetation, and wasted fish food. Those most commonly offered are the ramshorn snail (*Planorbis corneus*), which has a spiral shell, and the black Japanese or trapdoor snail (*Viviparus malleatus*). The latter is the more desirable of the two because it won't snack on your prized plants. Trapdoors bear live young; other snails

Frog. Frogs will serenade you with their nighttime chorus, but males will often abandon the pond in search of a mate.

Mussel. Provide a little sand for them, and mussels or clams will obligingly serve as natural water filters. Be aware, though, that koi and raccoons both love to eat them.

Newt. A cousin of the salamander, the newt starts out life in the water, has a two-year hitch on land, and then returns to water.

Snail. Working hard as the pond's cleanup crew, snails take care of algae, decaying vegetation, and uneaten fish food.

lay eggs in jellylike masses on the undersides of leaves. Different species of snails may show up in your pond and will serve the same useful function, but they'll munch on live plants if they multiply too rapidly. Don't tolerate the presence of the great pond snail (*Lymnaea stagnalis*). Shaped like a 1-inch ice cream cone, it will quickly overpopulate your pond. You can attract snails by floating a lettuce leaf on the pond—remove the leaf when enough snails have boarded it. To further keep their numbers in check, wipe egg masses off of leaf undersides. Stock eight to ten small snails or six to eight large snails per square yard of water surface area.

Turtles (Order *Testudines*). A turtle that does laps in your pond will also add its waste to the water. But you may need to learn to coexist, as many turtles are endangered; moving them to another habitat is illegal in many states. Fortunately, snapping turtles—the ones most likely to cause problems—are not endangered, and it's legal in some areas to hunt them. Discourage turtles by making sure they don't have an easy way into your pond.

Snakes. You shouldn't have to worry about snakes moving into your pond unless you live near another body of water where aquatic snakes are at home. The most common are the water snakes (*Nerodia sipedon* and other *Nerodia* species), nonpoisonous snakes native to the eastern United States and into Canada. Other species, such as garter snakes, may stop for a drink and eat your fish when they do. The dangerous water moccasin, or cottonmouth (*Agkistrodon piscivorus*), is native to the southern states. It holds its flat head well above water when it swims (unlike other water snakes); fortunately, it's rarely active during the day. If you have any reason to suspect that the snake in your pond is a water moccasin, call your local animal-control official. Snakes can eat your fish and frogs. With the exception of the aggressive water moccasin, snakes you'll find near water are afraid of humans and will try to retreat, unless they feel threatened. If you encounter one, always leave the snake an exit.

Turtle. Because they need air to breathe, turtles may avoid your pond if they don't have an easy way in and out. They are destructive and can harm both plants and fish.

Snake. Most snakes, such as this banded water snake, are harmless and should be tolerated in your garden. Aquatic snakes aren't likely to visit your pond unless you live near water.

Attracting Birds

A water feature of any kind or size can be a magnet for birds. The most irresistible will be those that provide a shallow area where birds can drink or bathe with ease. Birds are especially drawn to moving water, even if it's only a tiny trickle.

Birds need two other things if you want them to hang around for any length of time: food and shelter. You can pro- vide food by putting bird feeders near your pond and by growing food-bearing plants. Feeders are easy but do have disadvantages. Some people feel that feeders can make birds lazy about looking elsewhere for food, so they become dependent on you to keep them fed. Feeders can also be a source of bird diseases. You need to keep them clean. (Scrape out old seed, or wash out hummingbird feeders, before refilling them.) Sterilize them yearly with one part bleach to nine parts water.

BIRD FOOD

If you want to attract a variety of species whether you have feeders or not, you should fill your garden with plants that offer seeds and berries. In summer and fall, birds will flock to seeds of sunflowers (*Helianthus* species), black-eyed Susans (*Rudbeckia fulgida* or *R. hirta*), purple coneflowers (*Echinacea purpurea*), and many ornamental grasses. Garden staples such as zinnias (*Zinnia* hybrids) and marigolds (*Tagetes* hybrids) are also good seed producers.

Some good berry plants include eastern red cedar (*Juniperus virginiana*), black cherry and chokecherry (*Prunus serotina* and *P. virginiana*), mulberry (*Morus rubra*), hollies of all types (Ilex species), dogwoods (*Cornus* species), and viburnums (*Viburnum* species). The larger, more prolific berry producers such as red cedars and mulberries should be kept a good distance from your water garden so that scooping up uneaten berries won't add to your pond-maintenance chores. This is rarely a serious problem with smaller trees and shrubs; just try to find a leftover of something you might also like to eat, such as a juicy blueberry or black cherry!

Birds appreciate a garden that's a bit untidy. Among good sources of berries are many "weeds" such as sumac and Virginia creeper (both of which are gaining in appreciation as garden plants), wild blackberries, wild grapes, and even poison ivy. A slightly overgrown garden will harbor more insects, which is good news if you want to attract insect-eating birds. Branches or stumps along the water's edge, or a rock jutting out of the water, let birds land and possibly hunt small water insects.

Mulberries. Mulberries will attract songbirds, but plant the tree well away from the pond so the fruit won't fall in the water.

Black-Eyed Susans. Seeds from these flowers are good for migratory birds. Other possibilities are sunflowers and purple coneflowers.

BIRD SHELTER

Shelter is just as important as food for luring birds. Give them dense plantings of leafy shrubs where they can hide from enemies and maybe even build nests; include evergreens for year-round shelter. Grasses provide cover for ground birds. If you don't mind some raised eyebrows among the neighbors, create a brush pile with fallen and pruned limbs. (You can always drape it with a berry-producing vine.)

Serious bird lovers let dead trees stand if they won't create a safety hazard. Dead trees are a big draw for woodpeckers, which want the insects in them; when the woodpeckers finish, small birds can nest in the cavities. If kingfishers are in your area, though, and you've stocked your pond with fish, dead trees make a perfect diving platform for these adept fishing birds.

Shelter. A birdhouse may persuade feathered friends to stay. Plant shrubs and tall grasses where they can hide from enemies.

AVOIDING CHEMICALS

One of the required trade-offs for luring wildlife is giving up garden chemicals. Pesticides will kill the creatures that many birds eat, including worms and grubs in the lawn, and birds may be harmed by pesticides on insects and plant parts that they eat. Herbicides used to control lawn weeds will harm water plants if they wash into the pond. Even common fertilizers, if they get into your pond, will upset the healthy balance you've tried to create for your water, plants, and fish. Seek out nontoxic control options for garden pests. If you must fertilize near a water garden, use as little as possible and try organic or slow-release formulas to cut runoff. You will be rewarded with the songs of old friends every summer morning and new species every spring and fall.

Visiting Foragers. The red-winged blackbird may drop by to forage. Avoid garden chemicals, which kill bugs that birds eat.

PART 4

Water-Garden Maintenance

There are routine tasks that you will have to undertake to keep your water garden thriving, including consistently maintaining the water quality. Keeping pond water clear for fish and plants will also make it more attractive to humans. Other tasks involve seasonal maintenance and troubleshooting. We'll start by addressing water quality, which is one of the greatest challenges in water gardening.

CHAPTER 10

Ecological Balance

Factors that affect the ecological balance of your pond include its size and depth, the amount of sun it receives, water temperature and movement, pollutants from runoff, and the kind and number of plants and fish you have. Because of this complicated ecological interplay, your pond can take anywhere from several weeks to several months to achieve an ideal balance. Then the pond can stay balanced indefinitely unless any of these factors changes appreciably.

How Your Pond Works

Your pond or water garden is a small, self-contained ecosystem. When you introduce aquatic plants, they draw nutrients (especially nitrates and phosphates) from the water and, if they're potted, also from the soil. These nutrients, combined with sunlight, are what nourish plants, enabling them to grow and thereby release oxygen into the water as a result of photosynthesis.

When fish are introduced into this ecosystem, they consume the oxygen produced by the plants. Fish derive other benefits from plants. Surface plants such as water lilies help keep water from overheating by providing shade from the hot summer sun. Plants also give fish a place to hide from other fish, cats, raccoons, birds, and other predators.

In turn, fish provide gases and nutrients that plants need in order to grow: carbon dioxide from their breathing, and nitrogen and other chemicals from their wastes. Fish also help control populations of plant-eating insects. To some measure, they likewise consume some of the plants and thus keep excessive plant growth in check.

When the numbers of fish and plants in the pond reach a stable relationship (not too many of one or the other), the pond is in biological balance. The reason balanced ponds are relatively clear is because plants and fish in tandem help control the algal growth that can turn the water cloudy. Scavengers such as snails and tadpoles also help balance the pond by consuming algae and organic debris.

Water Problems. The most common water problems are caused by having too many fish or feeding the fish too much. A buildup of dead plant material, having too many living plants covering the surface, prolonged hot weather, or

A waterfall, left, helps maintain the water quality in this pond and keeps it well aerated.

Surface plants such as water lilies provide shade for the fish in this pond, opposite bottom, preventing overheating.

an excess of algae can deplete oxygen and lead to more problems. Your water may also contain pollutants from pond-building materials and toxic chemicals that may have been washed or blown into the water from outside sources.

Incorporating a waterfall or a fountain in your pond design will promote good water quality. Either of these features will aerate your pond and help ensure that fish have all the oxygen they need. Lack of oxygen will bring fish to the surface, gasping for air. This sometimes happens with little warning after long periods of hot, dry weather. But it can also occur in stormy weather, when water may turn and decrease available oxygen in the pond's top layer, or when prolonged cloudy weather disrupts photosynthesis by your pond's plants. You can rescue gasping fish quickly by oxygenating the pond with spray from a garden hose. Or you can have on hand a separate aeration kit that includes an air pump. If the need for aeration arises, you simply place the pump about an inch below the water surface, screening the pump's intake so that it doesn't suck in small fish or other tiny pond creatures while in operation. When fish behavior returns to normal, these measures can be discontinued.

This idyllic setting, above, was achieved over months of getting the water, plantings, and fish to coexist in a balanced environment.

Nitrogen Cycle

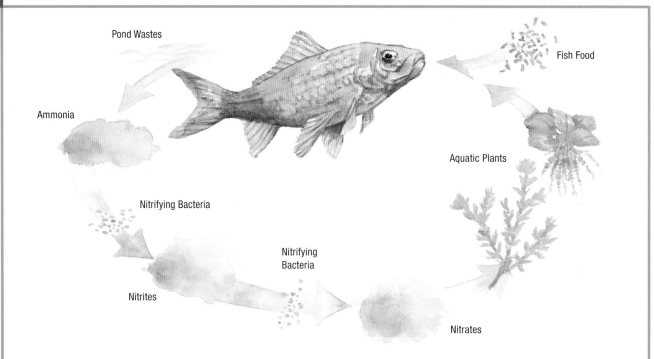

Pond Wastes

Fish Food

Ammonia

Aquatic Plants

Nitrifying Bacteria

Nitrifying Bacteria

Nitrites

Nitrates

Ammonia from pond wastes can be fatal to fish. Bacteria in biological filters and some algae convert ammonia first to nitrites (also harmful), then to nitrates that plants can consume.

ALGAE: FASCINATING AND SOMETIMES HELPFUL

Algae may look unappealing in your pond, but they can be beautiful under a microscope. Under magnification, their usual colors of green, brown, and yellow can give way to reds, blues, oranges, and other hues.

Algae lack flowers and the leaves, stems, and roots that circulate nutrients in "higher" plants. They range from the single-celled forms that can cloud your pond to sea-dwelling kelp more than 200 feet long. The type that turns a pond murky is called planktonic, a term that covers all forms that are suspended in water. Under a microscope, you would see that these algae have threadlike "tails" (flagella) that allow them to move through the water.

Planktonic algae thrive when it's warm and sunny. When the weather cools in fall, you might see more filamentous algae—the type that forms long, hairy-looking strands. Some of these algae are yellow or gold. Spirogyra, the melodic name of which derives from its spiral

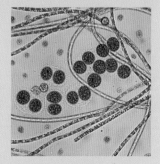

bands of chlorophyll, consists of long strings of cells that attach themselves to the pond bottom and other surfaces.

Not all algae live in ponds. One called Haematococcus prefers shallow water such as birdbaths. (You might see its telltale reddish color if you have the Japanese water basin called a *tsukubai*.) Others grow on moist stones or even in soil. Some of these soil dwellers are the blue-green algae, or cyanobacteria, that have become such a popular item in many health-food stores.

Mosslike algae that grow on the sides of the pond are beneficial and a sign of good pond health. Because they harbor the same kind of bacteria found in an artificial biological filter, they help to remove toxic chemicals from your water.

CONTROLLING ALGAE

When you first fill your pond, the water will be crystal clear. After a few days, however, the water will turn murky and take on a greenish tinge. This is caused by microscopic, single-celled, free-floating algae. Their presence is to be expected until aquatic plants have established themselves. Submerged (oxygenating) plants eventually starve the algae by outcompeting them for available nutrients. Floating plants and water lilies likewise help starve the algae; they not only consume nutrients but cut off the sunlight that algae need to grow. To a lesser degree, fish, snails, and accidentally introduced algae eaters such as water fleas also help.

Algal Concentration. You can expect to have some algae in the pond, even after it's balanced. At a level that causes only a slight discoloration, algae are not harmful to fish or plants; they help conceal the artificial-looking liner or shell as well as any planters or pump on the pond bottom. As the pond matures, most of the free-floating algae will eventually be replaced by various visible forms of filamentous, mossy, and slime algae growing on the sides and bottom of the pond, as well as on plants, rocks, and any other convenient surface.

When algal growth becomes excessive, however, it's worse than unsightly. Not only do algae consume the pond's oxygen in the process of decaying, but in excessive amounts they will cut off sunlight to oxygenating plants below the surface, reducing the oxygen supply even further. Algae can also coat the floating leaves of water lilies and other plants so that they lose their ability to help balance pond gases. When pond water is depleted of oxygen, fish begin to gasp for air and eventually die.

Natural Control. Make every effort to control algae naturally with oxygenating plants and pond scavengers such as tadpoles and snails—or mechanically. Algae that forms a scummy mat on the surface, sometimes called filamentous algae, can be removed with a fine-mesh net or by twirling it around a long-handled brush or rake as you would twirl spaghetti on a fork.

Chemical Control. You can buy chemicals called algicides to kill algae. Many people use algicides for initial algal control after they install a pond or to control the algal blooms that tend to occur in spring. But like any garden chemical, algicides are just a temporary remedy and not a cure. Moreover, they can cause other problems. Some algicides are toxic to fish, and those sold in pet stores for use in aquariums, in particular, will affect the growth of other water plants. (Always check the package label.) Furthermore, these products do not guard against the growth of new algae, which is inevitable. A much better, long-term solution, in addition to the natural controls mentioned above, is adding one or more filters to your system. (See "Filtration" on page 180.) If algal growth continues to be a problem even after some type of filtration has been installed, consult a pond specialist.

Algae removal. Excess algae is unsightly and unhealthy for your pond. It's easily removed with a stick, rake, or long-handled brush.

Balancing a New Pond

Once you've done all the hard work to install your pond, you'll be eager to populate it with plants and fish. But a bit of patience now will pay off with fewer problems later. Do your homework by calling the local water authorities so that you will know what chemicals your water supply contains; then you can obtain test kits and any chemicals you will need to correct chlorination or any other anticipated imbalances. (See "What's in Your Water" on the next page.) Follow the steps below to create a natural biological balance in your brand-new pond.

Rinse and Fill the Pond. If you've used pool paints, wood stains or preservatives, pipe-joint glues, or similar wet materials on your pond, let them dry thoroughly, because otherwise they can contaminate pond water and poison fish and plants. Treat mortar, concrete, and cement with an acidic solution to prevent lime from leaching from these materials, which would make the pond water too alkaline. (See "Constructing a Lined In-Ground Pond," Step 6 on page 71.) After you've rinsed the solution off, drained the water, and rinsed out any debris remaining from pond construction, fill the pond with fresh water. If you've installed a filter, run it continuously for the first few days before introducing plants. Depending on your situation, you may have to drain and refill your pond several times.

Test the Water. When you first fill the pond, the water may contain chemicals and minerals that are toxic to fish and plants. Well water may contain hydrogen sulfide (also produced by decaying organic matter and detectable by a slight rotten-egg smell), which requires extra aeration. Tap water from public supply systems may contain chlorine, chlorine dioxide, chloramine, or ammonia; well water won't. Allowing tap water to stand for a few days will get rid of most free chlorine, but chlorine dioxide and chloramine require chemical treatment. (See next page.)

After filling the pond but before introducing plants or fish, test the water. You can buy kits from pond dealers, garden suppliers, and pet shops to test for most problems. The kits usually include instructions for correcting any problems you find. Some pond dealers and pet shops provide water-testing services and can advise you on proper treatment.

Correct Water Conditions. Follow instructions included with the test kits to correct any problems that have been detected. Some fish and plant dealers recommend giving the pond a dose of a general-purpose water conditioner

INTRODUCE FISH TO THE POND

Two to three weeks after you've introduced plants and corrected any adverse water conditions such as the presence of chloramine (next page), it's safe to add fish, snails, and tadpoles. The size and number of plants and fish a pond will support will vary with the amount of available oxygen and sunlight and the water quality. A pond with good water circulation and filtration will support a larger population of fish than will a stagnant pond with no filter.

before adding fish or plants, just to be on the safe side. But just as you shouldn't use chemicals in the rest of your garden unless there's a good reason, you shouldn't use water conditioners in your pond unless tests show that they're actually needed. Even if you use a conditioner to achieve your initial water balance, try to determine the source of the pollution to prevent future problems.

Introduce Plants. Once water tests show that you've removed chloramines and that other measures are within a safe range—and the danger of frost is past—you can add plants. The sooner you add them, the sooner they can begin their balancing act of helping to prevent algal buildup, and providing oxygen and food for fish. The pond water will likely start to turn green right then, but it will probably clear up in a few weeks as plants become established.

WHAT'S IN YOUR WATER

Water-garden suppliers offer kits you can use to test water for potentially harmful chemicals or unhealthy situations. Here's a quick explanation of what you might find. (For more on monitoring contaminants, see "Water Quality" on page 158.)

■ **Ammonia.** Ammonia is present in fish waste, so the usual explanation for high levels of ammonia is having too many fish. But some public water supplies contain ammonia if they've been treated with chloramines. Decaying organic matter will also contribute to ammonia levels. Ammonia will stress your fish, and too much will kill them. Clean out the pond bottom, and change at least 50 percent of the water. The best control for an ongoing problem with excess ammonia is having a biological filter installed.

■ **Chlorine.** The most common additive in municipal water supplies, chlorine is also fortunately the easiest to deal with as it dissipates within 24 to 48 hours. If you are adding chlorinated water to an existing pond, however, avoid adding more than 20 percent of the pond volume at one time to keep from harming the fish.

■ **Chloramine.** Also used to purify municipal water supplies, chloramine is a combination of chlorine and ammonia. It's more toxic to fish than chlorine and does not dissipate on standing. Find out from local water suppliers whether it's used in your tap water. If so, always have on hand the chemicals needed to neutralize it.

Fish need a pH level that is near neutral—between 6.6 and 7.5—so you should test the water periodically.

■ **Nitrites.** Resulting from the breakdown of ammonia, and so are most likely to be present when there are too many fish, nitrites suffocate fish. Control nitrites by changing half the water and treating it with 2½ pounds of dissolved pond salt per 100 gallons of water. (Dissolve the salt in a small amount of water first, and remove as many plants as possible.) You can make emergency filters by putting an absorbent substance called zeolite, sold by water suppliers, into mesh bags and dragging this around the pond.

■ **Nitrates.** Harmless compounds that result from the breakdown of ammonia or nitrites, nitrates serve as nutrients for plants. Their presence can show that your pond is going through a healthy process of converting those harmful compounds into the harmless form that plants can use. An excess of these nutrients can feed algae, however, and may indicate the need for more submerged plants (oxygenators) and other plants. In general, you won't need to test for nitrates.

■ **pH.** Short for "potential hydrogen," pH is a measure of acidity or alkalinity. The scale ranges from 1.0 (highly acidic) to 14.0 (highly alkaline), with 7.0 being neutral. Healthy pond water ranges in pH from 6.5 to 8.5. Tap water is more likely to be within this range than well water in some areas. Alkaline water can be caused by leaching from concrete or limestone rocks; fish tend to raise acidity. You can buy commercial products to adjust your pond water's pH, but use them carefully because a rapid change in pH is harmful to fish.

■ **Hardness.** Hard water, which has an excess of minerals, is not in itself harmful, but it can affect pH. If your tap water is hard, it may be alkaline; if your tap water is very soft, it's probably somewhat acidic. While there are kits available for testing hardness, you won't need them. If you suspect hard or soft water, just test the pH.

■ **Oxygen.** Maintaining high levels of oxygen in your pond keeps everything in balance. You might want to test for dissolved oxygen before adding fish or if the fish you have seem ill. If oxygen levels test low and you already have a waterfall or a fountain, add an aerating device to provide more oxygen. Oxygen can be depleted by having too many fish.

Filtration

If your goal is to have a small ornamental pond with a few plants and fish and you don't mind slightly cloudy water from time to time, you may not need a filter. If on the other hand, you have a large pond with many fish and want clear water for viewing them, a good filter will certainly help. Koi ponds, particularly, require clear, relatively pure water.

There are two basic types of filters: mechanical and biological. Mechanical filters trap algae and other particles, while biological filters convert chemical pollutants into harmless substances. When you're shopping for any type of filter, it's a good idea to seek out the advice of an independent dealer who carries several brand names.

Filters require pumps to move water through them. If the pump will be used for filtration only (and not also for a waterfall or fountain), arrange the system so that the pump intake is at one end of the pond—preferably the deepest—and the discharge is at the other. This will produce a slight current across the bottom of the pond, which will aid in recirculating the water to remove sediment and other water impurities.

A skimmer removes leaves and other large debris before they fall to the pond bottom and start decomposing.

STOCKING FORMULA FOR A BALANCED POND

It will take time and experimentation to achieve a balance between plant and animal life. For starters, use the following formula for stocking your pond. More detailed information is provided in "The Roles Plants Play" (see page 200) and "Pond Critters" (see Chapter 9, page 150).

■ Two bunches of submerged (oxygenating) plants per square yard of pond surface.

■ One medium to large water lily for each square yard of surface area, or enough water lilies, lotuses, or floating plants to cover 50 to 70 percent of the pond surface during the summer months. Most water plants go dormant during the winter months and then reestablish themselves during the spring. After they are established, you will have to divide or prune water lilies and other water plants occasionally to prevent them from overcrowding the pond.

■ Two inches of fish (length) for each square foot of pond surface in a pond 18 to 24 inches deep, or one koi for every 25 square feet in pond surface. When you are stocking your pond, keep in mind their eventual size, rate of growth, and the possibility that they will produce fry.

■ Eight to ten small snails or six to eight large snails per square yard of pond surface.

MECHANICAL FILTERS

Don't confuse mechanical filters with the filter screens and prefilters attached to pumps. Those screens are meant only to keep debris from clogging the pump impeller and fountain jets; they won't have any effect on water quality. Debris- or algae-filled water will be hard on your pump, however. (And a good mechanical filter will keep the screen or prefilter from clogging with mats of algae.)

The primary purpose of a mechanical filter is to trap large particles of suspended matter that can cloud water. This material includes fish waste, decaying organic matter, floating algae, and leftover fish food. Mechanical

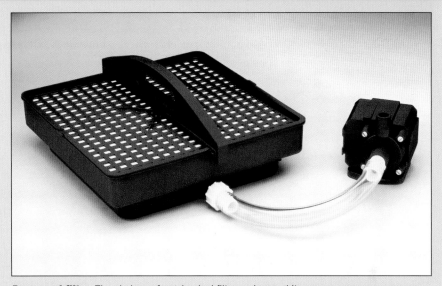

Pump and filter. The choices of mechanical filter and pump kits are numerous. They are generally rated for pond duty by the number of gallons in the pond.

filters are less expensive than biological filters, and they start filtering your pool immediately, whereas biological filters are not effective for several weeks. Their main drawback is that they require frequent cleaning—at least once a week, and usually daily during the summer. Some mechanical filters (suction filters) are plumbed into the pump inlet, while others (pressure filters) are plumbed to the pump outlet. Some go inside the pond, and others are placed outside. An in-pond cartridge-type filter is sufficient for most small ponds (those with a capacity of less than 1,000 gallons). These devices use a corrugated polyester filter medium, which looks and works much the same as an automobile oil filter. Other small filters strain the debris through screens, foam, or woven fiber pads or wraps. Some let you add activated charcoal or a mineral called zeolite to remove ammonia and other chemical impurities from the water. None of these filter media has any particular advantage over another. The effectiveness of the filter depends more on its overall size, which is usually expressed as the surface area of the filter medium (in square feet) and the amount of water pumped through it (in gallons per hour). Manufacturers generally provide performance capacities for their filters—for example, "for ponds up to 300 gallons."

Very large ponds (1,000 gallons or more) require more substantial filters. Options include a diatomaceous-earth filter or a high-rate sand filter, like those used in swimming pools. These large filters must be placed outside the pond and require a large pump and extensive plumbing.

Skimmers. A variation on the mechanical filter, called a skimmer, removes debris before it can sink to the bottom of the pond, holding it in a bag that you remove, much like a vacuum cleaner bag, a couple of times a month. Water gardeners with numerous deciduous trees find them indispensable. Skimmers are installed in the ground at the perimeter of the pond. Dealers recommend that they be run with a separate pump so that all of the water, not just that on the surface, is circulated regularly.

To be effective, a mechanical filter needs a high flow rate. The filter should be combined with a pump that can circulate all of the water in the pond once every two hours. If you've installed a fountain or waterfall, be sure you have a pump large enough to operate that feature and still provide sufficient circulation through the filter. Your water-garden dealer can advise you. If your budget allows, select a filter that exceeds the minimum requirements for your pond. The larger the filter, the less often you'll have to clean it. Fortunately, cleaning generally takes only a few minutes: you simply remove the filter pad, cartridge, or screen, and wash it off with a garden hose.

BIOLOGICAL FILTERS

The main function of biological filters is not to remove debris or even algae but to convert organic pollutants into relatively benign substances. Primarily this means converting ammonia from fish wastes (and to a lesser extent, from decaying plant matter and uneaten fish food) into nitrates, which can be absorbed by plants as a nutrient. If you have an excess of nitrates, however, you are more likely to have algae. To avoid this situation, be sure to include a sufficient number of oxygenating (submerged) plants. (See page 205 for descriptions.) They are particularly good at absorbing nitrates.

How They Work. Biological filters contain two or more layers of gravel or other medium that harbor large concentrations of beneficial nitrifying bacteria naturally found in ponds. As water slowly flows through the medium, these bacteria break down toxic ammonia (and nitrites, which result from the partial breakdown of ammonia) into nitrates. Other specialized microorganisms feast on single-celled algae passing through the filter. More complex types of biological filters may incorporate mechanical prefilters or compartments filled with activated charcoal, zeolites, or other media.

Look for a filter that includes an aeration tower, which provides additional oxygen for beneficial bacteria. Dirty water is pumped from the pond through the aeration tower to the bottom of the filter, where it slowly percolates up through the gravel filter medium (giving the bacteria a chance to eat their fill). It exits near the top of the filter and through a return pipe to the pond. (The return pipe can be hooked up to a waterfall.)

You can grow submerged plants in the top layer of gravel to provide additional oxygen for the bacteria and to absorb nutrients. The layers of gravel also serve as a crude mechanical filter to trap some suspended particles in the water, further clarifying it. If you still have problems with debris, add a mechanical filter to the filtering system.

Cleaning. About once a month, drain the filter by opening a drain valve at the bottom to remove accumulated silt and sediment. (You can use this to fertilize garden beds.) Then lightly rinse the filter medium to dislodge trapped particles. Don't use heavy sprays of chlorinated tap water, as that would tend to dislodge or even kill the beneficial bacteria in the filter medium; a small bucketful of rainwater is better. Give the filter a more thorough cleaning at the end of the season. (The bacteria won't survive below 55°F anyway, so once it gets cold, you don't have to worry about chlorinated water.)

Unlike mechanical filters, biological filters do not require a high flow rate to operate efficiently. The pump needs to turn over the total water volume only once every four to six hours. So even though they are initially more expensive than mechanical filters, they use less electricity. Biological filters need to be run constantly and don't start working efficiently until several weeks after they are installed—unless you give them a dose of "starter" bacteria, purchased from your water-garden supplier. Most of them are large, unsightly tanks placed outside the pond above water level and will need to be disguised somehow, such as behind a shed or under a deck. Several manufacturers have recently introduced small in-pond biological filters, but their capacity is limited to ponds of 300 gallons or less.

Basket for
Additional Plants

Anchored
Lava Rock

Filter Media

Filter Media

Water Passages

Waterfall box and biological filter. This upflow biological filter is used to convert organic wastes into nontoxic forms. As water flows through various media, harmful substances are broken down and rendered harmless.

OTHER WATER-CLEANING DEVICES

Mechanical and biological filters will be sufficient for most ponds. Where algae or fish diseases are an ongoing problem, consider adding one or more of the following devices.

Ultraviolet Sterilizers. Ultraviolet (UV) water sterilizers are sometimes used in conjunction with a biological filter. Plumbed into the inlet side of the filter, these units consist of an ultraviolet bulb encased in a transparent, waterproof sleeve, which in turn is placed inside a tube plumbed into the system. When microscopic organisms are exposed to concentrated ultraviolet light, the UV energy causes the cell content (protoplasm) of the microorganisms to explode. Algae, bacteria, viruses, and certain fish parasites can be killed in this manner. The light also encourages minute organic particles to clump together so that they can be trapped in the filter. UV sterilizers usually aren't needed if you have a good biological filter. But if you're constantly dealing with fish diseases or parasites, they may help.

Ozone Generators. Converting oxygen from the air into ozone and infusing it into the water, where it breaks down chloramines, ammonia, nitrites, and phosphates into harmless gases that escape the pond, ozone generators purify water and reduce bacteria and fish parasites. Like UV light, ozone promotes the clumping of minute toxic waste particles so that they are more easily trapped by other filters. Used for many years to sterilize water in swimming pools and spas, ozone generators are becoming popular among koi hobbyists. Although they are costly, they may be a good investment if you want a crystal-clear fish pond with few or no plants to remove nitrates from your water.

Natural Plant Filters. Another option for ponds with few or no plants, a natural plant filter is nothing more than a separate small pond or a large tub densely planted with such plants as water hawthorn, watercress, water lettuce, or water hyacinth placed between a biological filter outlet and the main pond. Because the plants consume nitrates and other nutrients produced by the biological filter, they reduce the algal growth in the main pond. They can also be incorporated as an attractive part of the overall landscape design. The expense of ultraviolet sterilizers and ozone generators probably can't be justified unless you are raising valuable fish. Using natural plant filters to remove excess nutrients is a low-tech, relatively inexpensive option.

In addition to lily pads, which are natural oxygenators, your pond needs an efficient filter system.

CHAPTER 11

Routine Tasks

nce your pond is established, you'll need to clean and maintain it on a continual basis. But caring for a pond isn't the drudgery you may think. There are many time-saving devices available. Pond maintenance can actually be a pleasurable pastime, getting you closer in touch with the plants and animals that live in your water garden.

Fish are susceptible to stress after their winter fast. Give them a closer look, right, if they show any signs of illness.

You'll need to tend to plantings, too. Summer flowers, below, should be deadheaded to encourage new blooms.

Season to Season

Maintaining a clean, healthy pond is like a cross between keeping up a garden and caring for an aquarium. Even during the summer months, when your pond requires the most attention, it shouldn't take you more than an hour or two every week to keep it in good shape.

Your pond will go through seasonal cycles, but while residents of temperate climates can almost forget their perennial beds for a few months during winter, they need to be vigilant year-round when it comes to their ponds.

The sequence of routine maintenance tasks is the same everywhere, even though spring comes sooner to North Carolina than Vermont.

Fish are especially vulnerable to diseases casued by bacteria, fungi, and parasites during hot weather.

SPRING

The advent of warmer weather is a time for inspection and remediation. Early spring, before plants have leafed out, is a good time to check your pond's edges for any settling or shifting and repair them if needed. Grounds softened (but not soggy) by spring rain make landscaping easier. Check your electrical connections, lights, and pumps; repair any loose connections. Make sure ground-fault circuit interrupters are working by hitting the "test" button. If you stored your pump and filters for the winter, bring them out, reconnect them, and make sure they're in working order.

Clean out any pond debris that accumulated over the winter. Start biological filters once the water temperature remains above 50°F. When you put a biological filter back in service, it will take several weeks for the beneficial bacteria to reestablish a presence in the filter medium. You can buy starter bacteria from a water-garden supplier to speed up the colonization process.

As the weather warms, you may notice excessive algae (called an "algal bloom"). This problem will usually take care of itself once water lilies and other aquatic plants leaf out and begin providing shade and consuming nutrients.

Spring is the traditional time to add new plants to your water garden and to transplant or tidy up existing ones.

Chemical Adjustments. Spring is a good time to check pH and water chemicals. If tests indicate that your water is polluted, you should replace a third of the water volume. Don't do this if the pond is undergoing an algae bloom, however, as that could make the problem worse. If you make the water change, do it over a few days. If you add more than 5 percent of your pond's volume in a week, then dechlorinate the tap water.

Late spring is the time to introduce new aquatic plants and to remove any dead foliage from existing ones. If you overwintered tropical water lilies, put the tubers in a shallow pan of water on a sunny windowsill about two months before the expected last frost in your area so that they can begin sprouting. Don't put them back in your pond before the water temperature reaches 70°F.

Divide water lilies, lotuses, and marginals with roots that are filling their pots. The best time to do this is after danger of frost has passed and before rapid growth resumes. Start giving lotuses fertilizer pellets twice a month; water lilies, once a month. Weed and mulch peripheral beds.

Frogs will begin singing and laying eggs. Fish, at first lethargic and weak from winter hibernation, will start to feed as the water temperature climbs toward 50°F. In the middle of the day, when their digestion is most active, offer them small amounts of high-carbohydrate foods containing wheat germ. Koi will like fresh salad greens.

Weather Changes. If the weather turns hot before water lilies have leafed out to provide shade, create temporary shade at one end of the pond with a tarp, or other fabric held down with rocks. Because the fish have gone many weeks without food, they have a heightened susceptibility to stressors of all kinds. That means they're more likely to become ill, so check them frequently for unusual symptoms. Watch for blotchy or discolored skin, missing scales, or lethargic or erratic behavior. (See "Fish Diseases," on page 160.) If you treat your pond with a fungicide because your fish are ill, do so before starting a biological filter because fungicides will also kill the beneficial bacteria that make the filter work. In mid- to late spring, you may see fish bumping and chasing each other because it's spawning time. To assist the process, you can buy spawning mats to place in the pond.

SUMMER

As fish become more active in warming weather, you can give them high-protein foods such as chopped worms and daphnia (water fleas). In established and well-balanced ponds, they may get all the protein they need from insects and other small water creatures. Never overfeed fish: the rule of thumb is to give them no more food than they can eat within five minutes.

Oxygen. Because flora and fauna will be flourishing and multiplying, you should inspect the pump once a week and clean it as often as necessary. As the water heats, it's a good idea to run the pump continuously. Oxygen levels will drop, especially at night or during a thunderstorm. If you have fish, it's worth investing in a kit to test for dissolved oxygen. Blackened water, a foul smell, or fish gasping at the surface of the water is a sign that the oxygen level is dangerously low. For emergency aeration, you can spray the pond with a garden hose or use a separate aerator, which many pond owners find to be a worthwhile investment.

Spend a few minutes each day snipping off faded blossoms and keeping plants trimmed; such maintenance chores can be relaxing and give you additional quiet moments to enjoy your water garden. Insects will start to appear on plants, but avoid the use of insecticides in or near the pond. Handpick larger insects and dispose of them. Use a garden hose to spray aphids from water lilies, or wipe plant leaves with a damp cloth periodically. Once the water temperature reaches 75°F,

In summer, you'll need frequent access to water for aerating the pond, topping it off, and spraying pests off plants.

increase your fertilizing of water lilies to twice a month. Blanketweed, a filamentous alga, may be a problem in hot weather; if you twirl a long stick under it, it will wrap around the stick like cotton candy for easy removal.

Evaporation. As the weather becomes hotter, water evaporation will increase, so you'll need to top off the pond every day or two. It's best to add a little water each day rather than a large amount once a week. Otherwise, if you use tap water, you'll need to dechlorinate it. You may find it helpful to store tap water in rain barrels, since chlorine will dissipate from the stored water. You can also set out plastic barrels to capture rainwater for topping off your pond. Remember to check it for pH, though, because rainwater can be highly acidic. Be vigilant about testing your pond's water quality at least once a month, or more frequently if you suspect a problem.

Heat brings greater incidence of fish diseases caused by bacteria, fungi, and parasites. Check fish regularly for signs of illness. (If you think you might forget, schedule a routine weekly check.) Immediately move sick fish from the pond to an aquarium, and treat them with the appropriate fish medicine. Seek treatment advice from a book on fish or from your aquarium supplier.

Hotter weather means lower oxygen levels. For healthy fish, consider buying a kit to test for dissolved oxygen and an aerator to rescue fish in emergencies.

AUTUMN

Keep falling leaves from collecting in your pond or they'll decay and pollute the water. If the pond is under a tree, stretch netting over the pond and weigh it down with bricks or rocks. If leaves tend to blow in from one direction, you may be able to keep them out with a line of netting or other temporary fencing. Scoop up floating leaves and other debris with a net. Remove any leaves that sink to the bottom of the pond with a soft plastic rake, pool sweep, or spa vacuum. (A pool sweep circulates water from your garden hose, so it may require you to dechlorinate your pond.)

Autumn is a good time to rein in rampantly growing oxygenating plants, which should be thinned and cut back severely. Don't remove the turions, or overwintering buds, from plants such as frogbit. Cut back other aquatics as they go dormant; water lilies can be trimmed to about an inch above the container. Do not cut marginals below the water level. Remove tropical water lilies and other tender aquatics and discard them or store them in their containers for the winter. If your pond has several depths, move water lilies to a level where the water will not freeze. If your pond might freeze below their crowns, you'll need to overwinter them in a frost-free place. Cattails and many of the ornamental grasses are beautiful in winter; don't cut them back until early spring.

Fish Food. As fish metabolism slows in preparation for winter, you should switch back to fish foods containing wheat germ. Gradually taper off the feedings to once every two to three days. Cease feeding as the fish become more lethargic and the water temperature drops to 50°F. When the water temperature drops below 45°F, fish become inactive and stop eating; you won't need to feed them again until the following spring. Refrain from feeding if fish become active during brief warm spells. In warmer climates (where water temperatures remain above 50°F), continue to feed fish all year, or as long as they remain active. As floating plants and water lilies die back, the fish will lose cover from predators, so lay down some sections of 4-inch drainpipe where they can hide. (Black plastic is less visible than drain tiles, but it may need to be weighted down with a rock.)

A well-maintained pond won't need an annual stem-to-stern decontamination. But if yours is filled with grit and debris or tests show it to be polluted, autumn is the best time to drain and clean it. As days shorten and temperatures drop, most water plants are on their way to dormancy and the increasingly drowsy fish are less likely to be stressed by a temporary relocation. (See "How to Drain and Clean the Pond," on page 192.)

If you won't be running the pump during the winter, remove it from the pond, and clean all parts before storing it. Drain all pipes to keep them from cracking. Even if you'll be using your pump to keep the water from freezing as suggested on the next page, detach and clean fountain nozzles. External pumps should also be removed and tended. To avoid damage to a biological filter, drain, rinse, and store it.

In autumn, installing a net over the pond will keep out falling leaves that can decay and pollute the water, which will cause more work next spring.

WINTER

If you live in a warm climate where freezes are rare, your pond duties won't change much in winter. Anywhere else, your main concern is to keep your pond from freezing for long periods. When ice forms on the pond, it can cut off oxygen to the fish and trap toxic gases beneath the surface. If the pond is frozen for more than a few days, fish may suffocate. (You should never break the ice, however, because the vibrations can injure your fish.) Ice can crack a concrete pond and may also damage inexpensive shells or the vertical sides of lined ponds.

Ice. Raised ponds are particularly susceptible to freezing. Plants and fish can't survive the winter in aboveground ponds except in frost-free areas. Protect a raised pond from ice damage in short freezes by covering it with boards and a tarp or similar heavy material. You can also keep ice from exerting pressure on the sides of the pond by floating something in it—rubber balls, wooden planks, a couple of milk jugs. This will work for in-ground ponds, too, where freezes are infrequent or of short duration.

In mild climates, where ice is a temporary condition, you can place a pot of boiling-hot water on the ice to melt a hole in it. Use a pot with a hole in the handle and run a heavy string through the hole so you can retrieve the pot if it melts clear through the ice.

In moderately cold climates, raise a circulating pump off the pond bottom (so it doesn't circulate cold water into the bottom where fish and plants are keeping warm) and direct the outward flow up with a short tube or pipe; this will keep ice from forming in that part of the pond. The easiest way to keep a pond ice-free, and the only way in extremely cold climates, is to buy a floating pond deicer to keep a hole open in the ice all winter. These devices are controlled by a thermostat, so they run only when needed, and (of course) should be plugged into a circuit with a ground-fault interrupter. Keep snow off the ice surface so light reaches the bottom of the pond.

Planning. Use winter downtime to your advantage. Make observations about your pond's microclimates; consider planting shrubs to block stiff cold winds; or figure out where to move slow-growing water lilies so they get more sun. Winter is the traditional time to order plants for the coming spring. Also replenish your supply of snails or tadpoles if necessary, and any testing kits or plumbing supplies you expect to need. Suppliers will wait to ship plants and animals until it's safe to put them outside in your area.

Many types of fish can spend winter in your pond as long as the surface doesn't freeze solid. Ice cuts off their oxygen and traps toxic gases. A pond deicer is the most reliable solution.

In climates where freeze-ups are relatively brief, balls or other floating objects will keep ice pressure from damaging the sides of your pond.

Troubleshooting

Your ability to observe and respond to small changes in the pond environment—whether it's a different color to the water, altered behavior in your fish, or a slight shift in your edging—can save you more expense and heartache down the line. The solution to serious problems may involve emptying the pond of water and quickly refilling it with the least amount of trauma to its inhabitants.

MAINTAINING THE POND

A well-maintained pond should only need cleaning every three or four years. You should avoid cleaning wildlife ponds if possible, because the microorganisms and small creatures in the water are all important to the ecosystem you want to maintain. It can take many months to reestablish a good balance.

But if the water is choked with algae, filled with sediment, or severely polluted, you may have to completely drain the pond, scrub it down, and refill it with fresh water. Draining may also be necessary to find and repair a leak in the pond liner or shell. (See "How to Repair a Pond Foundation," on pages 194–195.)

The best time to clean the pond is during late summer or in early autumn. If you clean the pond in the spring, you might disrupt spawning fish and amphibians or destroy the eggs, or damage emerging plant shoots. And cleaning a pond in the middle of summer is like trying to make a bed with people still lying in it; it's much harder, in addition, it upsets the sleepers!

Quick Guide to Common Problems

PROBLEM	SOLUTION
Pond stays green into summer	Remove debris from bottom Add more oxygenating and floating leaved plants
Fish gasping at surface	Add more oxygen to water with garden hose or aerator
Fish act frantic	Spring: this is normal spawning behavior Other seasons: check for diseases (see page 146)
Fish disappear	Suspect predators (see page 150)
Water level drops after topping	Suspect a leak (see page 179)
Water level turns black, smells unpleasant	Oxygen is low: aerate quickly with garden hose or aerator Add more submerged plants to prevent in future
Lotuses don't bloom	Climate too cold; choose a more appropriate plant
Water lilies don't bloom	Not enough sun; look for shade-tolerant varieties

Make it a daily habit to snip off faded blossoms. This "chore" can actually be a way to relax and enjoy your water garden.

how to

Drain and Clean the Pond

DIFFICULTY LEVEL: MODERATE

When it's time to clean your pond, arrange to do it when you can drain and refill it as quickly as possible. Although it's important to do a thorough job, you don't want to leave a flexible liner exposed or aquatic plants out of the water any longer than absolutely necessary. Be sure to run the pumped out water into a nearby garden that can benefit from the water's nutrients.

Tools and Materials: holding tubs (plastic wading pool or trash can); plastic buckets; fish net; newspaper or burlap (for water plants); plastic dustpan; aquarium air bubbler (for lengthy cleaning/repairs); garden hose and adapter for pond pump (if available), or sump pump; soft-bristled brush (optional); water purifier or dechlorinating agent; thermometer

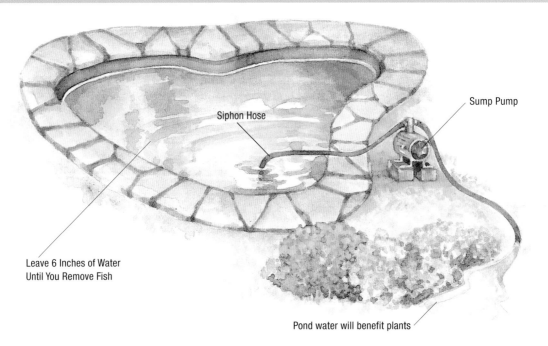

Siphon Hose

Sump Pump

Leave 6 Inches of Water
Until You Remove Fish

Pond water will benefit plants

Remove the water. Use a siphon hose, the pond pump, or a high-capacity sump pump to drain the pond.

1 Drain the Pond. Before you start, prepare one or more holding tubs for your fish. You'll need about a gallon of water for each inch of fish (for example, one 5-in. fish in a 5-gal. bucket). If you have a lot of fish, a children's plastic wading pool or 50-gal. plastic trash can works well. Place either in the shade; fill with some of the pond water; and add a few bunches of oxygenating plants to the tank.

Drain the pond to about 6 in. above the bottom; then carefully net out the fish and put them in the holding tub. If the fish will be out of the pond for more than a few hours, place an aquarium air bubbler in the tank to provide additional oxygen. If your property slopes and your pond is situated slightly uphill, you can use a garden hose to simply siphon out the water to a lower area of your yard. Otherwise, you can use your pond's pump to pump the water out.

Garden hose adapters are available for many pond pumps. If you can't get an adapter for your particular pump, or if you can't use the pump to remove the water for some other reason (it's a slow process, and it may be that you simply can't spare that much time), you can rent a high-capacity sump pump at most tool rental shops or home centers.

Run the pumped out water into a nearby garden area; the nutrients it contains will benefit your plants. Don't allow the pump to run dry, or the motor will burn up. At this point, you will be glad if you have followed the advice to create a sump area when building your pond. (See page 60.) It will ensure that your motor does not run dry before you have most of your water pumped out, and will also leave you a smaller area of water and muck to bail out by hand. To avoid damaging your liner or shell, always use a plastic bucket to bail out any remaining water.

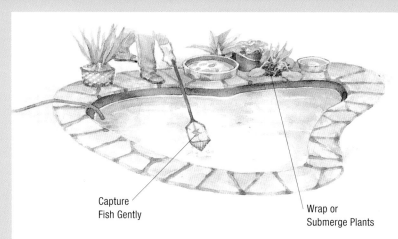

Capture
Fish Gently

Wrap or
Submerge Plants

Preserve fish and plants. Place fish, snails, and other pondlife in tubs filled with pond water. Aerate the water. Submerge or wet-wrap plants as appropriate.

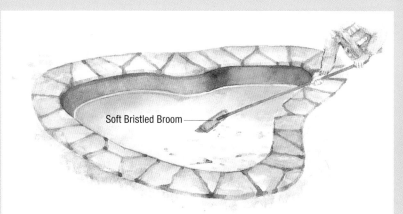

Soft Bristled Broom

Clean pond gently. Use soft tools that won't damage your liner or shell.

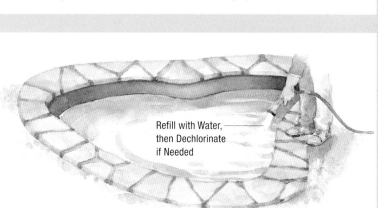

Refill with Water,
then Dechlorinate
if Needed

Refill pond. Treat any water imbalances; reintroduce plants; then add fish when water warms.

2 **Remove the Wildlife.** You'll have to take measures to preserve the fish and plants. All of your oxygenating plants will have to be submerged in holding tanks or buckets; it's often easiest to make new bunches of stems and repot them in fresh soil. Water lilies and marginals need to be kept moist and out of the wind. Wrap them in wet newspapers or burlap sacks; put them in a shady location; and spray them occasionally with a garden hose.

When the pond is drained, sift through the silt, and pick out as many snails as you can find. (You probably won't get them all.) Put these snails in the holding tank with the fish. Use a plastic dustpan to shovel out the silt on the pond bottom.

3 **Clean the Pond.** Carefully scrub the sides and bottom with a soft-bristled brush or a strong jet of water from a garden hose; don't use chemical cleaners; and be careful not to tear or puncture the liner or pond shell. Rinse and drain the pond several times in order to remove any remaining muck. Once the liner is completely clean, inspect it carefully for leaks. This is a good time to make liner repairs.

4 **Add Fresh Water.** Refill the pond with fresh water. Unless you are using well water, add a dechlorinating agent or water purifier. Pour a few buckets of the original pond water back into the pond to help establish the biological balance. Reintroduce your plants now, but don't put the fish back into the pond until the water temperature returns to within 5 deg. of the temperature in the holding tank. Don't forget: as with new ponds, you can expect increased growth of algae until the ecological balance is reestablished in the pond.

Repair a Pond Foundation

DIFFICULTY LEVEL: MODERATE

If you've been careful installing a liner or shell, not introduced a 200-pound statue with no footing, and avoided wading across the pond in your golf cleats, the chances are good that your foundation will meet or exceed its life expectancy. But accidents happen to even the most careful pond keepers: big branches fall, big dogs drop by for an uninvited romp, big rocks tumble from the edging. Here's what to do if your pond is leaking.

Flexible Liners. If flexible liners develop punctures or tears before the end of their life expectancy, it's worth repairing them with patching kits available from water-garden dealers. The kits usually contain a small can of adhesive and a piece of liner for making patches; some come with double-sided tape rather than adhesive.

Tools and Materials: scissors or utility knife; milk or food coloring; buckets (for fish); wet newspaper (for wrapping plants); sand; liner underlayment; cloth; utility paint brush; liner patch material; liner adhesive; weight (sandbag, etc.)

A flexible liner can develop tears or leaks, which can usually be repaired.

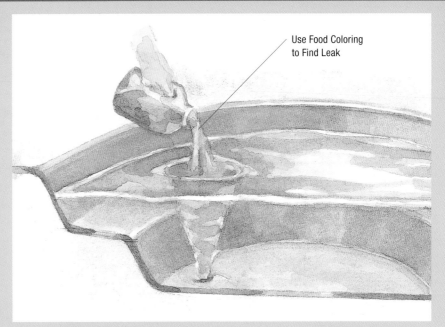

Use Food Coloring to Find Leak

1 **Locate the Source of the Leak.** Eliminate a leak in a waterfall by shutting it off, topping off the pond, and seeing if the level goes down. If not, check along the sides of the waterfall or in the tubing. Then check the pond's edges to make sure a spot hasn't settled lower than the water level. Add water to just above this level. Squirt milk around the edges of the pond; it will form a line toward a leak. Drain water to below the leak. Cushion the area behind the tear with damp sand or liner underlayment.

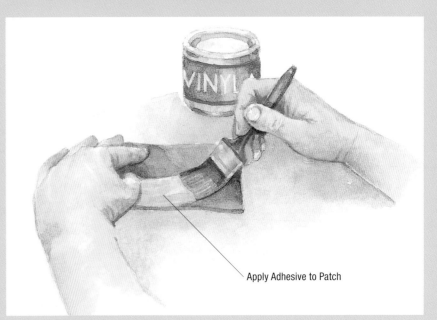

Apply Adhesive to Patch

4 **Coat the Patch.** Apply a coat of adhesive to the back of the patch, making sure you cover it completely. Allow the adhesive to become slightly tacky (about 2 to 3 min., or as recommended on the label directions).

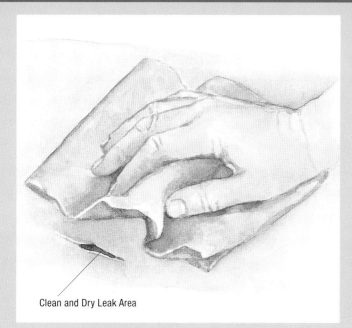

Clean and Dry Leak Area

Apply Adhesive to Liner

2 **Wipe off the Leak Area.** Make sure the tear or puncture is completely clean and dry. This is important because otherwise the adhesive you will be using on the liner material and the patch will not adhere properly.

3 **Brush on Adhesive.** Cut a patch from the same material as the liner (PVC plastic or rubber) that is about 2 in. wider and longer than the tear. Apply a thin, even coat of adhesive over and slightly beyond the torn area.

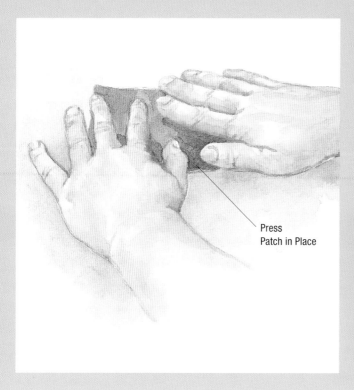

Press Patch in Place

5 **Adhere the Patch.** Firmly press the patch down, and smooth it to remove wrinkles. If possible, weight the patch with a bag of sand. Allow the adhesive to dry thoroughly.

Rigid Ponds. Leaks in rigid pond shells usually indicate an uneven base (in which case you will find the leak along the rim) or a sharp stone under the shell (in which case you'll find a leak farther down). You can repair the leak with a fiberglass-boat repair kit, which has resin and a catalyst you will have to mix.

After locating the leak, drain the pond and either level the shell bottom or remove any object that may have caused the puncture. You can patch the shell before or after returning it to the hole, whichever seems easier. Using sandpaper, roughen the area around the leak so that the patch will stick. Spread the adhesive mixture on the patch, and apply the patch to the leak. Follow the manufacturer's directions for drying.

Concrete Ponds. You may be able to patch a few small cracks with a caulk and neoprene rubber coating. Or install a flexible liner on top of the concrete. Sand down rough spots; fill deep crevices; and install an underlayment before lining.

PART 5

Selecting Your Plants

Now you're ready to choose plants for your water garden. There are absolutely no limits to your choices. In fact, you can decide not to have any plants at all! A small formal pool set into a stone patio is not a place where most plants will thrive—such a design is often just about water. From that extreme, there is a spectrum of possibilities.

CHAPTER 12

Plant Encyclopedia

A ny pond with some area of still water can be home to a few water lilies or an elegant lotus. Most water gardeners will grow underwater plants because of the important biological functions they perform. On the margins of your pond, you can plant a single clump of exquisite Japanese irises or a vast collection of wetland plants and cattails. If the rest of your garden is rose beds, a formal pool surrounded by rose topiaries might be wholly appropriate. On a sweeping lawn, the answer might be a slightly less formal water feature with a single dramatic clump of ornamental grasses or a huge swath of them—depending on the size of both the yard and pond.

Pickerel weed's tiny blue flowers grow on spikes and bloom from late spring to autumn. It thrives in full sun and in water up to 5 in. deep or alongside a wetland or pond.

Choosing Plants

Look for plants that blend with the design of your water feature and the rest of your yard. Whether your design is formal or informal will affect the way you use plants. Formal gardens employ plants in ways that make human intervention obvious—in geometric beds or in planters, or carefully pruned. To complement a formal pool, limit your choices to a few plants. You can choose a single dramatic specimen—a solitary bonsai on a pedestal or a weeping cherry tree. An informal pond calls for a planting area with sweeping curves and a relaxed mix of plants in a variety of shapes, textures, and colors.

Chapter 2 (pages 24–47) describes some practical uses of plants around your water garden: for reducing wind, discouraging predators, framing views, and defining paths. You'll certainly want to take advantage of your pond's ability to reflect plants with colorful foliage and dramatic shapes, and to situate fragrant plants near benches or other stopping places.

To make your water garden an integral part of your landscape, you may want to choose flowers with colors that echo those elsewhere in your garden. Light affects how we see color. In a bright sunny garden, hot colors such as reds, oranges, and bright yellows stand out. If your garden is somewhat shady, or if you're designing an evening garden (one that you won't usually visit until the sun is low), cool blues, pinks, and especially whites will seem to glow in the fading light and create a tranquil atmosphere.

But many people concentrate too much on the color of flowers. Most plants won't bloom all season (except for annuals), so try to include plants with attractive foliage to provide interest when the flowers have faded. Foliage can serve as more than a backdrop to flowers; you can design a gorgeous all-season display by featuring plants that are handsome primarily for the color, shape, and texture of their leaves. Water-lily leaves have interesting patterns that change daily; those of lotuses are fluted and waxy so they capture raindrops. Leaves of floating plants can look like lettuce, clovers, or green snowflakes.

Around your pond, go for variety: big bold leaves such as those of ligularia, vertical leaves such as those of irises and grasses, lacy and delicate ferns, and creeping plants that will spread and even drape over the edge of your pond to help hide its edge. Avoid going overboard by trying to plant one of everything. Repeating one or two plants—or echoing one or two colors, textures, or shapes—in several spots will make a variety of plants look like a coherent design.

No garden is ever finished. Some plants may die, and others may simply fail to satisfy. But if you're like most people who discover gardening, every year will bring the discovery of new varieties that you would like to try. Approach your garden design as an adventure—an exciting exploration of the vast world of plants.

Flowers and foliage play both an aesthetic and practical role with respect to your water garden.

THE ROLES PLANTS PLAY

Most water gardeners will choose at least some of the traditional water-garden plants, which fall into the four categories that are described next.

▪ **Submerged plants** are those that grow below the water surface. Also called oxygenators, these plants act as natural filters to help keep your pond in chemical and biological balance, making it more hospitable for fish and less inviting to algae. In fact, submerged plants are a necessity if you want fish and aren't going to invest in a biological filter. (For more on biological filters, see page 182.)

▪ **Floating plants** either float freely on the surface of the pond or are rooted in containers on the bottom and send up leaves that float. They help to discourage the formation of algae by keeping the water cool and shady. Floaters include lotuses and water lilies, which many people consider a must for a pond.

▪ **Marginal plants** are those that like to grow in very shallow water or at the mucky edge (margin) of a pond or lake. You can grow most of them right in your pond if you plant them in containers raised on shelves or blocks to their preferred level. Plants in this category are especially useful for creating the look of a natural pond and help conceal the edge of a flexible liner or rigid shell.

▪ **Moisture-loving and bog plants** make up a broad category that includes almost any plant that likes very moist to slightly soggy soil (more moisture than is found in the average garden, but not standing water). In a natural environment, a lake, pond, or stream will be surrounded by a transitional zone of relatively wet soil that supports a fascinating array of plants. Include some of these plants if you want to create as natural-looking a pond as possible.

Even beside a decidedly less "wild" pond, some of these plants—willows, irises, and ornamental grasses, for example—simply look right located near a bog pond. These are described in the section, "Plants for the Periphery," which begins on page 228.

True bog plants are a subcategory of moisture lovers. These species require a more specialized environment of very acidic soil and low oxygen. Bog plants, and how to create their specialized environment, are described in Chapter 8, "Wetland Gardens," which begins on page 134.

Most water gardeners choose a combination of submerged, floating, and marginal plants.

Successful design means both varying and repeating textures and shapes.

Lovely waterlilies have a practical purpose: they discourage algae and protect fish.

Water Garden Planting Profile

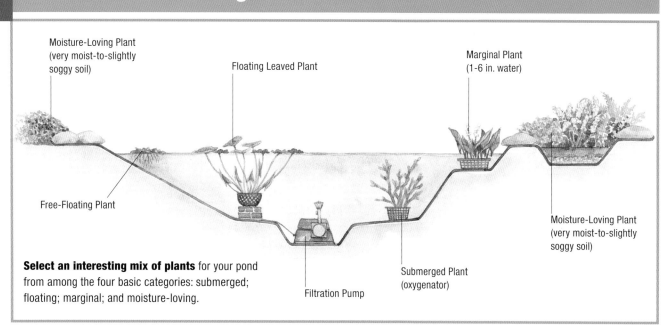

Moisture-Loving Plant
(very moist-to-slightly
soggy soil)

Floating Leaved Plant

Marginal Plant
(1-6 in. water)

Free-Floating Plant

Moisture-Loving Plant
(very moist-to-slightly
soggy soil)

Select an interesting mix of plants for your pond
from among the four basic categories: submerged;
floating; marginal; and moisture-loving.

Submerged Plant
(oxygenator)

Filtration Pump

Lythrum salicaria

Eichhornia crassipes

Hydrilla verticillata

Myriophyllum spicatum

Beware of Invasive Plants

There are a number of plants that biologists consider truly evil, and some of these are, unfortunately, still recommended and sold for water gardens. Nearly all of these space invaders originated in other countries and have no natural controls in their new home (biologists call them "aliens"). They reproduce in an uncontrollable manner and escape to natural areas, where they wipe out more delicate plants, diminish food sources for birds and other animals, and interfere with boating and other water sports by clogging waterways.

Don't be fooled by arguments that such plants are "safe" in urban gardens, where they are far from natural areas and are carefully controlled by the garden's owner. Many of these species have succeeded with their takeover because they are aided by the wind, birds, or other animals, which spread their seeds from gardens to parks or along waterways, where they can be carried for many miles.

BEAUTIES VERSUS BEASTS

As you'll see in the pages that follow, there are vast numbers of beautiful and well-behaved water garden plants to choose from. You can easily find the perfect plant for your needs while avoiding invasives.

The plants pictured on this and the opposite page are considered pests in various regions of North America. Plants that can wreak havoc in one area may be meek as lambs in others. For more information on invasive plants where you live, contact your local chapter of The Nature Conservancy or your local native-plant society; also see page 173. Acquiring knowledge of what to avoid planting may save you considerable time and aggravation later.

One of the most diabolical, and most familiar, invasives is eye-pleasing purple loosestrife (*Lythrum salicaria*). This Asian perennial bears spikes of magenta flowers from mid- to late summer, making it appealing to gardeners who want long-lasting color. But its ability to spread both by its millions of tiny seeds and by even a fragment of its roots has helped it choke out other wetland species in the Northeast and Upper Midwest. It has no food value for animals. Research has shown that even named cultivars of the plant, once thought to be sterile, will also spread. If you want similar color in your garden, choose a blazing star (*Liatris* species) or one of the purple selections of great blue lobelia (*Lobelia syphilitica*).

Another gorgeous villain is water hyacinth (*Eichhornia crassipes*), which looks like a floating orchid. A native of South America, it chokes waterways of all sizes in the Gulf States, California, and other warm areas throughout the world. Some consider it "safe" for gardeners north of Zone 8 because it will not survive winters north of there. But gardeners in the warmest areas of Zone 7 who live near waterways should avoid it. Instead, provide blue flowers for your pond with tropical water lilies or pickerel rush.

Two other aquatics that are well known as troublemakers are hydrilla (*Hydrilla verticillata*) and Eurasian water milfoil (*Myriophyllum spicatum*), a cousin of the popular marginal called parrot's-feather. Government agencies are spending millions of taxpayer dollars trying to kill hydrilla and milfoil and keep them from spreading in waterways, where they make the areas unusable by boaters or swimmers. Fortunately, reputable nurseries have stopped selling these plants. Don't buy them if you see them and don't introduce them into your own pond by collecting plants from infested ponds or waterways.

The beautiful yellow flag iris (*Iris pseudacorus*) is making least-wanted lists in the Mid-Atlantic states. If you live in that region, consider other species or hybrids such as Louisiana or Japanese irises for your pondside garden; both are available in several colors. Or consider a yellow daylily, which will be happy in moist or dry soil.

One of the most troublesome grasslike plants is common reed (*Phragmites australis*), which botanists call a "cosmopolitan" plant because it occurs worldwide. Common reed moves into areas that have been disturbed by humans or changed in other ways and it is almost impossible to eradicate.

Trees can be pests, too. Melaleuca (*Melaleuca quinquenervia*) is taking over Florida's Everglades. In western states, tamarisk trees (*Tamarix* species) are invading riverbanks and draining precious water resources, increasing the salinity of the soil, and displacing native plants that feed wildlife.

Iris pseudacorus

Melaleuca quinquenervia

Phragmites australis

Tamarix species

USING THE ENCYCLOPEDIA

There are six plant categories in this chapter: Submerged Plants, or Oxygenators; Floating Plants; Water Lilies; Lotuses; Marginal Plants; and Plants for the Periphery. Each category lists plants that are proven performers or have outstanding features (wonderful scent, spectacular flowers, dramatic leaves, etc.). Plants are listed alphabetically by botanical name (genus and species), which appears in italics in parentheses. Common name, if there is one, appears in capital letters above the botanical name. Cultivar name, if there is one, appears in single quotes. Some plants are listed by the genus and nonspecific species, for example: Ludwigia species, to indicate that several different species of Ludwigia are worthy of consideration.

Water lilies all belong to the genus Nymphaea and so are listed alphabetically by species or cultivar name. Similarly, all lotuses belong to the genus Nelumbo and are also organized by species and cultivar name.

Example: COMMON NAME
(*Botanical name* **'Cultivar'**)

Submerged Plants, or Oxygenators

Catalogs often refer to submerged aquatic plants as "oxygenators," because during the day they produce oxygen that helps support your fish and tadpoles. Submerged plants also remove mineral salts and fish wastes that feed unsightly algae. A few of these plants produce flowers above the waterline. Yet it is for their oxygenating and filtering services that they should be the first you buy. Place them in the water a few weeks before any fish to allow them time to get established and get your water's chemical balance on an even keel.

Many of the submerged plants have forms that resemble bird's plumage, inspiring common names such as parrot's-feather and making them beautiful additions to aquariums. When it comes to your pond though, availability and cold hardiness will dictate your plant choices; their appearance will affect your selection only if your pond is relatively clear. Use the zones given in the plant descriptions that follow as a general guide, and be prepared to re-

place plants after unusual winters. All of the plants described on the next few pages are efficient oxygenators, and you can plant one species or several. You may also find that some grow better than others in your pond conditions. The general rule is that you need one bunch (six stems) of submerged plants for each 1 to 2 square feet of pond surface. You can plant two or three bunches of these plants in a pan 1 foot in diameter.

PLANTING OXYGENATORS

Submerged plants obtain their nutrients from the water. You can plant them in sand or gravel and they will never need fertilizing. (Don't ever plant them in rich soil, manures, or composts, as nutrients will leach out of these and upset the ecology of your pond.) In fact, oxygenators don't even need containers. Bundle a half dozen plants and weigh them down on the bottom of the pond with a rock.

If you're using containers, fill them with sand almost to the top. Then use your finger to poke each stem an inch or two into the sand. Plant one stem for roughly each inch of pot diameter. Top the sand with clean gravel, which will help hold sand and plants in place, and add some water to help displace air bubbles. If you have koi or other ravenous feeders, you may want to protect your plants with mesh, which you can buy from aquatic suppliers.

Lower the pots slowly into your pond. There should be 1 to 2 feet of water over the roots of the plants. If you have a deeper pond, set the containerized plants on blocks to ensure that they get enough sun. They'll tolerate semi-shade, but they'll die if the sun is blocked by too many floating plants or by algae. Keep the pots well away from your pump; most water-garden plants don't like much agitation.

Once the plants have grown about a foot long, you can cut off half their length and reroot the tops in new pots. Once you have the recommended number of oxygenating plants for your pond's size (and have shared cuttings with all of the water-gardening friends who can possibly use them), you'll probably want to keep their growth in check. Some oxygenators can grow 3 feet long and may quickly choke a pond, robbing it of oxygen. If you have enough fish, they may do an efficient job of controlling plant growth. Inspect your oxygenators periodically and trim them back if they get out of hand. Bear in mind that algae or decaying plant material floating in the pond can cling to the submerged plants and eventually smother them. If you see this, pull the pots out of the water and hose off the plants.

RECOMMENDED OXYGENATORS

WATER HYSSOP
(*Bacopa caroliniana*)
Native to coastal areas of southern and central North America, water hyssop has a stiff, round stem 2 feet long that is covered with fine hairs. Egg-shaped leaves are about an inch long and hairy underneath. Light blue tubular flowers about ½ inch long appear above the water in the leaf axils (where leaves are attached to the stem). **Zones 8–10.**

FANWORT CAROLINA WATER SHIELD
(*Cabomba caroliniana*)
This plant is native to ponds and streams from Michigan to Texas and south to Florida. Underwater, its leaves are feathery, in a fan shape 1½ inches across. Leaves that grow above water are linear, pointed, and ¾ inch long. Flowers are usually white with yellow spots. **Zones 6–11.**

HORNWORT
(*Ceratophyllum demersum*)
Hornwort develops stems 1 to 2 feet long, clothed in whorls of forked leaves, which remain completely underwater. Like some other aquatic plants, it reproduces from turions, buds that drop to the pond bottom in winter. You can pot up these turions when they start to grow in spring. **Zones 6–9.**

ANACHARIS
(*Egeria densa*, also sold as *Elodea densa* or *Anacharis densa*)
This is a widely available submerged plant, but suffers from name confusion. It goes by many botanical names, and its common name may be used for Canadian pondweed. Sometimes it is called Brazilian waterweed. This plant is semi-evergreen and produces branched stems up to 3 feet long. In summer it has small but pretty white flowers above the water surface. **Zones 6–11.**

HAIR GRASS
(*Eleocharis acicularis*)
You can use this aquarium plant to create an underwater lawn. (And it will never need mowing.) Pale green needlelike leaves grow to 8 inches tall and spread to form a mat that looks like prairie grass or green hair. Flowers are little brown spikes. Avoid using it in earth-bottomed ponds, where its vigorous roots can quickly turn it into a nuisance. (Other species of *Eleocharis* that need water only a few inches deep are described under "Marginal Plants," on page 224.) **Zones 7–10** (but often hardier; some northern gardeners report that it usually winters well in ponds that freeze over).

CANADIAN PONDWEED
(*Elodea canadensis*)
Whorls of translucent leaves on each stem are dense and curl downward. Found in Quebec, it will also grow in the Deep South. In fact, it's so obliging that it can become a pest where it can spread out, but it may be a good choice for a water gardener who has trouble growing other oxygenators. Some catalogs call this anacharis because of its resemblance to *Egeria densa*. **Zones 5–11.**

MILFOIL
(*Myriophyllum* species)
Some of the milfoils are extremely invasive, and others aren't winter hardy. Avoid *M. spicatum*, which is a waterway pest in states from Wisconsin to Massachusetts and down to Florida. *M. aquaticum* ('parrot's-feather'), which you'll find with marginal plants on page 224, can grow in or out of water but is hardy only to **Zone 9.**

Farther north, substitute myriad leaf (*M. verticillatum*), which has 3-foot-long graceful stems with whorls of bright green leaves; above the water the leaves are little comblike tufts. In summer, it bears 6-inch spikes of tiny yellow flowers.

Floating Plants

Like submerged plants, floaters play an important role in creating a healthy natural balance for your water garden. The leaves of these plants float on the surface and shade the water, making it less hospitable for algae, cooling the water for fish, and giving fish a place to hide and to lay their spawn. You may decide not to include floating plants in your water garden, especially if it has a fountain. A fountain or waterfall that churns the water of a small pond will create too much commotion for them.

Most floating plants prefer full sun but will tolerate at least partial shade. Water lilies, as a rule, require at least six hours of sun a day to bloom. Lotuses are less particular about the amount of sun they receive than they are about temperature. They will bloom in partial shade, as long as they have a sufficient stretch of warm weather. Other options for flowers in partial shade include water hawthorn and pond lilies.

Some of these plants literally float; all you need to do to establish them is drop them in the water, where they will obtain nutrients through roots that hang down from their leaves. You don't need to fertilize these floaters. When they become too vigorous, they reduce light to submerged species, which in turn reduces the filtering and oxygenating functions of the underwater plants. Don't let floating plants cover more than 70 percent of your pond's surface; a large pond of 1,000 square feet or so should be only half covered. Skim free-floating plants off the surface using a net. These excess floaters can make a posthumous contribution to your compost pile. Don't ever release them into open bodies of water. Certain floating species, such as water hyacinth, have caused extensive damage to natural waterways.

Other species such as water lilies are more aptly described as floating-leaved plants. Plant these in containers of heavy garden soil and place the containers on a shelf or block anywhere from a few inches to a couple of feet under the water surface. Some of them can live either submerged or in shallow water toward the margins of a pond and will tolerate ponds with fluctuating water levels. Containerized plants need monthy aquatic fertilization. Remove spent plant parts to keep your pond clean.

Some of the plants listed here are not winter hardy in most of North America. You may want to experiment with growing them as annuals. Or over-winter them in an aquarium to start a new crop the following spring.

RECOMMENDED FLOATING PLANTS

WATER HAWTHORN, CAPE PONDWEED
(*Aponogeton distachyus*)
Tropical gardeners can try this South African perennial with 8-inch elongated oval leaves. Heavily scented flowers, which bloom in both spring and fall, are held on a double spike; their purple-brown anthers look like freckles on the rows of white petals. Give water  hawthorn a container 1 foot across and start it about 4 inches below the surface of the water, lowering it to 1 to 3 feet. **Zones 6–9.**

MOSQUITO FERN
(*Azolla caroliniana*)
Often called by the more charming name of fairy moss, this tiny fern with inch-long fronds floats freely on the water surface, each plant above its own little root. The dainty green snowflakes turn burgundy in autumn or in strong sunlight. Their delicate appearance is deceptive, though. This  native of subtropical America has naturalized in North America and Britain and easily becomes invasive. It can be useful if you need quick cover for a new pond and are willing to thin regularly. **Zones 7–10.**

WATER HYACINTH
(*Eichhornia crassipes*)
This is one of the most beautiful yet one of the most noxious water-garden plants. One of the worst pest plants in California, Florida, Georgia, and Louisiana, it can't be shipped across state lines anywhere. (If you want to grow it, you'll have to buy it from a supplier in your state.) Nevertheless, it  is considered safe to grow as an annual in **Zone 7** and north because it can't survive freezing temperatures. Its shiny round leaves bob in the water, supported by buoyant stems. The free-floating plants are topped by 6-inch spikes of exotic-looking lilac flowers. Each plant has a foot-long root and spreads by stolons. Be prepared: this rampant beauty can take over your water garden if you don't thin it regularly.

FROGBIT
(*Hydrocharis morsus-ranae*)
This free-floating species from Eurasia has shiny, 1-inch-diameter leaves shaped like a water lily's and handsomely veined. Delicate cup-shaped white flowers have three yellow petals near the base. New plants form on runners; in fall, turions (winter buds) drop  to the pond bottom to overwinter. Frogbit is a good choice for gardeners who don't have the time to do a lot of thinning. **Zones 6–10.**

WATER POPPY
(*Hydrocleys nymphoides*)

A Brazilian native, water poppy is worth growing as an annual for its 3-inch pale yellow flowers with red-and-brown centers. The three petals overlap slightly to form a shallow cup just above the water. Thick, glossy leaves are also about 3 inches across and look a lot like a water lily's. Plant it in rich soil and in shallow water, 6 to 9 inches deep; it likes acidic water. **Zones 9–11.**

COMMON DUCKWEED
(*Lemna minor*)

This free-floater is the water gardener's crabgrass. Each one of its light-green oval leaves has a root hanging beneath it, but plants will cluster in large communities. It is a nutritious food for goldfish. **Zones 3–11.**

Ludwiglia species. Taxonomists have made a serious muddle of this group of aquatic plants. Some of the plants are free-floaters and others are better adapted to the margins of a pond. The most attractive is probably tropical *L. sedioides*, which has red stems and floating diamond-shaped leaves that form kaleidoscopic patterns. Place it so its crown sits 4 to 12 inches under the water. **Zone 11.**

WATER CLOVER
(*Marsilea* species)

These plants are technically ferns, but they look like four-leaf clovers. The most colorful is *M. mutica*, from Australia; its quartet of 3-inch leaves has two shades of green separated by a dark band. The hardiest is *M. quadrifolia*, from Europe; its new leaves are downy. Water clovers can be grown in up to 12 inches of water, in which case their leaves will float. They can also be grown as marginal plants with only an inch of water above their crowns, and then their stems will stand a few inches above the surface. **Zones 9–11.**

BOGBEAN
(*Menyanthes trifoliata*)

In spring, bogbean produces a foot-tall spike of 10 to 20 white-fringed, star-shaped flowers that unfold from a pink bud and remain pink on the outside. Full sun produces more flowers. It has three-part leaves and can form a clump 3 feet or more in diameter. Bogbean will grow in a container 6 to 9 inches below the surface as well as in mud at the water's edge, where it will camouflage pond edges by creeping into the water with its spongy rhizomes. It likes the acidic environment of a true bog; it will grow better if you mix peat moss in the soil to increase acidity. It may not flower in the warmer parts of its range. **Zones 5–11.**

POND LILY, SPATTERDOCK
(*Nuphar* species)

These plants make a good substitute for water lilies where water is shaded, gently moving, or acidic. Globe-shaped flowers are followed by oval berries. Plants develop long thick roots—divide them in spring. *N. lutea* bears 2-inch flowers. Its translucent submerged leaves can be a foot long, while the 16-inch floating leaves are leathery and slightly more pointed. **Zones 5–11.** The best choice for an average-size water feature is *N. pumila*, which can be grown in water only a foot deep. **Zones 4–8.**

Japanese pond lily (*N. japonica*) has arrow-shaped leaves and flowers blushed with red; a variegated cultivar, 'Variegata', is suitable for small ponds and another, 'Rubrotincta', has reddish orange flowers. **Zones 6–9.**

FLOATING HEART
(*Nymphoides* species)

These plants are often compared to water lilies. Unlike water lilies, all thrive in relatively shallow water—plant them 3 to 12 inches deep in a container 18 inches across. The ¾-inch white or yellow flowers are usually fringed. Two native species are *N. aquatica* (banana plant), which bears ½-inch white flowers and forms tubers that look like tiny bananas, and *N. cordata*, which varies only in its tubers; both are hard to find. **Zones 6–9.**

N. peltata (water fringe, yellow floating heart), a European species that has naturalized in the United States, has rounded, 3-inch leaves with brown splotches and holds bright gold, fringed flowers several inches above the water all summer; it needs a large pond. **Zones 6–11.**

N. cristata has fragrant white, yellow-centered flowers. **Zones 7–11.**

WATER LETTUCE, SHELLFLOWER
(*Pistia stratiotes*)

It's easy to see where this subtropical free-floater got the name "water lettuce." Shaped like romaine, the 8-inch leaves are undulating, velvety fans that stick up from the water, near white on base and undersides. Little green flowers are negligible, but the roots—which mature from white to purple to black—hang 18 inches and make a great fish nursery. It is a noxious weed in southern states (it can't be shipped to California, Texas, Louisiana, or South Carolina); grow it as an annual north of **Zone 8.**

BUTTERFLY FERN
(*Salvinia* species)

Hairy, 1-inch paired leaves of these free-floating aquatic ferns inspired the name, looking like a butterfly at rest. In this genus they're grouped again into whorls of three, ranging from light green to brownish purple. Happy in even an inch of water, they reproduce fast and are pests in warm regions. **Zones 10–11.**

Water Lilies

Although it's quite possible to have a stunning and soul-satisfying water garden without water lilies, most gardeners plant at least a few. These plants are prized not just for the blossoms that open day after day, but also for the shiny pads that serve as landing strips for frogs and dragonflies. While not as colorful as the flowers, these floating leaves have a fascination all their own. When they first unfold, they are often purple or copper and show pronounced splotches and streaks. Some retain this mottling as they age. Most lily pads are roughly round, but some are more egg shaped. The edges are sometimes serrated, similar to a bread knife. All pads have an indentation, or sinus, which can be wide open in a triangle or closed so that the two lobes overlap. In some cases, one or both of the lobes may turn up, showing a flash of burgundy on the leaf's underside.

Adding to the visual interest of many water lilies are plant parts in colors that contrast with petals. These include the sepals, which while in many plants are unexciting green structures that simply protect the bud, in others such as water lilies develop another color as the plant matures. Providing color in the center of the water lily flower are the stamens (the male reproductive organ) and anthers (the part that holds pollen). They are most often yellow and orange, but in some water lilies can be white or bear touches of red or pink.

ANATOMY OF A WATER LILY

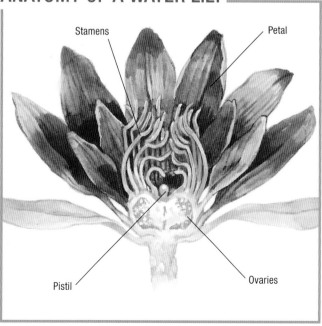

Stamens
Petal
Pistil
Ovaries

GUIDE TO WATER LILY ENTRIES

All water lilies belong to the genus *Nymphaea*. They are listed here alphabetically by their cultivar name or by their species name, within one of three categories: *Hardy Water Lilies; Tropical Varieties: Day-blooming; Tropical Varieties: Night-blooming.*

■ Hardy Water Lilies, page 212
■ Tropical Varieties: *Day blooming*, page 216
■ Tropical Varieties: *Night blooming*, page 219

The flowers also vary in shape. They are usually described as either cup-shaped—with the petals held upright and close together—or star-shaped—with the petals opening wider and flatter. Many open cup-shaped and then become star-shaped. They can also range from single, with a few elegant petals, to fully double, with so many petals that they look like floating peonies.

There are biological arguments for planting water lilies as well. They discourage algae and protect fish. To achieve both of these goals, you need to cover about half of your pond surface; in a small pond, up to 70 percent. If you're meeting these goals with water lilies alone, plant at least one water lily for each 10 to 20 square feet of surface. Water lilies vary in the surface area they will cover, from a single square foot to 10 or 12. Some are demure enough to grow in a small patio tub, whereas others are too frisky for anything smaller than a lake.

Water lilies are classified as either hardy, meaning that they will survive winters into Zone 4 as long as the pond doesn't freeze down to the level of their roots, or tropical, meaning that they can be left in your pond all year only if you live in Zone 10 or 11.

CHOOSING WATER LILIES

You can find hardy water lilies in white, pink, yellow, and red as well as the so-called changeables, which go through an array of sunset colors. Hardies open around 9 A.M. in midsummer and close between 3 and 5 P.M.

Tropical water lilies also come in blues and purples, shades that are unavailable in hardy water lilies. Tropicals are further divided into day bloomers, which close around dusk; and night bloomers, which open at dusk and close late the next morning. The flowers of the tropicals are bigger and more fragrant than those of hardy water lilies; they bloom two to three times as heavily, and their leaves are more heavily textured.

If you're a 9-to-5 worker, bloom time may be important. A few day-blooming water lilies reliably stay open a couple of hours later each evening, giving you a short time to enjoy them when you arrive home. The hardies' day-blooming habit is a good argument for having at least one night-blooming tropical, even if you have to replace it every year.

Your chief consideration when choosing a water lily is likely to be the spread of its leaves. Some varieties that get no more than 2 to 3 feet across will even restrict their growth further in a tub or patio water garden. Others will quickly zoom to 10 feet across, covering all the surface in a small pond and limiting options for other plants in a medium-size pond.

A medium-size pond is generally considered to be one about 100 square feet (10 x 10 feet) in area. Keeping this in mind, here's a rough rule for choosing the maximum size of your water lilies: tub, no more than 3 feet in diameter; small pond, 6 feet; medium-size pond, 9 feet; large pond, 10 or more feet.

GROWING WATER LILIES

Water lilies like full sun, at least six hours a day, and calm water. Although it's possible to build permanent beds for them on the floor of your pond, most water gardeners use plastic tubs. Water-garden suppliers sell specially-made baskets, but you can recycle plastic dish pans, trays sold for mixing concrete, or other containers. If you live in frost-free Zone 10 or 11, you can plant water lilies any time of year. Elsewhere, plant hardy water lilies when the danger of frost is past in spring, up until a few weeks before the first expected frost in fall (although if you plant them early in spring, you'll get to enjoy their flowers the first year). Plant tropical water lilies once the water in your pond has warmed to 70°F.

Keep your hardy water lilies moist and cool until you plant them. Tropicals should be planted as soon as you receive them from the nursery. Suppliers will ship mail-ordered water lilies at the appropriate time for planting in your area.

The container you use needn't be deeper than 6 to 8 inches, but most water lilies need a diameter of 12 to 18 inches; vigorous hardy water lilies and tropicals need more width. Err on the too-big side and you may be able to divide the plants less often—but then they will be more difficult to lift from the pond.

Heavy garden soil—even clay that's not good for other plants—is the ideal planting medium for water lilies. Lighter soil may float away, and manure or compost may foul the water. Fill your container about half full of soil and lay the water-lily rhizome on top. The rhizome can be either a "pineapple" type, with growth coming from the top, or more similar to an iris rhizome, with growing tips running along the rhizome's length. In both cases, add soil around the rhizome until just the growing tip appears above the soil surface.

Potted Plants

Top with an inch of gravel to hold the soil. Now lower the container into the pond, so the first few lily pads easily reach the surface. If your plant has already unfurled leaves, put the container on bricks or blocks so leaves can float. (Avoid concrete blocks, which can make water more alkaline.) Otherwise, place so the growing tip is about 6 inches below the water surface. As leaves grow taller, lower the container gradually to a maximum depth of 18 inches.

A 1- to 3-gal. dishpan or special container lined with burlap and filled with heavy garden soil

Gravel (1-in.)

To keep your pond clean, your only ongoing chores will be to remove dead foliage and fourth-day flowers (which usually stay underwater) and fertilize the container once a month in spring and fall and twice monthly in midsummer. Fertilizer tablets sold by aquatic dealers are the most convenient way to feed your water lilies without polluting your pond or breaking the plants' fragile growing tips.

Divide water lily pads every two to three years, and possibly every year in the Deep South. Spring is the best time to do this. Gently upend the container and pull the rhizome from the soil. Cut the rhizome into sections 3 to 6 inches long, using a clean knife, and replant.

TROPICAL WATER LILIES: NYMPHAEA SPECIES AND CULTIVARS

Flowers of almost all tropical water lilies are fragrant and stand above the water. They should bloom for at least a short time anywhere in North America except for the Northwest, where summers don't get hot enough. They need air temperatures over 65°F.

Some tropical water lilies are viviparous, meaning that they develop perfectly formed baby plants on their leaves. All you have to do to have more plants is pull off the babies, press each into a container of garden soil, and lower the containers gradually into your pond to a depth that allows the first leaves to reach the surface.

WINTER CARE

If your pond doesn't freeze entirely, you can leave your hardy water lilies out all winter. If your pond is very shallow or your climate is cold, you need to winter over your hardies by lifting their containers from the water and storing them in a cold place such as a garage. Put containers in plastic bags, and make sure they don't dry out completely.

Although most people just let their tropical water lilies die and buy new ones the following spring, you can try storing them for the winter. Lift each container, pull the rhizome out, rinse it, and let it air-dry for a couple of days. Brush off remaining dirt and pull off excess roots; store the rhizome in a container of distilled water in a cool but frost-free place. In early spring—a couple of months before you expect your pond water to reach 70°F—pot up the rhizome and place the pot in a pan of water in a sunny window to start the growth process.

Most water lilies on the market are hybrids that are sold under a cultivar name often without indicating a species. However, in a few cases, you will find species offered.

Little Lotuses

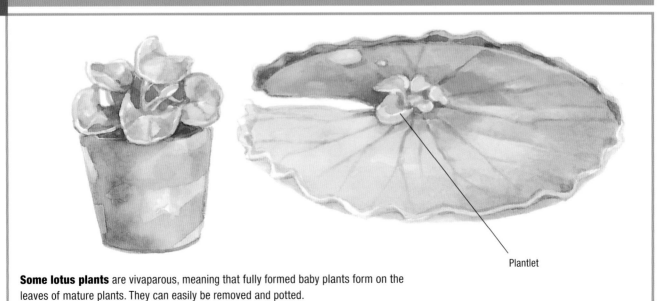

Plantlet

Some lotus plants are vivaparous, meaning that fully formed baby plants form on the leaves of mature plants. They can easily be removed and potted.

Hardy lily pads growing above the water need to be divided.

HARDY WATER LILIES

Nymphaea cultivars

'Arc-en-Ciel'
Described as a "moderate" bloomer, this beauty would be worth having even if it never flowered at all. Developed at the turn of the twentieth century by the great French hybridizer Joseph Bory Latour-Marliac and named for the rainbow, it has foliage that rivals that celestial phenomenon: deep and pale pink, purple, yellow, green, cream, and bronze. The fragrant flowers are soft pink and have slim petals. **Flowers 5 inches, light pink, fragrant; leaves 9 inches, variegated; spread 4 to 5 feet.**

'Attraction'
These flowers are among the biggest of the red hardies. Opening in a cup shape and spreading to a star, they are a deep, rich garnet red with slightly paler outer petals, set off by orange stamens. Blooming is vigorous. Oval leaves often have one lobe raised. This, like other dark red water lilies, can burn in intense sun; it tolerates a little shade and in the South even benefits from it. **Flowers up to 8 inches, garnet red; leaves up to 12 inches; spread 4 to 5 feet.**

'Charlene Strawn'
Kirk Strawn, a hybridizer at Texas A&M University, named this deliciously fragrant water lily after his wife. Large, star-shaped yellow flowers with long pointed petals are held several inches above the water surface. Leaves often keep some of their purple markings as they age. 'Charlene Strawn' is a generous bloomer with a longer flowering season than most water lilies. **Flowers up to 8 inches across, yellow, fragrant; leaves 9 inches; spread 3 to 5 feet.**

'Chromatella'
Sometimes listed as *N.* x *marliacea* 'Chromatella' or 'Golden Cup', this reliable water lily is small enough for a tub only 2 feet across and 1 foot deep; it will take some shade as well. The broad petals of the canary yellow flowers curve up at the edges; anthers in center are slightly darker yellow. **Flowers 6 inches, semidouble, canary yellow; leaves 8 to 9 inches; spread 3 feet.**

'Chrysantha'
(formerly **'Graziella'**)
This changeable cultivar has spoon-shaped petals, and its little flowers remain cup shaped. Their color alters from an apricot-yellow to a reddish orange; the overall effect is a steadily deepening apricot. Olive green leaves remain splotched with maroon. 'Chrysantha' flowers freely and will work in a tub, but it doesn't like hot summers. **Flowers 3 to 4 inches, apricot to red-orange; leaves 6 inches, mottled; spread 2 to 3 feet.**

'Comanche'
This is one of the largest changeable water lilies. First a cup-shaped golden yellow, it spreads to a rosy apricot star that turns deep coppery orange with redder inner petals and pale yellow tips. The leaves change, too, from bronze to olive green. 'Comanche' is a bit more susceptible to crown rot than some other changeables. **Flowers 5 inches, gold to copper; leaves 12 inches; spread 4 to 5 feet.**

'Darwin' (formerly 'Hollandia')
This cultivar starts life with pink inner petals and white outer petals, all becoming pinker as it ages—usually for more than the standard three days. Profuse flowers are fully double and goblet shaped with a tidy habit. Fragrance is slight, but 'Darwin' makes good cut flowers. **Flowers 7 inches, double, pink, lightly fragrant; leaves 11 inches; spread 4 to 5 feet.**

'Ellisiana'

Looking for a fragrant, bright red water lily for a small pond? 'Ellisiana' will stop blooming in hot weather, but if you garden in **Zones 3–7,** it may be perfect. Its star-shaped flowers are a rich purple-red hue. The mid-green leaves have open sinuses. **Flowers 5 inches, purple-red; leaves 8 inches; spread up to 3 feet.**

'Escarboucle'

If you miss seeing your water lilies bloom during the work week, this one will cut you some slack by staying open a couple of hours longer than most. A vivid vermilion red with white-tipped outer petals, yellow anthers, and dark orange stamens, it offers a spicy fragrance, too. Flowers change from cup- to star- shaped. Leaves age from copper to deep green. **Flowers 6 inches, white-tipped red, spicy fragrance; leaves up to 11 inches; spread 4 to 5 feet.**

'Firecrest'

The name was inspired by the flaming orange-and-yellow center, which contrasts strikingly with the soft lavender-pink petals. From spring until fall, stems hold blooms just above the water; the outer petals hang down like a bed ruffle, while the central petals form a perky egg cup. Leaves are dark purple when they unfold and keep some dark purple specks as they turn dark green. Give it a container at least 2 feet across and 1 foot deep for lots of flowers. **Flowers 6 inches, lilac-pink; leaves 9 inches; spread 4 feet.**

'Froebelii'

This little gem can handle water a mere 6 inches deep. Burgundy flowers perch jauntily above the water; contrasting stamens are orange-red. It first looks almost like a tulip and flattens to a star. Leaves mature from bronze to pale green and have open sinuses. Like 'Ellisiana', it does best where summers are relatively cool. **Flowers 4 inches, burgundy; leaves 6 inches; spread 3 feet.**

'Gladstoniana'

Sometimes sold as 'Gladstone', this vigorous water lily is for large ponds. It is as interesting for its foliage as for its large flowers, which are pure white and semidouble. Leaves are somewhat waxy looking and have crinkly margins. **Flowers to 7 inches, semidouble, white; leaves 12 inches; spread from 5 to 8 feet.**

'Gloriosa'

The many red petals of this cuplike flower get redder with age and sometimes have darker flecks. The white sepals are flushed with pink; stamens are orange-red. Oval leaves mature from a dark-blotched light purple to bronze-green. 'Gloriosa' is susceptible to crown rot, one of the few diseases to trouble water lilies. But you'll still see it on lists of the best water lilies because of its abundant flowers. **Flowers 5 feet, red, fragrant; leaves 8 inches; spread to 5 feet.**

'Gonnere' (also sold as 'Crystal White' and 'Snowball')

This pure white cultivar has two to three times as many thick, curved petals as most others. The flowers stand out among the relatively small, light green pads, are fragrant, and stay open late into the afternoon. 'Gonnere' can adapt to small, shallow ponds, but it doesn't do well in the summer south of **Zone 7. Flowers 4 to 6 inches, white, fragrant; leaves 6 to 9 inches; spread 3 to 4 feet.**

'Helvola'
(sometimes listed as N. x *pygmaea helvola* or 'Yellow Pygmy')

Want to enjoy a water lily on your patio after work? This gem opens late in the afternoon and stays open later, too. Plus it can be grown in a tub only 6 inches deep. It produces clear yellow, semidouble flowers and mottled oval leaves. **Flowers 2 to 3 inches, semidouble, clear yellow; leaves 5 inches long; spread 2 feet.**

(continued on next page)

HARDY WATER LILIES

(continued from previous page)

'Hermine'

While double flowers are voluptuous, there is a classic simplicity to singles such as pure white, long-petaled 'Hermine'. Held above the water, when fully open each flower looks almost like a snowflake with a yellow center. This cultivar blooms reliably its first year and profusely after that, always for a long season. It tolerates shade and

various water depths but is restrained enough to grow in a tub, where you can more easily catch its light fragrance. **Flowers 5 inches, double, white, slightly fragrant; leaves 6 to 7 inches; spread 2½ feet.**

'James Brydon'

This longtime favorite was developed by a Philadelphia nursery at the turn of the twentieth century and named for a customer. Double rosy red flowers— cupped and peony-like, the center a range of oranges —often open several at a time. Purple-brown new foliage has darker blotches and then turns bronze. With small features and a tidy disposition, this plant

makes a great water lily for a tub just a foot deep. It resists crown rot, too, but like most reds it appreciates a temperate climate. **Flowers 4 inches, double, rosy red, fragrant; leaves 7 inches, purplish to bronze; spread 3 to 4 feet.**

N x marliacea 'Carnea' ('Marliacea Carnea')

While many water lilies have paler sepals than petals, this one is reversed, with light pink petals and deeper pink sepals that have even darker rose markings. The central petals remain upright, embracing their yellow stamens and anthers like a flesh-colored egg cup. 'Carnea' tolerates some

shade and adapts to any size pond, but it does best in medium to large ones. **Flowers 5 inches, semidouble, pale pink; leaves to 8 inches; spread 4 to 5 feet.**

'Masaniello'

This water lily is as starkly two-tone as a '57 Chevy. Rose-pink petals are dabbed with red; sepals are white. The dual colors are accentuated by the way the petals remain in a cup while the sepals spread down toward the water. Although subject to crown rot, 'Masaniello' takes some shade and adapts to small ponds. A high-contrast choice that adds flair. **Flowers to 6 inches, bright pink; leaves 9 inches; spread 4 feet.**

'Mayla'

There aren't many water lilies that can touch this fairly recent Kirk Strawn introduction for drama when it unfolds its flamboyant fuchsia flowers above the water. Inner petals have gold tips that match the stamens. Redolent of musk, 'Mayla' has bronze-maroon leaves. **Flowers 6 to 7 inches, bright pink, fragrant; leaves to 12 inches; spread 5 to 6 feet.**

'Pearl of the Pool'

Fragrant double flowers are baby-girl pink with pinkish-orange stamens and stay slightly cupped. 'Pearl' can handle fairly shallow water but needs a big container that will allow it to develop a lot of shoots. Round bronze leaves mature to deep green but often flash their coppery undersides by turning up a lobe. Aside from a classy moniker, it is a choice without

disappointments. **Flowers to 6 inches, double, pink, fragrant; leaves to 10 inches; spread 4 to 5 feet.**

'Pink Sensation'

Extra hours of flowers—and a lot of them—make this intense pink Perry Slocum selection a good choice for any size pond. The fragrant flowers have long oval petals, slightly darker in the center, with both pink and yellow stamens. Leaves mature from purple to green. **Flowers 5 to 6 inches, rich pink, fragrant; leaves 10 inches; spread 4 feet.**

'Rose Arey'

Deep pink, semidouble flowers are star-shaped and smell of anise. You may notice some orange-pink along the edge of the long, narrow, pointed petals, which curve in slightly. Leaves are bronzy-green. A container 2 feet square and 1 foot deep will allow it to form a large colony. This cultivar may need a year or two to establish itself. **Flowers 7 to 8 inches, semidouble, deep pink, fragrant; leaves up to 9 inches; spread 4 to 5 feet.**

N. odorata 'Sulphurea Grandiflora'

Its flowers are among the biggest of all the hardy water lilies. Bright yellow semidouble stars, they have long narrow petals and stay open late. This is a heat lover; north of **Zone 6**, flowering is sparse and leaves can be deformed until weather warms in spring. **Flowers 9 inches, semidouble, bright yellow; leaves 11 inches, oval; spread 4 to 5 feet.**

'Texas Dawn'

This is such a new cultivar that its cold hardiness is still being tested, but it already has an award from the International Water Lily and Water Gardening Association. Semidouble, lemon-scented flowers are golden with a touch of pink on the outer petals that may become more pronounced in fall and a hint of green in the sepals. 'Texas Dawn' can produce seven or eight blooms at a time, held high above the water. It is hardy at least to **Zone 6. Flowers 7 inches, semidouble, yellow, fragrant; leaves 8 Inches; spread 3 to 5 feet.**

'Virginalis'

This water lily is still considered one of the most dependable, generously blooming whites. It's a good choice for short-season gardeners because it starts blooming early and keeps blooming longer than many others. The flower is a pure white cup; its broad petals may have a faint rosy glow. Pale green

leaves are flushed with purple and have a downy covering. It needs water at least 15 inches deep. **Flowers 5 inches, white; leaves 9 inches; spread 3 to 4 feet.**

'Virginia'

Maryland water-lily expert Charles Thomas named this one after his mother. It's such a pale yellow that it's always categorized as white (most of the yellow is in the center). This buxom bloomer is a starry semidouble; long narrow petals make it look full as a pom-pom. Open later than most in the afternoon, it also has a long bloom season. Leaves start out purple and age to green, but some of the purple remains around the edges. **Flowers to 8 inches, semidouble, white to palest yellow; leaves 10 inches; spread 5 to 6 feet.**

'William Falconer'

Dark red center petals, slightly rounded at the tips, are set off by cherry pink sepals. The outer stamens have a touch of burgundy on them. Leaves, maroon at first, keep some purple veining as they mature to green. Like most red water lilies, this one does not like heat and will wilt in temperatures above 95°F. **Flowers 5 inches, deep red; leaves 8 inches; spread 4 feet.**

OTHER HARDY LILY CHOICES

■ **'Vesuve'**
  Flowers 7 inches, gorgeous bright red; leaves 9 to 10 inches; spread to 4 feet.

■ **'Sultan'**
  Flowers 6 to 7 inches, deep red; leaves 10 to 11 inches; spread 4 to 5 feet.

■ **'Carolina Sunset'**
  Flowers to 8 inches, deep-to-light-yellow to blushed peach; leaves to 11 inches; spread 4 to 5 feet.

■ **'Florida Sunset'**
  Flowers to 8 inches, yellow with a peach-color center; leaves 11½ inches; spread 4 to 5 feet.

TROPICAL LILY VARIETIES

DAY BLOOMING

'Afterglow'
Bred a half century ago, this is one of the tropical water lilies described as having "sunset" colors, in this case golden yellow toward the center, blushing to orange-pink at the tips. Wonderfully fragrant, the flower is somewhat flat and floats in the water. Leaves are nearly round with wavy edges.

'Albert Greenberg'
Similar in color to 'Afterglow', this 1969 selection has slightly smaller flowers and more of a cup shape. Leaves are much bigger, are heavily streaked with purple, and have a wavy edge and one raised lobe. It will bloom well into fall. **Flowers 6 to 7 inches, yellow with pink tips; leaves to almost 20 inches; spread 5 to 8 feet.**

'Aviator Pring'
George Pring, a hybridizer at the Missouri Botanical Garden, named this flower after a son who died in World War I. The many deep yellow, cup-shaped flowers are eye-popping semidoubles, a full foot out of the water. Mottled leaves have toothed, wavy edges. **Flowers 10 inches, semidouble, deep yellow; leaves to 12 inches; spread 6 to 8 feet.**

'Blue Beauty'
Heady-scented, semidouble flowers are blue set off by yellow stamens with violet anthers. Star-shaped, they're often 10 inches across and profusely borne 8 inches above the pond. Oval leaves are wavy edged, and flecked with brown. Wait until the water is 75°F before you set the plant out in spring. **Flowers 10 inches, semidouble, rich blue, fragrant; leaves to 15 inches; spread 4 to 8 feet.**

N. capensis
('Cape blue' water lily; also sold as 'Blue Capensis')
Picture a periwinkle flower with more petals, then a yellow center, and make it the size of a dinner plate. This semidouble species is native to southern Africa. Round, speckled, mid-green leaves are toothed and have wavy margins. It thrives in water anywhere from 10 inches to 3 feet deep. **Flowers 9 inches; leaves 10 to 16 inches; spread 6 to 10 feet.**

N. colorata
Gardeners with small ponds or tubs will find several wonderful choices among blue day bloomers, and this is one of them. Even with only three to four hours of sun a day, it will be generous with its cup-shaped flowers of a violet shade similar to wisteria. It needs just 6 inches of water over its roots and will bloom well into fall—all year in frost-free areas. **Flowers 5 inches; leaves 8 to 9 inches; spread 3 to 5 feet.**

N. x daubenyana also sold as 'Daubeniana' or 'Dauben'
Considered the easiest of the tropical water lilies to grow, it's prolific, tough, and can grow in just 4 inches of water! Intensely fragrant, cup-shaped flowers have dark margins but overall are not as bright a blue as *N. colorata* and can fade to near white. It makes up for this by cranking out three and even four generations of new plants on its leaves. It needs just three to four hours of sun. Oval leaves are olive to bronze and have wavy margins. **Flowers 5 inches, pale blue, very fragrant; leaves 12 inches; spread 3 to 4 feet.**

'Director George T. Moore'
Named for a former director of the Missouri Botanical Garden, this is possibly the richest violet-blue of any water lily. Flowers are fragrant and abundant, too, with centers that are dark purple and gold. It tolerates lower light levels (5-6 hours) than other water lilies. Leaves are slightly flecked with purple. This one is happy in any size pond. **Flowers 7 to 9 inches, deep violet-blue, fragrant; leaves 10 to 12 inches; spread 5 to 8 feet.**

'Evelyn Randig'

You just have to pay attention when a breeder names a flower for his wife, as Martin Randig of San Bernardino, California, did with this water lily. The raspberry-sherbet color will have you smacking your lips. Green leaves are heavily marbled with both purple and brown. **Flowers 8 inches, deep pink; leaves up to 15 inches; spread 5 to 7 feet.**

'General Pershing'

A general arrayed in delicate lavender-pink? This double-flowered variety earns a salute with its size, strong sweet scent, and periodically dawn-to-dusk bloom. The flowers, which keep coming well into autumn, open as a cup and then are nearly flat. Wavy-edged leaves are mottled with purple. 'General Pershing' doesn't mind some shade and can adapt to any pond bigger than a tub. **Flowers up to 11 inches, double, lavender-pink, fragrant; leaves 10 inches; spread 5 to 6 feet.**

'Madame Ganna Walska'

This cultivar was named for the Polish opera singer who developed amazing Lotusland, once her home and now a public garden near Santa Barbara, California. It's considered the most profuse bloomer among pink tropical water lilies. The color is bright lavender-pink with an intense yellow center. Petals are narrow and pointed, forming star-shaped blooms. Leaves are mottled and have round sinuses. **Flowers 3 to 8 inches, lavender-pink; leaves up to 12 inches; spread 6 to 12 feet.**

'Margaret Mary'

This lady is a standout for her intensely rich blue color and ability to bloom almost nonstop in considerable shade. The cup-to-star flowers produce an appealing scent. The leaves are lightly mottled and plants are somewhat viviparous. It has a long bloom season and will adapt to small ponds and tubs. **Flowers 6 inches, rich blue, fragrant; leaves 9 inches; spread 4 to 5 feet.**

'Marian Strawn'

Texan Kirk Strawn honored his mother with this 1969 pick, a super-fragrant white star held boldly above the water's surface. Yet its big blooms are almost dwarfed by the serrated pads, which have purple blotches that radiate from the centers. **Flowers 9 inches, white, fragrant; leaves 15 inches; spread 7 to 8 feet.**

'Mrs. George H. Pring'

This Joseph Marliac pick has been on the market for almost 80 years. It earns its keep by producing up to a half dozen flowers at one time. They stay open all day as well. Star-shaped, they are cream-colored with gray-green stripes on some of the outer petals. Oval leaves usually lose most of their speckles with age. **Flowers 8 inches, cream; leaves to almost 17 inches long; spread 6 to 9 feet.**

(continued on next page)

TROPICAL LILY VARIETIES

(continued from previous page)

'Mrs. Martin E. Randig'

The flowers of this cultivar are haunting in both their fragrance and color, which deepens from a rosy purple to an intense lavender-blue. Leaves are edged in maroon. Like other viviparous tropicals, 'Mrs. Martin E. Randig' is tough and will tolerate a bit of cold weather and adapts well to water gardens of all sizes and depths. **Flowers 6 inches, violet-blue, fragrant; leaves 9 inches; spread 5 feet.**

'Pamela'

The color of these flowers is slightly more purple than an October sky, while the size can be immense. There are always a lot of them, too. The huge oval leaves are heavily mottled with chestnut and have raised lobes. **Flowers 8 to 13 inches, lilac-blue; leaves to 15 inches long; spread 6 to 8 feet.**

'Panama Pacific'

These star-shaped flowers open a claret red and deepen to a more plumy purple. Their yellow stamens are tipped with red-violet. This cultivar will be content in a tub garden and, like other viviparous tropicals, will bounce back from a slight chill. **Flowers 5 inches, red-violet; leaves to 11 inches; spread 3 to 6 feet.**

'Pink Platter'

The name reflects the way these mid-pink flowers, composed of many long, tapering petals, open almost flat. Anthers in the center are yellow touched with pink at the tips; outer anthers are pink and orange. Olive leaves have some purple mottling. 'Pink Platter' is not as viviparous as some of the tropicals, but it does share their tolerance to chills. **Flowers 10 inches, pink; leaves 10 inches; spread 5 to 6 feet.**

'Yellow Dazzler'

A clear chrome yellow with an appealing scent, these double flowers open late but stay open until dusk. The way they lie flat on the water makes these large flowers seem even larger. This can make the huge bronze-speckled oval leaves look small in comparison. **Flowers 10 inches, double, bright yellow, fragrant; leaves to 17 inches; spread 6 to 8 feet.**

NIGHT BLOOMING

'Emily Grant Hutchings'

A slightly paler center gives greater depth and sheen to this cultivar's long, slightly curved, rose-pink petals. Star-shaped flowers are semidouble and sometimes bloom in clusters. They lack the usual pungent aroma of night-blooming tropicals. Easy to please, 'Emily' has green leaves with wavy edges and a bronze sheen. **Flowers 7 inches, semidouble, rose; leaves 12 inches; spread 6 to 7 feet.**

'H.C. Haarstick'

Here's a night bloomer with an extra-long season. Its dark scarlet petals have a touch of purple at their bases, while the reddish-brown stamens shade to amber at the bottom. Leaves are burnished bronzy-red. **Flowers 12 inches, dark red, fragrant; leaves 16 inches; spread 6 to 12 feet.**

'Missouri'

White flowers will be the most visible in your pond at night, especially in moonlight or under artificial light. This broad-petaled beauty is a great choice for a big pond. With an ample container and regular feeding, it will develop creamy white flowers the same size as its toothed and fluted leaves. **Flowers to 14 inches, white, fragrant; leaves 14 inches; spread from 6 to 10 feet.**

'Mrs. George C. Hitchcock'

The narrow petals on this reliable bloomer are a soft pink. 'Mrs. George C. Hitchcock' should keep blooming late into the summer. The stamens are burnt-orange, and the copper-green foliage is specked with darker green. **Flowers 10 to 12 inches, pink, fragrant; leaves up to 15 inches; spread 7 to 8 feet.**

'Red Flare'

When this cultivar rises a full foot above the water and opens its glowing red petals wide, the effect is a lot like a tumultuous Fourth of July fireworks. Maroon leaves, which retain their reddish tinge, have a toothed, crimped edge and open sinuses. 'Red Flare' turns up the temperature in any pond. **Flowers 10 inches, deep red; leaves 12 inches; spread 5 to 6 feet.**

'Wood's White Night'

A fragrant, semidouble, star-shaped, creamy-white flower touched lightly with yellow on the tips of its stamens. The scalloped leaves grow large, but the plant stays compact enough for a medium-size pond. **Flowers 12 inches, semidouble, white, fragrant; leaves up to 16 inches; spread 8 to 10 feet.**

OTHER TROPICAL LILY CHOICES

■ **'Bagdad'**
Flowers 8 inches, light-blue petals with lavender sepals, day-blooming; leaves 10 to 12 inches; spread 6 to 7 feet.

■ **'August Koch'**
Flowers 4½ to 5½ inches, blue petals with purple sepals, day-blooming; leaves 12 inches; spread 4 to 6 feet.

■ **'Midnight'**
Flowers 6 to 8 inches, dark violet-blue, dayblooming; leaves 9 to 10 inches; spread from 4 to 6 feet.

■ **'Antares'**
Flowers 6 to 10 inches, deep red petals and sepals, night-blooming; leaves 10 to 12 inches; spread 5 to 7 feet.

■ **'Trudy Slocum'**
Flowers 6 to 8 inches, flat white, night-blooming; leaves 13 inches; spread 5 to 6 feet.

Lotuses

The history and lore surrounding lotuses have left a lot of people with the impression that they are tropical or at least hard to grow. While it's true that they are showstoppers and may overwhelm a small pond, they don't need any more care than a water lily once they're established. All they absolutely require is two to three months of daytime temperatures over 80°F. All lotuses are hardy to Zone 4, and some will survive in Zone 3.

There are only two species: the sacred East Indian lotus (*Nelumbo nucifera*), which can be pink or white, and our native American lotus (*N. lutea*), which is yellow. But hybridizers have wrung vast variety from the genes of these two, so lotuses can range in height from less than 2 feet to more than 8 feet.

Lotus flowers are fragrant and can be as big as a basketball. Most bloom for only three days, many of them changing color each day. These are flowers for early birds. The first day, they open before dawn and close again by the time most of us are at work. The second day, they are open from midmorning to noon, and on the last day the petals fall by midafternoon.

The show still isn't over, though. The cone-shaped seedpod, which during bloom has gone from yellow to green, expands and turns brown—offering itself for dried arrangements. And lotuses remain impressive when not in bloom,

Plant or transplant lotus tubers as early in spring as possible, before they turn into a maze of runners.

with both floating leaves and upright leaves that look like parasols. Up to 2 feet across, the leaves have a waxy coating that catches raindrops and holds them for hours.

Lotus seeds and tubers are edible. This fact is reflected in one of the older names for American lotus: pond nuts. Another of its names is water chinquapin, chinquapins being nuts related to chestnuts.

ANATOMY OF A LOTUS

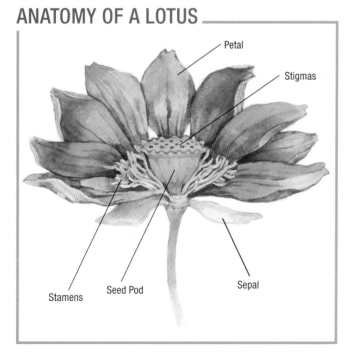

Petal

Stigmas

Stamens

Seed Pod

Sepal

The roots of this lotus are planted in the soil at the bottom of the pond; the leaves float on the surface of the water.

GROWING LOTUSES

For each lotus tuber, you will need a round planting tub about 18 inches in diameter and at least 9 inches deep. One 3 feet in diameter and 1 foot deep is even better. When you receive your lotus tuber, you'll probably notice one or more buds, or growing tips. Be careful not to break them. In fact, most experts recommend against planting lotuses in square containers because the buds are so delicate that they can break just by jamming into a corner as they grow. You can plant lotuses in March in Zone 9, but wait until May in Zone 4. Gardeners in between should plant in April.

Fill your tub to within 2 to 3 inches from the top with heavy garden soil. Lay the rhizome on the soil horizontally, and add a couple more inches of soil, leaving about ½ inch of the lotus's growing tip above the surface. Add ½ inch or so of clean gravel to hold the soil down, keeping it away from the bud. Lotuses are heavy feeders; add four to six fertilizer pellets at this point to ensure a good display. Fertilize once or twice a month after planting, until a month before your first frost date.

Place your tub in the pond with just 2 to 3 inches of water above the growing tip. Lotuses can handle about 1 foot of water over their tips, but less is better. You should see your first floating leaves three to four weeks after the water has reached 80°F.

If your pond will freeze in winter, store your lotus container in a plastic bag in a cool, frost-free place (ideally around 55°F). Lotuses grown in tubs may be overwintered if you can bury the tub in the ground.

To start your own lotuses, collect seeds when the pod has turned brown; dry them; and save them until early spring. Then nick a hole in the hard seed covering and drop the seeds in water, where they should germinate in 10 to 20 days. Transplant the seedlings to soil once the third leaf has appeared. Move the container to a sunny location for several days prior to moving the container into the pond water. Avoid burning the tuber with too much fertilizer when planting initially.

Lotuses

Dramatic and relatively shade tolerant, lotuses make a wonderful addition to a pond. They are cold-hardy throughout much of the United States and southern Canada, but require two to three months of 80° temperature in order to flower. You will need to rise early to see their flowers.

READILY AVAILABLE LOTUSES

(*Nelumbo* species and cultivars)

AMERICAN LOTUS, WATER CHINQUAPIN
(*N. lutea*)
This American native is easy to grow. Its sunny yellow flowers usually bloom 10 inches above the water. Round blue-green leaves can reach 2 feet. It likes shallow water and can adapt to fairly small ponds. **Flowers 7 to 11 inches, yellow; leaves 12-18 inches; height 2½ to 5 feet.**

SACRED LOTUS, (EGYPTIAN)
(*N. nucifera*)
This Asian species is bigger all around than our native species. The flowers, most typically a rose-pink but sometimes red or white, have an arresting aroma, especially when they first open. **Flowers 12 inches, usually rose, fragrant; leaves to 3 feet; height to 6 feet.**

ASIATIC LOTUS ('Alba grandiflora')
This classic and vigorous lotus is sometimes called the "magnolia lotus" because of its flower's resemblance to that tree's substantial white blossom. The frill of anthers around the seedpod is especially showy. Bluish green leaves have wavy edges and can sometimes hide the flowers. **Flowers 12 inches, white; leaves 16 to 23 inches; height to 6 feet.**

'Angel Wings'
You may imagine a band of angels in these white, pointed petals, which curl in slightly. As each flower first opens, the central seed capsule is chartreuse with a green rim. The wavy, concave leaves may expand to 2 feet wide, but the plant itself rarely reaches 4 feet tall. **Flowers 9 inches, white; leaves 18 to 24 inches; height under 4 feet.**

'Baby Doll'
You'd be hard-pressed to find a better choice for a tub than this miniature lotus: dainty flowers that look like white tulips, seedpods not much bigger than a thumbnail, and petite in stature. In a bigger pond it will show off with a dozen flowers at once. **Flowers 5 inches; leaves 9 to 11 inches; height 2½ feet.**

'Charles Thomas'
Just a bit bigger than 'Baby Doll' but still adaptable to a small pond, this selection is unique for the lavender-pink color of its flowers, which smell sweetly of anise. **Flowers 6 to 8 inches, lavender-pink, fragrant; leaves 14 to 22 inches; height 2 to 3 feet.**

'Momo Botan'
The rosy pink flowers have yellow at their base and a yellow center. With more than 100 petals, each looks like a double peony and that's what its name means. But 'Momo Botan' is most famous for blooming for a week, twice as long as other lotuses. The fragrant flowers may stay open all night and are produced over a long season. It's another cultivar that will be happy in a small pond. **Flowers 6 inches, rose-pink; leaves 12 to 15 inches; height 2 to 4 feet.**

'Mrs. Perry D. Slocum'
This has become America's favorite lotus. Its colors are often compared to those of a favorite rose, 'Peace'. First yellow blushed with pink, the flowers fade to equally lovely cream and pink. Each bloom is subtly different, and a single plant can have several differently tinted blossoms at once. The flowers have more than 80 petals and a strong anise scent. Felty leaves grow large and the plant is over 4 feet tall, so it will need a medium to large pond. **Flowers to 12 inches, pink with yellow or cream, fragrant; leaves to 23 inches; height 4 to 5 feet.**

Marginal Plants

Marginal, or shallow-water, plants occur naturally along the edges of ponds and streams and usually like water over their roots at least part of the growing season. These are the ones to plant just inside the margin of your water garden. If your pool or pond doesn't have built-in planters or plant shelves, you'll need to raise the plants' containers on blocks to the depth where they grow best. Except for the rampant spreaders, marginals generally make excellent plants for tub gardens. Some species also thrive in garden beds if the soil is well amended with organic matter and kept moist.

A few plants described under "Grasses and Grasslike Plants," page 235, also grow well as marginal plants. Soft rush (*Juncus effusus*, page 237), bulrush (*Schoenoplectus*, page 237), and woolgrass bulrush (*Scirpus cyperinus*) can grow in water up to 6 inches deep (either in containers or planted in a natural or earthen pond) as well as in constantly moist soil. Other grasslike plants have been included in this section because of their preference for standing water. Be sure to include some of these species, or other spiky-looking plants such as sweet flag or true irises, for strong vertical interest at your pond edges.

The irises are another group of plants with many members that grow either in shallow water or moist soil. Beginning gardeners are most likely to be familiar with bearded irises, and there's no reason these can't be wonderful choices for well-drained soil along the edge of a lined pond. But the irises most closely associated with water gardens are beardless irises in the category called "*Laevigatae* irises." These need moist, acid soils or even a couple of inches of standing water. They will be happiest in a wetland garden, or in a bed that is heavily amended with peat moss and watered frequently. These species differ from bearded irises, and each other in the shape of their upright petals (called "standards") and their horizontal or drooping petals (called "falls"). Descriptions of several species of moisture-loving irises begin on page 225.

You will want to mix these vertical plants with low-growers—moneywort or water mint, for example. Look for interesting leaf shapes, such as those of the aptly named arrow arum and arrowhead. While the colors of some marginal flowers are subtle, they have interesting shapes as well. Some, such as skunk cabbage and golden club, have a hoodlike modified leaf called a spathe enclosing a flower spike or spadix, similar to the woodland flower called "jack-in-the-pulpit."

'Red Lotus'
(*N. nucifera* var. *rosea*)
A naturally occurring variety in China and Japan, this is among the bigger lotuses. Its medium-size, anise-scented flowers are a rosy pink similar to 'Rosea Plena' (below) but with fewer petals, so that on the first day each looks like an unfolding rose. The leaves are held more than 4 feet over the water. **Flowers 8 to 10 inches, rose-pink, fragrant; leaves 18 inches; height to 6 feet.**

DOUBLE ROSE LOTUS
('Rosea plena')
The flowers of this cultivar resemble a peony or a full, open rose with up to 100 deep rose-red petals, which are yellow at their base. Its 1-inch seed capsules almost disappear inside the blossom. If well fertilized, this cultivar can grow shoulder high to most gardeners. **Flowers to 13 inches, deep rose; leaves 18 inches; height to 5 feet.**

TULIP LOTUS
('Shirokunshi')
This pure white flower looks even more delicate because it has a mere 16 petals. This one is a good patio choice, since it stays relatively petite. **Flowers 8 inches, white; leaves 18 inches; height 30 inches.**

'Shiroman' ('Alba Plena')
Here's a peony look-alike for those who want a pale lotus. The blossoms are fluffy and cream colored. It will spread rapidly, so choose this lotus only for a medium to large pond. **Flowers 10 inches, cream; leaves 24 inches; height to 5 feet.**

RECOMMENDED MARGINALS

SWEET FLAG (*Acorus calamus*)
The strap-shaped foliage of this perennial looks for all the world like that of an iris, or "flag," but its midsummer flowers are underwhelming 2-inch horns. The leaves smell like cinnamon if you crush them, and can be 4 feet tall. The cultivar 'Variegatus' is striped from top to bottom with white or cream. Grow sweet flag in water up to 9 inches deep or a well-watered flower bed. **Zones 4–11.**

WATER PLANTAIN, MAD-DOG WEED
(*Alisma plantago-aquatica*)
The baby's breath of marginals, water plantain will self-seed and is too vigorous for all but large ponds. Lance-shaped, gray-green leaves about 1 foot long form spiky rosettes, which are topped with frothy sprays of tiny pink or white flowers that reach up to 30 inches. Plants do best in water 6 inches deep. **Zones 5–8.**

FLOWERING RUSH
(*Butomus umbellatus*)
Native to North America, Europe, and western Asia, this 3 to 5 footer has twisted, strongly vertical leaves ½ inch wide, which are bronzy purple when they're new. Fragrant, cup-shaped, rose-pink flowers appear in 4-inch-wide clusters in late summer. It can grow in water up to 5 inches deep. Divide it frequently if you're growing it in a container. **Zones 5–11.**

BOG ARUM, WILD CALLA
(*Calla palustris*)
Bog arum, in the same family as jack-in-the-pulpit, has a flower similar to that of the South African calla lily. A nearly round spathe cups the green-and-yellow club of the spadix; after a long season of bloom, flowers are followed by red-orange berries. Its 6- to 20-inch rhizome (modified stem) creeps along the soil surface with

shiny, leathery, heart-shaped leaves, spreading to about 2 feet. Give it full sun and water to a couple of inches deep, or plant it in wet pondside soil heavily amended with peat moss to increase its acidity. **Zones 3–8.**

MARSH MARIGOLD
(*Caltha palustris*)
The bright yellow flowers of this spreading native look more like buttercups than what we usually call marigolds. Growing from rhizomes to about a foot tall, it has toothed kidney-shaped leaves. The cultivar 'Flore Plena' (also sold as 'Multiplex') has double flowers. Marsh marigold likes water only a few inches deep. **Zones 3–7.**

GREEN TARO
(*Colocasia esculenta*)
Every water garden deserves at least one elephant-leaved perennial, even though most can be challenging. Cultivated as a root vegetable in Southeast Asia, taro has 2-foot arrow-shaped leaves on 3-foot stalks. Look for the cultivar 'Fontanesii', which has violet stalks and

leaves that glow with dark red veins and margins. 'Hilo Beauty' has white mottling; 'Illustris' has dark purple mottling and stalks. All like high humidity and filtered sun and can be planted 12 inches under water. In **Zone 8** and north, store the tubers (dry) over winter in a place where they won't freeze. **Zones 9–11.**

UMBRELLA SEDGE
(*Cyperus* species)
These grasslike plants are topped with tufts of brownish flowers, some radiating like the ribs of an umbrella. You can grow the smaller ones in containers and enjoy them indoors in winter. Giant papyrus or Egyptian paper reed (*C. papyrus*) is an African native that can grow 12 to 15 feet tall. Long thin leaves sprouting from the top look like green dust mops. It needs a huge container (20-gallon), lots of sun, and protection from wind. **Zones 10–11.**

Dwarf papyrus (*C. profiler*, formerly *C. isocladus*), from South Africa, is at the other end of the spectrum at only about a foot tall. Grow it in 2 inches of water. **Zones 9–10.**

Umbrella palm (*C. alternifolius*), from Madagascar, which is often sold as a houseplant, grows 1 to 3 feet tall; it has a daintier cultivar, 'Gracilis', and one with lengthwise stripes, 'Variegatus'. It tolerates a bit of shade and thrives in up to 6 inches of water. **Zones 9-11.**

SPIKE RUSH
(*Eleocharis montevidensis*, also sold as *E. palustris*)
This plant also goes by the name of fiber-optic plant (as do a couple of completely different plants with a similar shape). Spike rush occurs naturally over much of the United States and grows a foot high, producing a quill of little brown tufts. It likes 2 to 4 inches of water. **Zones 6–11.**

If you enjoy Asian cuisine, try related Chinese water chestnut (*E. dulcis* or *E. tuberosa*) for its edible tubers. It also offers graceful stems up to 3 feet tall and can grow in water up to 1 foot deep. **Zones 9–10.** (Another species, *E. acicularis*, grows completely underneath the water.)

HORSETAIL
(*Equisetum* species)
These grasslike plants have jointed hollow stems and brown cones at the tip. Common horsetail (*E. hyemale*) is also called scouring rush. It usually grows 3 to 4 feet tall. Dwarf horsetail (*E. scirpoides*) may stop at 6 inches and is less hardy. Other species range to more than 6 feet. Grow them in containers in up to 8 inches of water or in a wetland area. **Zones 3–11.**

COTTON GRASS
(*Eriophorum* species)
A field of cotton grass looks almost surreal when it opens its 2-inch balls in midspring. The plant is about 18 inches tall; height doubles with the flowering spike. Two widespread and similar species are common cotton grass (*E. angustifolium*) and the aptly named broad-leaved cotton grass (*E. latifolium*). Both will grow in up to 2 inches of water in full sun but don't like hot summers. **Zones 4–7.**

CHAMELEON PLANT
(*Houttuynia cordata*)
Like many ground covers, this native of eastern Asia can be invasive, but it is useful for wet shade. Heart-shaped leaves exude an orange scent if bruised. The true flowers are tiny yellow-green knobs, with four white petal-like bracts (modified leaves). Look for the cultivar 'Chameleon', which has yellow and red mixed with the green on its leaves and is less invasive. Grow it in a container under 1 to 2 inches of water in sun or partial shade. **Zones 5–11.**

JAPANESE IRIS
(*Iris ensata*) and cultivars
Many people consider these the most beautiful of irises. These plants have been bred over centuries so that their standards have all but disappeared, but the almost horizontal falls are huge and often double. This makes them look somewhat flat, best viewed from above. The many selections, 2 to 3 feet tall and in almost every color but green, frequently bear Japanese names. They can grow in an inch of standing water and should not be allowed to dry out during the growing season. **Zones 4–9.**

RABBIT-EAR IRIS
(*I. laevigata*) and cultivars
This Asian native is similar to the Japanese iris in its rather flattened flower, which is 2 to 3 inches across and lavender. Flowers are larger when grown in a few inches of water than when grown in moist soil. Cultivars are available in white and shades of violet, blue, or rose; one variety has variegated leaves. Soil for these also should be constantly wet but can be more alkaline than for other water irises. **Zones 4–9.**

LOUISIANA HYBRIDS
You're more likely to find hybrids for sale than any of the species, which are becoming rare. The five species (*I. brevicaulis*, *I. fulva*, *I. nelsonii*, *I. giganticaerulea*, and *I. hexagona*) are always grouped together because they have the same habitat and requirements. Their flowers have no beards, and both species and hybrids tend to have drooping standards and narrow falls. Hybrids offer larger flowers than the species and are unusual among irises in the fact they come in reds as well as blues, purples, yellows, and white. They thrive in hot summers, but breeders have made them adaptable much farther north than the state for which they're named. **Zones 4–9.**

YELLOW FLAG
(*I. pseudacorus*)
It's hard to imagine this graceful perennial as a pest, but it has escaped and run roughshod over natives in the Mid-Atlantic states. As with all such plants, a gardener may end up loving it for its toughness or detesting it for its rambunctiousness. Yellow flag averages 3 feet tall, has ribbed gray-green leaves, and in early to midsummer bears 3- to 4-inch yellow flowers with slightly darker falls and brown or violet markings. It can grow in up to a foot of water. **Zones 4–9.**

SIBERIAN IRIS
(*I. sibirica*) and hybrids
In May or June, this elegant flower bears small flowers of a dark, rich lavender-blue. Slender leaves up to 4 feet tall continue to provide a punctuation mark after the flowers are gone. There are innumerable cultivars in many colors, including bi-colors. Disease-free Siberian irises can survive with average moisture and go several years without being divided. While they bloom well in a few inches of water, they'll overwinter better if the pots are removed and buried in well-drained garden soil until spring. **Zones 4–9.**

(continued on next page)

RECOMMENDED MARGINALS

(continued from previous page)

BLUE FLAG

(I. versicolor)
Native to the United States from New York to Texas, blue flag has dramatically narrow falls of lavender-blue, each with a white splotch veined with purple. A few cultivars in other colors are available. Similar to yellow flag in shape but only 2 feet tall, it blooms in late spring or early summer. Unlike the other species described here, it doesn't grow in standing water. **Zones 3–8.**

WESTERN SKUNK CABBAGE

(Lysichiton americanus)
Musky-smelling skunk cabbages are a favorite harbinger of spring. This western native produces rosettes of glossy, heavily textured leaves 2 to 4 feet long. A banana yellow spathe forms a vertical dish 16 inches long around a club (spadix) of tiny yellow-green flowers. It will tolerate moving water, but no deeper than an inch over its crown. It will also thrive in deep, rich, moist soil. **Zones 7–9.**

MONEYWORT, CREEPING JENNIE

(Lysimachia nummularia)
This central European creeper can grow in or out of the water; it usually ends up right on the edge. It has escaped into the wild in much of eastern North America. Moneywort has small round leaves and bears bright yellow, cup-shaped flowers with dark red spots. The yellow-leaved cultivar 'Aurea' is less likely to get out of bounds. **Zones 4–8.**

WATER MINT

(Mentha aquatica)
The leaves are much like those of dry-land mints—slightly hairy, serrated, and aromatic—and have reddish stems. In summer, tiny tubular lavender flowers appear in globes. Native to Eurasia, it will grow 3 feet high and wide and can be useful for stabilizing a bank, but like other mints it can gallop all over the garden. Grow it in a container in 6 inches of water. **Zones 5–9.**

PARROT'S-FEATHER

(Myriophyllum aquaticum)
This versatile plant from the Southern Hemisphere is sometimes categorized with submerged plants. (It's related to the milfoils described under "Submerged Plants" on page 205.) But it will creep from the water's edge to make itself at home on a muddy bank; even in the middle of a pond, it waves its brushy whorls of blue-green leaves high above the water surface. The underwater leaves are yellow-green, and its stems can grow up to 5 feet long. It can sometimes overwinter beneath the ice in frozen ponds north of its usual hardiness range. **Zones 7–11.**

GOLDEN CLUB

(Orontium aquaticum)
"Odd but endearing" describes this flower, a 7-inch skinny white spadix tipped with yellow, like a miniature club or poker, blooming from late spring to midsummer. Its 18-inch lance-shaped leaves are blue-green and velvety. You can plant it as deep as 12 inches under water or on a muddy bank. **Zones 6–11.**

ARROW ARUM

(Peltandra species)
These native marsh dwellers can become invasive, but it's hard to resist their arrowhead-shaped foliage. White arrow arum (*P. sagittifolia*) has white spathes that open wide, followed by red berries. **Zones 7–11.**

Green arrow arum (*P. virginica*) is twice as big, at 3 feet tall, and produces green, nearly closed spathes and green berries. Grow them in containers in up to 8 inches of water. **Zones 5-9.**

PICKEREL WEED

(Pontederia cordata)
If you love blue flowers, you'll want to have several plants of this wonderful native growing on the edges of your pond. Its tiny baby blue flowers are clustered on spikes up to 6 inches long, blooming from late spring to autumn. Plants can grow to more than 4 feet tall and spread to 2 feet and offer shiny, upright, lance-shaped leaves. Grow it successfully in full sun in water up to 5 inches deep or along the sides of a wetland garden or pond. **Zones 4–11.**

ARROWHEAD, SWAMP POTATO
(*Sagittaria* species)

These plants have even more dramatically arrow-shaped leaves than arrow arums and look poised to be shot into space. Three-petaled white flowers have yellow centers. A common native is the vigorous duck potato (*S. latifolia*), which grows 1½ to 3 feet tall and offers 1½-inch flowers and variously shaped leaves 4 to 12 inches long. Waterfowl love to snack on its walnut-size tubers. **Zones 4–11.**

Also native is the smaller-flowered awl-leaf arrowhead (*S. subulata*), which is 2 feet tall and has 3-foot submerged leaves and egg-shaped floating leaves. **Zones 5–11.**

Japanese arrowhead (*S. sagittifolia*) has 18-inch leaves and purple-blotched flowers on 3-foot stems, but it can spread too eagerly; its double-flowering form, 'Flora Pleno', is better behaved. **Zones 5–11.**

Giant arrowhead (*S. montevidensis*), a tropical species, reaches to 30 inches; they are marked with red at the base of each petal. **Zones 9–11.**

LIZARD'S TAIL
(*Saururus cernuus*)

Despite the common name, the spikes of tiny fragrant white flowers look more like big caterpillars standing on end. One fan compares them to swans' necks. A southeastern U.S. native, it grows 1 to 2 feet tall and has bright green, heart-shaped leaves. The species name means "nodding"; if you give lizard's tail moisture and shade, it will reward you by romping about and producing hundreds of these bobbing "tails" more than 6 inches long. **Zones 4–9.**

HARDY CANNA
(*Thalia dealbata*)

This plant will be the showpiece of a water garden. It has long fishing-pole flower stalks topped with 8-inch panicles of violet flowers. The leaves grow on stalks, too: oval or more lance shaped, 20 inches long, and gray-green with a white powdery coating. Sometimes called "hardy canna," the plant can reach 10 feet tall and spread 6 feet wide. Give it an appropriately large container (at least 5-gallon) and grow it in 6 inches of water along the margin of a sunny pond. **Zones 6–11.**

EASTERN SKUNK CABBAGE
(*Symplocarpus foetidus*)

The eastern skunk cabbage has a purple-brown spathe, fatter than that of its western counterpart, enveloping the spadix like a monk's hood. The flower generates heat to protect it when it emerges from pondside ice or snow as early as February. Despite its name, it only smells unpleasant if you handle it. The "cabbage leaves" emerge when the flower is gone. Give it a bog or shallow water. **Zones 4–8.**

CATTAIL
(*Typha* species)

Cattails are aggressive, but their flower spikes and long pointed leaves are invaluable for waterfowl. Two common native species are narrow-leaved cattail (*T. angustifolia*), which grows to 5 feet tall, and common cattail (*T. latifolia*), which reaches 10 feet. Both can be planted in water 6 to 12 inches deep and need at least a half day of sun. A variegated form of *T. latifolia* with stripes, called 'Variegata', is less vigorous and half as tall. Graceful cattail (*T. laxmanii*) has narrow leaves and grows 4 feet tall. The male (tan) and female (dark brown) "tails" are separated on its stem. **Zones 3-11.**

Dwarf cattail (*T. minima*) is less than 2 feet tall. Its leaves are slender and itsspikes are short. It can take lots of water but likes full sun. Flowers may be non-existent in warm climates. **Zones 4–9**

CALLA LILY
(*Zantedeschia aethiopica*)

Beloved by florists (and their customers), this 2- to 3-foot-tall bulbous plant from Africa can be grown as a marginal aquatic in warm climates—although it's almost too beautiful to look at home in an informal pond. Its shiny leaves are arrow-shaped. The cup-shaped fragrant white flower (spathe) surrounds a club, or spadix. Grow calla lilies in a container of heavy soil under a foot of water. They can also be grown in garden beds; they tolerate a wide range of soils provided the soil is moist or they get regular watering. **Zones 8–10.**

Plants for the Periphery

A pond stuck in the middle of a vast expanse of lawn may look artificial and barren. Use some of the plants described in this section to dress up the surroundings. Add some perennial borders, or use shrubs to define a pondside seating area. Larger shrubs and trees can serve as a pleasant backdrop to frame the pond, or they can mask views of property fences or a neighbor's house.

Remember that plantings need to be in scale with the pond and the rest of your yard. They should also blend with the overall style of your water feature and yard. Clipped evergreens will only look good next to the most formal pool; a mix of plants is best for an informal pond. The easiest way to make an informal pond, particularly a natural water gar-

den, look as though it belongs in its setting is to surround it with plants that occur near ponds in nature. That's why many of the perennials, shrubs, and trees described in this section are species native to North America.

The plants described here like moisture, but they also need soil that drains well. In their natural setting, you would find them on the banks above a stream or a pond, not right at the water's edge. If you're looking for plants to grow in constantly soggy soil, check under "Marginal Plants," beginning on page 223.

Well-chosen shrubs and trees can draw attention to your water garden, providing a lush border around it, or they can mask or draw attention away from a less-than pleasant view.

MOISTURE-LOVING PERENNIALS

All of the herbaceous perennials on pages 230 to 232 like moist soil, but some can tolerate more average garden conditions. As a rule, moisture lovers in shade can survive with less watering, but most will produce fewer flowers in those conditions. If you want to create a more hospitable environment for moisture-loving perennials, dig in a generous helping of peat moss, compost, or leaf mulch so that it will retain more moisture. A layer of organic mulch (shredded bark, chopped leaves, or compost) will also help keep soil moist.

Check the conditions around your pond before you decide what to plant. Moisture lovers may be perfect around a natural, earth-bottom pond in a low spot, but they may be totally inappropriate for ponds with liners. First, you're probably creating your pond in the middle of a lawn or otherwise naturally dry area, rather than in a zone of constantly wet soil. Second, many moisture-loving plants also like some shade, so they won't thrive next to a pond that's situated to get plenty of sun for water lilies.

The good news is that many wetland plants adapt easily to drier conditions. (It never seems to work the other way around.) In addition, many of these plants have "look-alike" relatives that don't require as much water. Look in standard garden catalogs and at nurs-

eries for other plants in the same genus (indicated by the first word of a plant's botanical name.)

Bulbs. These are nature's clever way of helping plants survive periods of unpleasantness: too wet, too dry, too hot, or too much competition. Because they can remain dormant for so long, planting them always seems a huge leap of faith, and their eventual appearance something of a miracle. A few of the bulbs described on page 233 have adapted to wet soils, but most require good drainage. If the soil where you want to grow them doesn't drain well (especially during the bulbs' dormant season), you'll need to plant the bulbs in raised beds to prevent rot. Corms, tubers, and rhizomes are always included in discussions about bulbs because they are handled in a similar fashion, although technically they're not bulbs but different types of underground storage organs.

Ferns. Ferns add welcome texture to any garden. Tucked in among rocks surrounding a pond or a waterfall, their featherweight fronds make a particularly refreshing contrast to the stone's hard surface. While some can prosper in full sun or slightly dry soil, none of them will live long in both; most benefit from some wind protection. Once in a happy home, ferns rarely need attention. Note in our descriptions beginning on page 234 that some can spread rapidly, so choose a species or location carefully if you don't want to have to control them.

RECOMMENDED PERENNIALS

JACK-IN-THE-PULPIT
(*Arisaema triphyllum*)
Jack is the flower (a tiny knob called the spadix) and the pulpit is the hooded spathe that surrounds him. The spathe is green, sometimes streaked with dark purple, and about 5 inches long; the spadix gives way to a stalk of bright scarlet berries. Either flower or berry is a delightful surprise to find in eastern woodlands. The leaves, which follow the "flowers," have three parts and reach 6 to 24 inches tall. Give this plant a cool, shady place with moist but well-drained soil. **Zones 4–9.**

GOATSBEARD
(*Aruncus dioicus*)
Goatsbeard grows 4 to 6 feet tall and in rich soil can spread 6 feet, but it's surprisingly delicate for such a large plant. Its five-part leaves are toothed and ferny, and in late spring plants develop flowing, creamy white "beards." Give goatsbeard afternoon shade if you live south of **Zone 5.**

The popular cultivar 'Kneiffii', at 3 feet tall, is more manageable for smaller ponds and its foliage is more threadlike. **Zones 3–8.**

SWAMP MILKWEED
(*Asclepias incarnata*)
Like other milkweeds, this has tough stems, a lot of branches which make it almost shrublike, and narrow elliptical leaves. Plants are topped by flat clusters of small flowers, each purple-pink with paler little upright "horns" and slightly fragrant. 'Ice Ballet', developed as a long-lasting cut flower, offers white blooms. Flowers give way to spiky pods that pop open to release

dark brown seeds on silky threads. The pods work well in dried arrangements. Despite its common name, swamp milkweed can grow in fairly dry soil. Milkweeds are slow to emerge in spring. **Zones 3–8.**

ASTILBE, FALSE SPIREA
(*Astilbe* species)
Some astilbes are native to North America, but most sold for gardens are *A.* x *arendsii*, hybrids of Asian species bred in Germany by Georg Arends. The plants' fuzzy plumes are usually in the white-pink-red range, with a few salmons and lavenders; the leaves are divided and lacy.

Plants range in height from about 1 to 4 feet. Astilbes will turn to toast before summer's end if they don't have fluffy, moist, neutral to slightly acid soil. **Zones 4–8.**

ASTILBOIDES
Astilboides tabularis; formerly *Rodgersia tabularis*)
The off-white plumy flowers are astilbe look-alikes, but most gardeners plant this for its bold leaves, which are round and slightly lobed and can be 3 feet across. Stems attach to leaves in the center, like umbrellas. Plants are about 5 feet tall and 4 feet wide. They demand cool

summers and moist but not soggy soil. **Zones 4–7.**

BLACK COHOSH, BLACK SNAKEROOT
(*Cimicifuga racemosa*)
This perennial grows naturally in damp places in the eastern U.S. Although black cohosh grows 4 to 7 feet tall and 2 feet across, its much-divided leaves give it an airy quality. Because side branches flower late, the long wands of little white flowers keep coming for weeks. 'Atrop-

urpurea' has purple foliage, and the flowers of American bugbane (*C. americana*) flaunt a touch of pink. Native Americans used black cohosh to treat a variety of ills; hence one of its common names. These plants like some shade, especially in the South, but are not fussy about moisture. **Zones 3–8.**

UMBRELLA PLANT
(*Darmera peltata*, formerly *Peltiphyllum peltatum*)
Round-topped clusters of pink or white flowers appear in spring on 6-foot stalks. In autumn, leaves turn copper. Umbrella plant forms mats that stabilize banks, in exchange for some shade and constant moisture. **Zones 5–8.**

JOE-PYE WEED
(*Eupatorium* species)
Joe-Pye was once used for medicinal purposes, but today it's planted to attract butterflies, which flock to its big frizz of flowers in mid- to late summer. Most common is spotted Joe-Pye weed (*E. maculatum*), which grows 2 to 6 feet with pink flowers; 'Gateway' is especially colorful. Similar E. purpureum is the biggest, at 9 feet tall. Sometimes called boneset, *E. perfoliatum* has white flowers and grows to about 5 feet. All prefer slightly alkaline soil that retains moisture but isn't soggy during the winter. Spotted Joe-Pye weed is the most cold hardy and may survive in **Zone 3**. Otherwise, **Zones 4–8.**

QUEEN-OF-THE-PRAIRIE
(*Filipendula rubra*)
Related to spirea, this native, with five-fingered leaves and fuzzy spires of peachy pink flowers grows 6 to 8 feet tall and spreads 4 feet across in **Zones 3-9.** 'Venusta' has more intense color. A Japanese relative, meadowsweet (*F. purpurea*), is usually pink but can be white. It's about 4 feet tall and grows in **Zones 4-9.** Both like moist, well-drained soil and will take some shade. A shorter relative is dropwort (*F. vulgaris*). It has white flowers. **Zones 4–9.**

BOG AVENS, INDIAN CHOCOLATE
(*Geum rivale*)
Bog avens, native to wet meadows and marshes, has strawberrylike leaves, but its flowers are usually a dusky pink. Cultivars include 'Leonard's Variety', having pink flowers flushed with orange; 'Lionel Cox', a yellow-orange; and bright orange 'Tangerine'. Give Bog Avens full sun and moist soil. It may take some hunting to find these. **Zones 3–8.**

GUNNERA
(*Gunnera manicata*)
Toothed leaves can grow 6 feet across, and the stalks to 8 feet tall. It will spread to the size of a small bedroom. Tiny red-green flowers appear in early summer on a 3-foot 'cob', followed by little round fruits. Gunnera needs protection from winds and dislikes heat. **Zones 7–10.**

SWAMP SUNFLOWER
(*Helianthus angustifolius*)
This is one of those swamp plants with many handsome cousins that can substitute in a drier pond margin. The sunflowers that most people know are annuals that require well-drained soil. Swamp sunflower is a perennial native to the eastern United States that produces rather sparse, 8-inch-long, narrow leaves on plants 5 to 8 feet tall. Its late-summer flowers are 3 inches across and have little dark purple centers. Like all sunflowers, it provides late-summer seeds for birds. Its natural habitat is moist and shady. It can grow in partial shade but will get tall and floppy; in full sun, it will be sturdier and produce more flowers. **Zones 6–9.**

COMMON ROSE MALLOW
(*Hibiscus moscheutos*)
The first time you see one of these growing in an eastern United States swamp, you may have trouble believing that some gardener didn't plant it. Lobed leaves 3 to 9 inches across give it a decidedly tropical look, as do the 8-inch funnel flowers in white, pink, or red. It grows 4 to 8 feet tall. Bright red 'Lord Baltimore' is a popular cultivar. Rose mallow needs full sun and consistently moist soil. **Zones 5–11.**

Swamp hibiscus (*H. coccineus*), which bears red flowers and has more finely divided leaves, is hardy only to **Zone 7**. It doesn't attract Japanese beetles like most mallows do.

BLAZING STAR, GAYFEATHER
(*Liatris spicata* and *L. pycnostachya*)
These wet-meadow natives have relatives that take drier conditions. All are recommended as a substitute for invasive purple loosestrife (*Lythrum salicaria*), which is banned in some states. Blazing star and gayfeather have a similar magenta color and upright shape, but the flower spikes are bottle-brushes, about 1½ feet long. The foliage is a grassy clump. Compact 'Kobold' is one of the best cultivars. All like full sun. **Zones 3–9.**

(continued on next page)

RECOMMENDED PERENNIALS

(continued from previous page)

LIGULARIA
(Ligularia species)

These imposing perennials can be difficult, but if you have a moist site with some afternoon shade, you may want to give them a try. Most people grow ligularia primarily for the big leaves, but some species also bear showy yellow flowers. *L. dentata* has heart-shaped leaves a foot across, and the plant can reach 5 feet tall with a 3-foot spread. The leaves of *L. stenocephala* are toothed; a popular cultivar is 'The Rocket', which produces dramatic 2-foot spires of yellow flowers. Both are hardy to Zone 4, but wilt quickly in the unrelenting heat of southern states. **Zones 4–8.**

LOBELIA
(Lobelia species)

The screaming red cardinal flower (*L. cardinalis*), a spike clustered with tiny three-lipped tubes, is astonishing to spot in an otherwise drab woodland. The shape and color (even brighter than the bird it was named for) make it a hummingbird magnet. A short-lived perennial, it can grow to more than 4 feet tall and produce dozens of flowers in the right conditions, namely unceasing moisture. **Zones 3–9.**

Big blue lobelia (*L. siphilitica*) isn't really any bigger than its relative; it's sometimes called "blue cardinal flower." It bears bright blue flowers and will tolerate somewhat drier conditions. It got its unfortunate species name because it was once thought to cure venereal disease. Look for new cultivars with magenta or dark purple blooms. **Zones 5–9.** You'll need to divide any of these every two to three years to keep them from dying out.

WATER FORGET-ME-NOT
(Myosotis scorpioides)

Like most other forget-me-nots, the aquatic version bears flat little sky blue flowers, each with an eye of yellow, white, or pink. It starts blooming in spring or early summer and will rebloom throughout the growing season. Creeping along the ground on stems as long as 18 inches, it will droop over the edge of a pond or waterfall. Grow it on a bank or in shallow water with afternoon shade. **Zones 4–9.**

PRIMROSE
(Primula species)

Among the moisture-lovers in this genus are the dramatic candelabra types, with several tiers of flowers whorled around their stems and rosettes of semievergreen leaves. *P. beesiana*, from damp mountain meadows of China, is 2 feet tall and wide and bears up to eight whorls of rosy red flowers. **Zones 4–8.**

P. japonica has purple flowers and is easier to grow, even in moving water. Cultivars with red or white flowers are available. **Zones 5–8.**

Drumstick primrose (*P. denticulata*) unspools both leaves and flowers in March or April. The leaves, eventually a foot long, are toothed and spoon-shaped. The round flowers that inspired its common name are purple with a yellow center. Many primroses loathe the hot dry summers common to much of the United States, but they can perform beautifully as long as they have partial shade or never dry out. They'll suffer without winter mulch in snow-free areas. **Zones 4–8.**

CHINESE RHUBARB
(Rheum palmatum)

This brawny perennial gives you the same satisfaction as Gunnera or Ligularia and is easier to grow. Dark-green, lobed leaves are 2 to 3 feet across; deep-red flower panicles look like 6-foot feather dusters. It spreads to 6 feet. 'Atrosanguineum' has leaves that are bright reddish-purple before they mature. Plant it in the fall, feed it in spring, and don't let its soil dry out. **Zones 5–9.**

RODGERSIA
(Rodgersia species)

One of these Asian plants will add drama to a pondside. They average 3 feet wide and up to 5 feet tall. They're easier to grow than some other big-leaved moisture lovers. Flower clusters, 2 feet tall, are like an astilbe's. Fingerleaf rodgersia (*R. aesculifolia*) gets its species name from textured leaves, with large "fingers" radiating from a central point. Its flowers are white, while those of featherleaf rodgersia (*R. pinnata*) are often pink or red. Leaves of the latter are more closely attached and look bronze in spring. *R. sambucifolia* usually grows only 3 feet tall; it has white or pink flowers. **Zones 5–8.**

RECOMMENDED BULBS

CHINESE GROUND ORCHID
(*Bletilla striata*)

Even if you tremble at the thought of growing fussy hothouse orchids, you can succeed with this temperate species. Plants have dark-green strappy leaves about a foot long and tuberous rootstocks. The bell-shaped magenta flowers last for a long time. Give plants a sheltered spot with rich, moist, well-drained soil, plus some shade in summer. **Zones 6–9.**

QUAMASH
(*Camassia* species)

More and more gardeners are including these blue beauties in their gardens. The spring flowers are six-petaled stars on tall spires. Cusick camas (*C. cusickii*) bears 2 to 3 feet tall with spires of steely blue flowers, while the flowers of common camass (*C. quamash*) are cup-shaped, brighter blue, and from 1 to 2 feet tall. Native to moist meadows, both do best with full sun and good drainage, and want ample moisture in spring. **Zones 4–10.**

WATER CANNA
(*Canna glauca*)

Cannas, once associated with Victorian-style flower beds, are making a big comeback. Unlike garden cannas, this species is a Brazilian native that has been bred to thrive in 6 to 12 inches of water. Plants will grow to 6 feet and produce gray, white-margined, lance-shaped leaves. Yellow flowers reappear throughout the summer. Cultivars include 'Endeavor' (flaming red), 'Erebus' (salmon), 'Ra' (yellow), and 'Taney' (orange-brown). Give cannas a sunny location in containers of fertile soil. **Zones 9–11**; north of **Zone 9**, unearth and dry the rhizomes in fall and overwinter them in slightly damp peat moss.

BOG LILY
(*Crinum* species)

These bulbs make striking specimens for a pond margin. Southern swamp lily (*C. americanum*), a native of Florida and the Gulf Coast, has leaves 2 inches wide and up to 2 feet long plus long-petaled, pungent white flowers. It will grow in 12 inches of water but prefers half as much. Plant so the neck of the bulb sits just above ground. The bulbs need to be overwintered indoors in all but frost-free areas. **Zones 10–11.**

CROCOSMIA 'Lucifer'

This increasingly popular bulb is native to South African grasslands. Its arching lance-shaped leaves and stems add a grace note to any pondside planting, and the flaming red flowers make a striking reflection on the water's sucrface. It grows 3 to 4 feet tall and tolerates partial shade. If you get tired of red, there are other cultivars with orange, yellow, or bicolored flowers. All need moderately rich, moist, and well-drained soil in full sun or partial shade. **Zones 5–8**; to **Zone 10** in the West.

ANGEL'S FISHING RODS
(*Dierama* species)

It's hard to imagine any flowers that would look more appropriate beside a pond than these 2 to 3 foot African natives, related to irises. Long, thin leaves are topped in summer by drooping wands of bell-shaped flowers, most often pink. Plant them in spring 2 to 3 inches below the soil surface. Zones vary with the species, either **Zones 7–9 or 8–10.**

SPIDER LILY
(*Hymenocallis* species)

White with six long petals, *H. caroliniana* is hardy. Its leaves grow about 18 inches tall and the flowers are up to 5 inches across. **Zones 6–9.**

The evergreen *H. liriosome* has 8-inch flowers that smell lemony. Plant in moist soil. **Zones 7–11.**

RECOMMENDED FERNS

MAIDENHAIR FERN
(*Adiantum* species)
These lacy ferns are tougher than they look as long as they have moist soil with good drainage. They grow naturally on cliffs along waterfalls, so they will look especially appropriate tucked into some soil pockets next to your pond. Both American maidenhair fern (*A. pedatum*; **Zones 3–8**) and southern maidenhair fern

(*A. capillus-veneris*; **Zones 8–10**) grow about 1 to 1½ feet tall and have black stalks. The former is deciduous and has triangular frond segments; the latter is evergreen, has fan-shaped frond segments, and needs consistently moist, alkaline soil.

LADY FERN
(*Athyrium filix-femina*)
Not demure in stature at 3 feet—even 5 feet in a marshy spot—this deciduous fern earns its common name with finely divided, light green triangular fronds, delicate enough for a lace curtain. It's easy to grow, too, provided it has some shade. It will survive drier soil conditions than many other ferns. **Zones 3–9.**

WOOD FERN
(*Dryopteris* species)
Members of this tough genus are common in eastern American woodlands. Crested wood fern (*D. cristata*) is the most moisture-loving; it grows 2 to 3 feet tall and has leathery blue-green fronds and leaflets that march up the stem horizontally. This species doesn't like heat, so give it cool shade. **Zones 4–8.**

Goldie's wood fern (*D. goldiana*) is an attention getter at 4 feet tall. Its deciduous pointed fronds are widest at the center and pointed at the tip. Its color is a light green verging on gold that glows in the shade that this fern needs. **Zones 4–8.**

OSTRICH FERN
(*Matteuccia struthiopteris*)
This is a giant of the fern world, at up to 5 feet tall, and is among those referred to as "shuttlecock" ferns because they have erect rhizomes topped by the plumage of the fronds. It has horizontal rhizomes, too, and spreads widely. Brown spore-bearing

fronds appear in late summer and last through the winter. Ostrich fern will tolerate some sun in northerly zones if it has consistently moist, well-drained, acidic soil. **Zones 2–8.**

SENSITIVE FERN
(*Onoclea sensibilis*)
The common name of this eastern native derives from its reaction to cold: it goes dormant at the first whisper of autumn. Its smooth broad leaflets are reddish in spring; the spore-bearing fronds appear in summer as a row of dark beads and often last through winter. Unlike most

ferns, it can grow in shallow, still water. If your soil is wet enough, sensitive fern can take a lot of sun. **Zones 3–9.**

Osmunda species
These deciduous native ferns will grow at least 3 feet tall and wide. Cinnamon fern (*O. cinnamomea*) has spore-producing fronds in spring. They fade away once the spores are shed, leaving green fronds up to 5 feet tall. **Zones 3–7.**

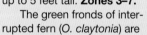
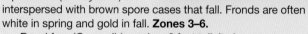
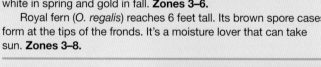

The green fronds of interrupted fern (*O. claytonia*) are interspersed with brown spore cases that fall. Fronds are often white in spring and gold in fall. **Zones 3–6.**

Royal fern (*O. regalis*) reaches 6 feet tall. Its brown spore cases form at the tips of the fronds. It's a moisture lover that can take sun. **Zones 3–8.**

CHRISTMAS FERN
(*Polystichum acrostichoides*)
Widespread in eastern forests, this fern forms a nest of dark-green 2-foot fronds that earn their common name by remaining green right through December. Each leaf segment has a little "boot" (think of Santa Claus) near where it branches from the

main stem. A cinch to grow, Christmas fern will spread rapidly in fertile, moist soil and even take some sun. **Zones 3–9.** Western sword fern (*P. munitum*) is the western equivalent. **Zones 5–9.**

MARSH FERN

(*Thelypteris palustris*)
On a sunny, never-dry patch of ground, marsh fern will spread 3 feet a year. The deciduous fronds are delicate and somewhat twisted, on black stems up to 2 feet or longer; they turn an appealing yellow in fall. **Zones 5–8.**

CHAIN FERN

(*Woodwardia* species)
These deciduous ferns creep assertively along the ground instead of forming clumps. The East is home to the 2-foot-tall netted chain fern (*W. areolata*; **Zones 4–8**) and slightly larger swamp-dwelling Virginia chain fern (*W. virginica*; **Zones 4–10**). Giant chain fern (*W. fimbriata*, also sold as *W. radicans*; **Zones 8–10**), which has fronds up to 7 feet long, forms large colonies in our western redwood forests. It needs constant moisture and protection from wind.

OTHER FERN CHOICES

- **Brittle Maidenhair Fern** (*Adiantum tenerum*)
  Evergreen fern; mid-green fronds; height to 2 feet; width to 3 feet. **Zones 9–10.**

- **Male Fern** (*Dryopteris filix-mas*)
  Deciduous fern; mid-green fronds; height 3 to 4 feet; width 3 feet. **Zones 4–8.**

- **Marginal Wood Fern** (*Dryopteris marginalis*)
  Evergreen fern; grayish-green fronds; height 2 feet; width 2 feet. **Zones 3–8.**

- **Licorice Fern** (*Polypodium glycyrrhiza*)
  Evergreen fern; mid- to dark-green fronds; height 1 foot; width 1 foot. **Zones 4–9.**

Grasses and Grasslike Plants. Grasses, like water, can add two powerful dimensions to your garden: movement and sound. All year, grasses sway in the breeze, helping you hear the wind if not see it and accompanying the music of your pond. In fall, when everything else is winding down, their iridescent flower heads catch the setting sun and provide food for migrating birds. Grasses make good hiding places for small animals, but also can create a barrier against predators such as raccoons and herons in search of fish. And the best news is that grasses need almost no care except for a crewcut back to the ground in spring and division every three years or so.

To make the mounds that you've created for waterfalls look more natural, plant them with broad sweeps of smaller grasses; include more broad sweeps around your pond. Taller grasses work best as one-clump specimens and make a good counterpoint to broad-leaved plants such as lotuses.

Although most grasses need well-drained soil, some grasslike plants grow well in standing water. You'll find the following species described in the section on marginal plants: spike rush (*Eleocharis montevidensis*, page 224), cotton grass (*Eriophorum* species, page 225), and cattail (*Typha* species, page 227). Soft rush (*Juncus effusus*), bulrush (*Schoenoplectus* species), and woolgrass bulrush (*Scirpus cyperinus*) can grow in water up to 6 inches deep, but they also grow well in moist soil, so they're included here.

Grasses and ferns add color and texture to your pond but require very little maintenance.

RECOMMENDED GRASSES

GIANT REED

(*Arundo donax*)
This hulking, bamboolike, eastern European plant, the reeds of which are used in reed instruments, is a noxious weed in California and other warm states. You might want to take a chance on it in colder areas, though. It will form pondside clumps 15 feet high and 5 feet wide of broad, cornlike leaves up to 2 feet long. The fluffy light green or purple flower heads can also be up to 2 feet long, but giant reed won't flower or set seed in the northern part of its range. 'Variegata' is a striped form. Giant reed will grow anywhere in wet soil; you may elect to slow it down by letting it go a bit dry. **Zones 6–10.**

COMMON QUAKING GRASS

(*Briza media*)
A knee-high grass with blue-green blades, quaking grass doubles in height when its flower stalks appear in spring. The tiny seedpods are slightly heart-shaped and remind some people of rattlesnake tails, others of puffed oats. This plant's charm lies in the way it nods, bobs, and shivers in a slight breeze. Native to wet meadows of the Mediterranean region, it tolerates a wide range of soil moisture, texture, and pH. **Zones 4–10.**

FEATHER REED GRASS

(*Calamagrostis* x *acutiflora*)
The 1-foot flower heads of this upright, graceful grass emerge narrow and bronzy purple, becoming more open and airy as they fade to tan. They bring the height of the clump to 6 feet. A popular selection is sold as 'Stricta' or 'Karl Foerster'. **Zones 4–9.**
Smaller 'Overdam', which has longitudinal creamy stripes, doesn't like heat. **Zones 5–8.**
A native wetland relative, Canada bluejoint (*C. canadensis*), is often burgundy in autumn; it tends to spread by rhizomes rather than clumping as feather reed grass does. You won't find this native for sale in ordinary garden catalogs; you'll need to seek out a nursery that specializes in prairie plants. **Zones 3–7.**
All like moist, well-drained soil, but feather reed grass shows its ability to please by tolerating less desirable conditions found in clay soil.

SEDGE

(*Carex* species)
There are some 1,000 species of sedges; as a general rule, if a grasslike plant reminds you of a mop head or the hairdo of the early Beatles, it's a sedge. Most sedges form tussocks rather than being strongly vertical like grasses. Since nearly all grow in damp places, there are many choices for pondside. Two cultivars of *C. elata* will brighten a shady area or cast a glowing reflection: 'Bowles Golden' has bright yellow leaves narrowly edged in green; 'Aurea' has yellow margins. About 2 feet tall and wide, both will grow in 2 to 3 inches of water. They like high humidity and a half day of sun. **Zones 5–9.**

Another multicolored selection of similar size is silver-variegated Japanese sedge (*C. morrowii* 'Variegata'). The white-margined blades are stiff, making it appropriate for a more formal pool. Its soil should be moist, not wet, but like 'Aurea' it sulks with exposure to hot drying winds and too much sun. **Zones 5–9.**

PALM BRANCH SEDGE

(*C. muskingumensis*)
From the north-central states, it gets its common name from the palmlike way its leaves radiate from the 2-foot stems. Somewhat floppy, it can look appealing over the edge of a pot or a pond. If it has shade, it can tolerate drier soil. **Zones 3–8.**

DROOPING SEDGE

C. pendula is unusual among sedges in that it is grown for its flowers. The leaves form a grassy fountain up to 5 feet tall, and then in midsummer the flower stems jut out another 2 feet, arching almost horizontally and seeming to drip with dark brown, catkinlike flowers up to 7 inches long. Give it light shade unless you can provide steady moisture. It may self-sow. Hard-to-find *C. crinita* is similar but tolerates drier soil in partial shade. **Zones 5–9.**

TUFTED HAIR GRASS

(*Deschampsia caespitosa*)
On stems that arch 2 to 3 feet out of the foliage, flowers glisten and catch early spring light, opening green and then changing to gold, bronze, or purple. A few cultivars offer flowers with different colors. Hair grass will survive wet, heavy soil. Buy plants locally. Northern plants don't like southern heat. **Zones 4–9.**

MANNA GRASS

(*Glyceria* species)
The most widely available manna grass is *G. maxima var. variegata*, the 2 to 3 foot blades of which emerge pinkish in spring and then turn cream-colored with green stripes. It will spread eagerly along your stream bank and take on a pink tinge again before disappearing in fall.
Zones 5–9.

RUSH

(*Juncus* species)
Rushes, like sedges, are generally residents of wet places, so they look and feel right at home next to a pond. They differ in having round stems with six-petaled, sometimes inconspicuous flowers at the end of the stems. Common or soft rush (*J. effusus*) grows 18 to 30 inches tall and bears round flower clusters that complement its vertical lines.

SWITCHGRASS

(*Panicum virgatum*)
Switchgrass sends up stems to 7 feet tall with 18 to 24 inch leaves. Flowers have a reddish cast that turn pale brown and continue to provide airy grace most of the winter. Leaves turn yellow in fall. The cultivar 'Haense Herms' is reddish-orange in fall; 'Heavy Metal' is straight and has blue-green leaves that turn yellow. Switchgrass will put up with almost any abuse. **Zones 5–9.**

BULRUSH

(*Schoenoplectus* species, still generally known by the earlier name *Scirpus*). If bulrushes make you recall the biblical story of Baby Moses, remember that he got big and went afar: these plants need to be restrained. *S. lacustris ssp. tabernaemontani* grows 4 to 9 feet tall and has brown terminal spikes; it will thrive in up to a foot of water. There are two popular, smaller cultivars: 'Albescens' is white with vertical green stripes; 'Zebrinus', also sold as zebra rush or zebra bulrush, has striking horizontal cream-colored bands. Both grow 3 to 6 feet tall. **Zones 5–9.**

PRAIRIE CORDGRASS

(*Spartina pectinata*)
Another constituent of our tallgrass prairies, cordgrass grows to 6 feet in moist situations, less in drier ones. The leaves, which arch gracefully, turn gold in fall. The cultivar 'Aureomarginata' has the thinnest of gold margins on its summer foliage. Cordgrass tolerates brackish water, wind, and both heavy and sandy soils. But it doesn't do well in dry conditions and spreads too eagerly in moist ones, so confine it in a wet garden. **Zones 4–9. Zones 3–9.**

OTHER GRASS CHOICES

- **Flowering Rush** (*Butomus umbellatus*)
  Long dark-green leaves; likes water no deeper than 3-5 inches. **Zones 3–11.**

- **Star Grass** (*Dichromena colorata*, also sold as *Rhynchospora colorata*)
  An evergreen sedge; arresting star-shaped flowers at the stem tips; 1 to 1½ feet tall. **Zones 9–10.**

- **Jointed Rush** (*Juncus articulatus*)
  Jointed, deep-green leaves; clusters of dark-brown flowers; height to 2½ feet; width 2 feet. **Zones 5–8.**

- **Hard Rush** (*Juncus inflexus* 'Afro')
  Spiraled blue-green stems; brown flowers; height to 2 feet; width to 2 feet. **Zones 4–8**

Shrubs

Shrubs will give shape and texture to your garden throughout the seasons, even after perennial plants have died to the ground and your pond is skinned with ice. Although you may decide to keep trees well away from your pond—to give water lilies plenty of sun or to avoid having leaves and twigs fall into the water—consider planting some shrubs nearby to define a path, to create a nice backdrop, or to serve as a wind barrier. If you want wildlife to visit your pond, plant shrubs where birds can perch, build nests, and steal berries. Many of the species listed bear showy flowers, and most offer interest when out of bloom—fragrant summer leaves, colorful fall foliage, interesting seedpods or berries, or eye-catching bark.

Most of the shrubs in this section prefer moist soil. To encourage them to thrive, dig plenty of compost or other organic matter into the entire planting area. After you plant them, spread at least an inch of compost or leaf mold over the soil. Keep the soil mulched throughout the year so it won't dry out. (You'll still need to water them during dry spells.)

'Blue Pacific' juniper has dense foloiage that provides a blue-green carpet near this pond year-round.

RECOMMENDED SHRUBS

BOG ROSEMARY
(*Andromeda polifolia*)
Here's a little evergreen shrub for northern pond gardens. Native to sphagnum bogs in Canada and the northern United States as well as in Europe and Asia, this slow grower bears bell-shaped, pale pink flowers in late spring. The long, stiff, leathery leaves (like those of rosemary) are dark green

and curve downward. Give it partial shade, work lots of peat moss into the soil, and make sure its soil stays cool and damp; moisture is especially crucial in spring. Only 1 to 2 feet tall, it's a spreading plant that works well between rocks used to create a waterfall or edging. **Zones 2–6.**

SWEETSHRUB
(*Calycanthus floridus*)
The main reason people grow this shrub (which also goes by the name of sweet bubby) is for the scent of its red-brown flowers: fruity fading to spicy. Two inches across, the pinwheel-shaped flowers appear first in May and then on and off through fall. Urn-shaped seed cap-

sules follow the flowers. Stems are fragrant when crushed; the bark was once used as a cinnamon substitute. It grows 6 to 8 feet tall and up to 12 feet wide. Native from southern Pennsylvania to Florida, it prefers acidic soil, but is adaptable. **Zones 4–9.** For western gardeners, there's California allspice (*C. occidentalis*). **Zones 6–9.**

BUTTONBUSH
(*Cephalanthus occidentalis*)
This is not a shrub that will adapt to dry soils, but it's worth looking for if you have a naturalistic swampy area. From Canada to Florida, through the Upper Midwest and into New Mexico and California, its natural home is wetland edges and shallow water. Unusual creamy-white, 1 inch flowers look more like prickly little golf balls than buttons; they ap-

pear in midsummer and last for several weeks. Pruning it to the ground every two to three years keeps it shapely and flowering heavily. The glossy leaves are slow to emerge in spring, so be patient. **Zones 5–11.**

SUMMERSWEET, SWEET PEPPERBUSH
(Clethra alnifolia)

Walking in a woodland in midsummer, you may detect summersweet's dreamy scent before you see the bush. The flowers are white to pink bottlebrushes 2 to 6 inches long. Growing 3 to 8 feet tall, summersweet spreads by suckers and makes a good hedge or windbreak. The leaves turn yellow in fall, leaving spikes of round seed capsules. This shrub will tolerate salt spray and dry soil, but needs acidity and some shade. There are several cultivars chosen for smaller size, such as 'Hummingbird', or for pinker flowers, such as 'Rosea'. **Zones 4–9.**

DOGWOOD
(Cornus species)

Most people are familiar with the native flowering dogwood tree that produces white bracts each spring. Its smaller cousins work well for a naturalistic pond planting. The most eye-catching of these may be redtwig dogwood (*C. stolonifera*). Most people buy it for its blood-red stems, arranged in a V, which brighten the garden in winter. Averaging 7 to 9 feet in height and spreading even wider, it produces late-spring clusters of whitish flowers. You can heighten the stem color by cutting off old branches that are fading to brown. This species is somewhat adaptable but does not like drought or heat. **Zones 2–7.**

Another dogwood for naturalizing is Tartarian dogwood (*C. alba*), which also has red twigs and offers variegated cultivars for more formal plantings. **Zones 3–7.**

Silky dogwood (*C. amomum*) grows 8 to 10 feet tall, tolerates poor drainage, and helps prevent erosion on banks. In nature, dogwoods grow under taller trees, so they can take some shade. **Zones 4–8.**

TITI, LEATHERWOOD
(Cyrilla racemiflora)

Gardeners and landscapers, especially those who admire native plants, seem to have discovered titi (pronounced TY-ty) in a big way. Its merits include 3 to 6 inch dangling tails of flowers that appear in groups in midsummer, lustrous leaves that turn flaming red and orange, and twisted stems for the winter garden. Growing 10 to 15 feet tall, it spreads equally wide and puts out suckers, so it needs lots of room and full sun. It will tolerate poor drainage—but not drought—and is evergreen south of **Zone 7. Zones 6–11.**

FOTHERGILLA
(Fothergilla species)

A relative of the witch hazel, it has similarly veined leaves. Dwarf fothergilla or witch alder (*F. gardenii*) grows 2 to 3 feet tall. Large fothergilla (*F. major*), as its common and botanical names hint, is 6 to 10 feet tall and bears larger flowers; it may also be a little more cold tolerant. Both require acid soil that is moist but fast draining and can prosper in sun or shade. **Zones 5–8.**

WINTERBERRY
(Ilex verticillata)

This deciduous holly is a must if you like both winter color and birds. Low-key all summer, it houts for attention in late summer or early fall when its berries turn icrimson. It likes slightly acid soil but tolerates dry or damp soil, sun or shade. Ask your nursery for both male and female plants in order to get berries. The usual height is 6 to 10 feet. There are hybrids and cultivars that grow faster and larger; 'Sparkleberry' (female) and 'Apollo' (male) are a top-rated pair. **Zones 4–9.**

ANISE TREE
(Illicium species)

Among Southern gardeners, the anise tree is hot—no pun intended. Native to Florida, Louisiana, and Georgia, it will flourish in moist shade farther north. The Florida or purple anise tree (*I. floridanum*) has pungent foliage and maroon, starburst flowers in spring. It needs damp to wet conditions and shade. The small anise tree (*I. parviflorum*) gets just as big—8 to 10 feet—but is more amenable to both sun and dry conditions. **Zones 6–9.**

SWEETSPIRE
(Itea virginica)

Here's a small shrub to choose for a site in deep shade, or for spectacular fall color. Native from New Jersey to Florida and west to Missouri, it grows 3 to 5 feet tall and bears fragrant white flowers, 2½ to 6 inches long in May or June. Sweetspire makes a great low hedge or edging. It prefers moist fertile soil but is fairly adaptable. 'Henry's Garnet', is a popular cultivar. **Zones 5–9.**

(continued on next page)

RECOMMENDED SHRUBS

(continued from previous page)

SPICEBUSH

(Lindera benzoin)
Most people love spice-bush for the clovelike scent the leaves give off when crushed. In the spring, fragrant little yellow-green flowers light up the woods for three to four weeks before the leaves appear. In fall, it often has yellow leaves and, if you have both male and female shrubs, bright red berries that birds appreciate. (Folks have used the berries as a substitute for allspice, and the stems and leaves to make tea.) It tolerates dry soil and deep shade, but performs better with some sun and moisture. Spicebush grows 6 to 12 feet tall and spreads up to 15 feet wide. **Zones 4–9.**

SWEET GALE

(Myrica gale)
This is a moisture-loving relative of the bayberry, and its deciduous leaves share the scent that many people associate with bayberry candles. Leaves are dense, glossy, and dark green; the lower limbs can be removed to show off the plant's almost white bark. Sweet gale bears yellow fruits that dangle in catkins. Growing 5 feet tall or less, it's a good choice for small gardens. It grows naturally at the edge of woods with sandy, acid soil, so it can take sun or part shade. **Zones 2–7.**

SWAMP REDBAY

(Persea palustris)
You might want to try this 6- to 18-foot, broad-leaved evergreen if you have a water garden near the coast, since it's a salt-tolerant native of the Atlantic seaboard. A hardy relative of the avocado, redbay grows naturally in swamps but adapts to drier, sandy soils. Aromatic leaves have a rusty brown fuzz on the underside. The plants develop blue-black, powdery-looking berries. This species is not available from standard nurseries; you'll have to track it down from regional plant specialists. **Zones 7–9.**

AZALEA

(Rhododendron species)
There are several native azaleas that like damp conditions. All need acid soil and protection from intense sun (but well-drained). Most are deciduous but make graceful and often fragrant additions to a garden, contributing flowers in spring or early summer. Sweet azalea (*R. arborescens*) produces white flowers (sometimes with a hint of deep pink) with a powerful heliotrope scent in late May or June. It can get 20 feet tall and will adapt to relatively dry soil. **Zones 4–7.**

Coast azalea (*R. atlanticum*) is only 2 feet tall and bears sweetly fragrant blossoms in midspring. **Zones 5–8.**

Rosebay rhododendron (*R. maximum*), an evergreen, is the state flower of West Virginia. It tolerates deep shade and earns its botanical name by growing 30 feet tall where it is protected from winds in the southern part of its range. Its late-spring to early-winter flowers are white with a pink blush. **Zones 4–7.**

Swamp azalea (*R. viscosum*) unfolds spicy-sweet white to pink flowers in late June. It averages 5 feet tall and wide. **Zones 4–9.**

WILLOW

(Salix species)
Most people find the sight of a weeping willow near a pond an irresistible combination. But weeping willow roots will make a beeline for a water source and can tear through a pond liner, plus willow trees also get too large for most gardens and then tend to drop litter and large branches. Here are a few small species to try with caution; install a root barrier between pond and willow to teach the plant its place. All of them like sun.

Most of us know pussy willow (*S. discolor*)—either in the garden or in flower arrangements—as a first sign of spring. It isn't beautiful, but it may be worth tucking away in an unobtrusive corner. It reaches 12 to 15 feet in height. **Zones 4–8.**

S. caprea is another species sold as pussy willow; it's a bit larger. **Zones 6–8.** A showier little shrub that likes moist soil is rosegold pussy willow (*S. gracilistyla*), which gets big, pinkish catkins in spring. It likes full sun, will tolerate clay soil, and grows 3 to 9 feet tall. **Zones 5–8.**

Black catkin willow (*S. gracilistyla var.*) has purple stems in winter and black catkins with touches of red and yellow. It will grow in any soil and may be useful in controlling erosion. This species grows 10 feet tall. **Zones 5–7.**

ELDERBERRY
(Sambucus canadensis)

You may want this eastern native near your pond if your interests include edibles, herbs, or birds. The flat white flower heads are used for fritters and herbal medicine and the fruits for jams, jellies, and wine. Butterflies are drawn to the flowers and birds to the purple-black fruits, which can sometimes bow the bush toward the ground. Severe pruning will help keep it in shape. Elderberry tolerates a wide range of soils and likes sun. **Zones 4–9.**

SNOWBELL
(Styrax americanum)

This 6 to 8 foot shrub will grow with its roots in water; they at least need to be both cool and moist. If you can give it those conditions, it will reward you in late spring with lightly scented white flowers, the petals of which are bent back (reflexed) like those of a tiger lily. Japanese snowbell (S. japonicum) is three times as big, but there are cultivars of this species that are the same size as the American snowbell; some of these are variegated. All snowbells appreciate some shade and moist soil. **Zones 5–9.**

VIBURNUM
(Viburnum species)

Once you get hooked on viburnums, you may want them everywhere in your garden for their flowers, fruits, fall color, or all three. There are many wonderful cultivars for ordinary soil. Those called double-files—for the way their white flowers march down the branches—are particularly beautiful. Wide-spreading 'Shasta' (6 feet tall by 11 feet wide) or 'Shoshoni' (which gets only half as big) would look beautiful reflected in a pond.

There are also several underused native species that are adapted to moist soils. Denizens of woodland edges, they will grow in shade but need some sun to flower well. Most of these species bear flat to rounded clusters of white flowers, followed by berries that are either dramatically colored or attractive to birds.

Hobblebush (V. lantanoides, formerly V. alnifolium), which grows 6 to 9 feet high, has veined and toothed leaves and white hydrangea-like flowers. Late in the season red fruits turn black against deep red leaves. **Zones 4–7.**

The 6-foot withe-rod (V. cassinoides) is the most moisture loving of the group. Its fruits start out hot pink and turn red, blue, and then black. Some clusters can have all these colors at the same time. Fall foliage is orange-red or purple. **Zones 4–8.**

Arrowwood (V. dentatum), a 10- to 12-footer, has toothed leaves that turn bright red in fall where it gets moderate sun. **Zones 3–8.**

American cranberry bush (V. trilobum) gets its common name from its edible, translucent orange-red berries. Leaves, shaped like a maple's, turn scarlet to purple-red in autumn. It grows 8 to 12 feet tall. **Zones 2–7.**

The similar European cranberry bush, V. opulus, is easier to find but somewhat susceptible to pests and diseases. Tough southern black haw (V. rufidulum) isn't quite as good looking as some of the others but will tolerate a slew of conditions, including heat, clay soil, and sun or shade. It bears 4-inch clusters of white flowers in May or June and then dark blue fruits. The leathery leaves on this 10- to 12-foot shrub turn burgundy in fall. **Zones 5–9.**

OTHER SHRUB CHOICES

- **Beautyberry** (Callicarpa americana)
  Deciduous native to 8 feet with small pink flowers followed by bright magenta berries. Tolerates some shade. **Zones 5–9.**

- **Winterhazel** (Corylopsis species)
  These deciduous species range from 6 to 12 feet tall and bear fragrant yellow flowers in early spring. **Zones 6–8.**

- **Ornamental Cherry** (Prunus species)
  Pink spring flowers, a tree associated with Japanese gardens. Look for small cultivars. **Zones 5–7.**

- **Snowbell** (Styrax species)
  Japanese silverbell (S. japonicum) grows to 30 feet. American species (S. americanum) to 10. Both have bell-shaped white flowers. **Zones 5–8.**

- **Bald Cypress** (Taxodium distichum)
  Deciduous native conifer that develops "knees" in standing water. Grows slowly to 70 feet. **Zones 4–11.**

- **Eastern Arborvitae** (Thuja occidentalis)
  Flat, scalelike evergreen leaves are fragrant. Grows slowly to 30 feet. Useful for windbreak or formal pool. **Zones 3–7.**

Trees

Unless you have a big, open landscape, your water-garden shopping list probably won't include a lot of trees. Of course, if you want water lilies and other sun-loving plants, you want to avoid creating too much shade over your pond. Trees can also drop leaves, twigs, and fruits that will add to cleaning chores, and their roots can damage pond liners. But there are many lovely small trees that reflect beautifully in ponds and can fit into almost any yard, and many wetland natives to consider for shading a bench or an adjacent patio, creating a windbreak, or attracting wildlife.

If you have room, you can plant several trees to create an inviting grove near the pond, or an allée (double row) to line a path toward the pond. For a formal pool, a single dramatic specimen can be perfect. The smallest trees can even be grown in large containers and moved to give the pond a bit of shade as the sun moves through the seasons. When you buy a tree, leave it in its container or burlap for a day or two and try it in several different locations to find the most effective one.

As mentioned in Chapter 2, you should consider the mature height and spread before choosing or planting a tree. Remember that the roots on trees don't go straight down like a carrot; they spread along the surface, generally to the width of the canopy (top branches). You want to plant the tree far enough from the pond that the roots won't tear through the liner, and so the canopy won't hang over and drop leaves, twigs, and other debris.

The deep red leaves of a Japanese maple tree provide visual contrast to the evergreens that surround this landscape.

RECOMMENDED TREES

JAPANESE MAPLE
(*Acer palmatum*)

A Japanese-style garden isn't complete without one of these exquisite small trees. The biggest problem with them is choosing one. You can have leaves that are almost threadlike, variegated foliage, leaves that are burgundy in spring and fall, and types that grow upright to 25 feet or others that stay small and weep almost to the ground. Many will suffer in hot sun, so some high shade is helpful. Height varies with the cultivar, but these trees generally spread equal to or greater than their height. **Zones 5–8,** depending on the cultivar.

RED MAPLE
(*Acer rubrum*)

This maple grows naturally in low, wet areas. Red maples vary a lot in heat tolerance and fall color, but they can provide some of the earliest and most intense autumn color for reflections in your pond. Fall color is generally not as good in the Southeast. Try to buy a tree grown in your area and plant it when dormant. There are many cultivars chosen for greater tolerance to cold or wind, or richer fall color. Two of the most widely available are 'October Glory' and 'Red Sunset'. Usually 40 to 60 feet tall and 50 feet wide, these are not for small landscapes. **Zones 3–9.**

SHADBUSH, SERVICEBERRY
(*Amelanchier* species)

The delicate white flowers of shadbush appear on the edges of woods in spring before dogwoods bloom. Several native species and hybrids offer subtle differences in growth habit or fall color, which can range from burgundy to orange or yellow. Flowers are followed by tiny, sweet, blue-black berries. As with other plants in the rose family, its leaves can be magnets for Japanese beetles. 'Autumn Brilliance', 'Ballerina', and 'Princess Diana' are cultivars of downy serviceberry (*A. arborea*) that get high marks. Most serviceberries grow with multiple trunks, about 25 feet tall, but some can be singletrunked and taller; the spread is roughly half the height. **Zones 4–9** (a few other species are even hardier).

PAWPAW
(*Asimina triloba*)

All of our native pawpaw's close relatives are semitropical fruit trees, and the pawpaw's foot-long leaves make it look tropical as well. Its spring flowers are dark red bells, not flashy but fascinating. You need more than one tree to get the custardy fruits. These trees grow naturally in deep shade, but need sun for better fruiting. With ample moisture they have bright yellow leaves in fall. Buy container-grown plants for more successful transplanting. Pawpaws rarely get more than 20 feet high and wide. **Zones 5–8.**

RIVER BIRCH
(*Betula nigra*)

Birches are usually grown for their striking bark and their frequently multitrunked form. These are some of the most effective trees for clustering in groves or planting in rows for an allée toward your pond. The popular cultivar 'Heritage' has good disease resistance and showy peeling bark. In autumn, river birches have yellow leaves and in spring, little catkins. They'll take either wet or dry soil, as long as it isn't alkaline, and adapt to heavy clay soil. They grow quickly, up to 70 feet high and spreading to 50 feet; some new compact forms grow more slowly. **Zones 4–10.**

REDBUD
(*Cercis canadensis*)

Native to woodland edges, the redbud has early-spring magenta flowers that will glow in a pond reflection. It's not a wetland plant, but it will thrive in well-drained soil of any type. It rarely grows more than 25 feet tall and wide. **Zones 4–9.**

ATLANTIC WHITE CEDAR
(*Chamaecyparis thyoides*)

This eastern native is a water lover. Atlantic white cedar grows slowly to about 45 feet high and 15 feet wide. Give it moist, sandy soil and full sun. **Zones 4–8.**

Two West Coast natives like moist well-drained soil: Lawson false cypress, also known as Port Orford cedar (*C. lawsoniana*), and Nootka false cypress (*C. nootkatensis*). These reach about 30 to 50 feet in cultivation and about a third as wide. Nootka needs moist air to thrive and has a weeping cultivar, 'Pendula'. **Zones 4–8**, but Lawson false cypress is subject to winter burn (browning caused by winter winds or sun) in Zones 4-5 and doesn't like areas of **Zone 8** with hot summers.

DOGWOOD
(*Cornus* species)

There are many native dog-woods worth growing, but undoubtedly the best known is the eastern flowering dog-wood (*C. florida*). Its horizontal branching pattern and up-turned white flowers (actually bracts) make it an inspiring sight in spring. It offers won-derful reflections in fall as well, with red foliage and berries that birds love and can reach 30 feet high and wide. **Zones 5–9.**

Pagoda dogwood (*C. alternifolia*) has horizontal branches in a pagoda-like form and grows 15 to 25 feet tall; it produces flat-topped clusters of small white flowers and blue-black fruits. **Zones 3–7.**

GINKGO, MAIDENHAIR TREE
(*Ginkgo biloba*)

This ancient Asian tree offers some of the most striking yellow fall foliage imaginable, made even more stunning by the leaves' unusual fan shape. It prefers sandy yet slightly moist soil, but is adaptable. Ask for a male tree, as females drop copious bad-smelling fruits. The mature height can be 50 feet or more and the spread half as much; if space is at all limited, look for 'Princeton Sentry', which grows upright rather than spreading. **Zones 4–8.**

SILVERBELL
(*Halesia* species)

These are among the best trees for a patio or a container because they really stay small and tolerate either sun or shade. One catalog aptly describes the hanging white bell flowers as "magical." Little silverbell (*H. parviflora*) is prob-ably the smallest, tending to form a shrub (with several main stems) less than 12 feet tall. **Zones 6–9.**

The easiest to find is most likely Carolina silverbell (*H. tetraptera*), which can get relatively large at 30 feet or more high and wide. Becoming more popular is the award-winning American snowdrop tree (*H. diptera var. magniflora*), which generally stays under 30 feet high and wide. **Zones 4–8.**

WITCH HAZEL
(*Hamamelis* species and cultivars)

Every landscape with ample room should have at least one witch hazel for the de-lightful surprise the spidery fragrant flowers bring when everything else seems dead or dying. The witch hazel's natural habitat is high up on riverbanks; give it moist but well-drained soil. Most of these trees grow only 15 to 20 feet tall but will spread almost as wide. Birds enjoy the exploding seeds. Vernal witch hazel (*H. vernalis*), a native with yellow, red, or orange flowers, is probably the smallest, averaging 6 to 10 feet. **Zones 4–8.**

Common witch hazel (*H. virginiana*), the largest at up to 30 feet tall and more than 20 feet wide, bears yellow flowers in mid- to late fall. **Zones 4–8.**

Cultivars developed from Asian species (*H. x intermedia*) can have reddish ('Diane'), copper ('Jelena'), or paler yellow ('Pallida') flowers in late winter. **Zones 5–8.**

SWEET BAY, SWAMP MAGNOLIA
(*Magnolia virginiana*)

Native to wetlands from New England to Florida, sweet bay is more demure than the more familiar southern mag-nolia, rarely growing as tall as 30 feet. It spreads 10 to 20 feet wide. Plant it near a resting spot where you can enjoy the delicate lemon scent of its 3-inch creamy flowers. The leaves, spicily fragrant when crushed, have silver under-sides that flash in a breeze. Sweet bay will shed its leaves north of **Zone 8** (a natural variety, *M. virginiana var. australis*, is evergreen farther north). It wants moist, acid soil and some shade. Several cultivars are available.

TUPELO, BLACK GUM
(*Nyssa sylvatica*)

You won't beat this Ontario-to-Florida native for brilliant red fall color, intensified by glossy leaves. When young, it has a handsome pyramidal shape, but may become ir-regular later, reaching 30 feet or more high, and almost as wide. Clusters of navy-bean-size, dark blue fruits are a hit with birds, and bees like the tiny early flowers. Salt resis-tance makes it good for seaside plantings, and it will tolerate wet or dry acid soil. **Zones 4–9.**

Glossary

Aeration. The infusion of oxygen into water, usually through a fountain, waterfall, or bubbling device.

Algal bloom. Sudden rapid growth of microscopic, free-floating algae, usually as weather warms in spring. The situation usually corrects itself in a well-balanced pond.

Algicide. A chemical treatment that controls algae growth. This should be used only after natural and mechanical controls have failed.

Allée. A double row of trees, intended to create a path.

Ammonia. A compound of hydrogen and nitrogen. Sometimes found in municipal water supplies, its presence in pond water is usually due to fish waste. High levels of ammonia are stressful and even fatal to fish but can be controlled with biological filters.

Anthers. The part of a plant's stamen, or male reproductive organ, that produces pollen. Anthers in water lilies are sometimes showy by virtue of being a different color than the stamen.

Backfill. Earth, sand, or gravel used to fill the excavated space under a pond shell or liner.

Bell fountain. A spray fountain that falls in a semispherical pattern.

Bentonite. Powdered clay made from volcanic ash, used to make dirt-bottomed ponds more watertight. You can also buy sheets of bentonite sandwiched between landscape fabric.

Berm. A mound of earth used in landscaping designs to help control the flow of water or improve drainage for plants.

Biological filter. A device that converts organic pollutants (primarily ammonia from fish wastes) into relatively harmless substances by utilizing large concentrations of beneficial bacteria.

Bog. A wetland in which soil is highly acidic and low in oxygen and nutrients.

Bubbler. A geyser-type fountain, usually less than a foot high, used in small water features or to mimic a spring in a natural-style pond.

Butyl. A type of rubber sometimes used as a pond liner.

Canopy. The overhanging branches of a tree that create shade around its trunk.

Carnivorous. Said of plants that obtain nutrition by trapping insects and other tiny creatures. Most are bog dwellers.

Cascade. The vertical part of a waterfall or stream, at which point the water drops to the next level.

Catch basin. The horizontal part of a waterfall or stream, where the water current slows briefly before reaching the next cascade.

Chicken wire. Flexible wire mesh used to reinforce thin concrete structures.

Chloramine. A mix of chlorine and ammonia, frequently added to public water supplies. It is toxic to fish and requires removal with chemicals.

Chlorine. A common additive to public water supplies. It is harmful to fish but dissipates after water has stood for 24 to 48 hours.

Coping. The individual stones, bricks, or other units that constitute the finished edging of a pond or pool.

Crown. In a piece of lumber, the edge that has a slightly convex curve. In a plant, the point at which plant stems meet the roots.

Daphnia. Water fleas, often used as high-protein fish food. They also help control algae.

Diverter valve. A device that allows outflow from a pump to be switched on or off, so that one pump can operate more than one water feature.

Ecological balance. In a pond, the situation attained when an ideal ratio of plants, animals, and water serve to prevent an excess of harmful chemicals. Oxygen levels are high, and both flora and fauna are healthy.

Ethylene propylene diene monomer (EPDM). A synthetic rubber. Flexible sheets of EPDM of varying thicknesses are formulated for lining ponds and waterfalls.

Fall. In an iris, one of the petals or petal-like structures that droop, or are held horizontally.

Float valve. A device that triggers automatic topping off of a pond when the water falls below a certain level.

Flow control valve. A device that allows control of the amount of water flowing through a pump to be turned up or down so that the height of a fountain or current of a stream or waterfall can be adjusted.

Footing. A poured concrete foundation for a heavy, more upright structure like a wall, statue, or stepping-stone.

Frost line. The maximum depth to which soil freezes in winter.

Fry. Newly hatched fish. Fry are vulnerable to predators, including the parent fish.

Geyser. A type of spray fountain having just a single jet of water.

Grotto. An artificial recess or structure made to resemble a natural cave, sometimes including water spouts, sculpture, and inlaid crystals.

Ground-fault circuit interrupter (GFCI). A safety circuit breaker that compares the amount of current entering a receptacle with the amount leaving it. If there is a discrepancy, the GFCI breaks the circuit and stops the current. The device is required by the National Electrical Code in areas that are subject to dampness.

Hard water. Water containing an excess of minerals. While not harmful in itself, it is usually associated with alkalinity in water and suggests the need to check pH.

Hardscape. The portion of a landscape that is made of non-living material, such as cement, stones, or lumber.

Head. Also sometimes called "lift." The vertical distance between a pump and water outlet, used to determine pump performance. Pumps are sized by how many gallons per hour they can deliver at different heads.

Jet. The outlet of a spray fountain.

Kakehi. A bamboo pipe used as a simple fountain in Japanese gardens.

Liner. A plastic or rubber sheet used to create a watertight foundation for a pond or pool.

Marginal plants. Those plants that grow along the edge of a pond or stream, with their roots under shallow water for at least part of the growing season.

Mechanical filter. A device for removing large particles of suspended matter from a pond.

Microclimate. A portion of a landscape with different growing conditions caused by variance in the amount of sunlight received, wind currents, topography, and other factors.

Milt. Sperm of a male fish.

Nitrate. A nitrogen compound that results in a pond from the breakdown of ammonia or nitrites. Nitrates are harmless and serve as nutrients for plants, although an excess may encourage algae.

Nitrite. A nitrogen compound that results in a pond from the chemical breakdown of ammonia. If not further broken down into nitrates, nitrites will be toxic to fish.

Ozone generator. A device that breaks down pollutants into gases that escape the pond. It also promotes clumping of other particles so they are more easily removed by filters.

Oxygenators. Submerged plants used in ponds primarily to aerate the water.

Parterre. A level area of low-growing ornamental plants and/or formal pools, usually enclosed with dwarf or closely cropped hedges.

pH (potential hydrogen). A measure of } alkalinity/acidity of soil or water in a range from 1 to 14, where 7 is neutral, above 7 is alkaline, and below 7 is acidic.

Photosynthesis. A process by which plants use sunlight, carbon dioxide, water, and their own chlorophyll to produce carbohydrates, which are needed in order for growth.

Plastic cement. A dry cement mixture with a powdered latex additive to make it more waterproof and resistant to cracking.

Polyvinyl chloride (PVC). A plastic formulation. Flexible sheets of PVC are used for inexpensive pond liners. Rigid PVC is used for water supply lines to ponds, streams, and waterfalls.

Pool sweep. A device used to clean algae and debris from ponds by suction created when attached to a garden hose.

Preformed shell. A rigid structure made of molded plastic or fiberglass and used as a pond foundation.

Rhizome. A specialized underground stem, usually horizontal, that acts as a storage organ and produces vertical stems at its ends and along its length. Water lilies grow from rhizomes.

Runoff. Surface water moving downhill after rain or irrigation. Runoff can wash dirt, organic matter, and pollutants into a pond.

Sinus. The area between the lobes of a water lily leaf, often used to distinguish one variety from that of another.

Skimmer. A type of mechanical filter that removes debris from the surface of a pond before it can fall to the bottom and begin to decay.

Spawn. The mating process of fish; also used to refer to their eggs.

Spray fountain. A fountain in which water spouts up from a jet or nozzle.

Stamen. A plant's male reproductive organ, which includes the pollen-producing anther. The size or color of the stamens often makes plants more showy.

Stand-alone fountain. A fountain that has its own reservoir and does not require a pond. (Also called a "self-contained" fountain.)

Statuary fountain. A fountain in which water issues from a sculpture such as a stone fish.

Subsoil. The layers of soil under topsoil, usually of poorer structure and texture than the topsoil.

Sump hole. A small depression created in the bottom of a pond for placement of a pump and to make draining and cleaning easier.

Shishi odoshi. A bamboo fountain, sometimes called a "stag scarer," designed to fill and refill accompanied by a clacking noise.

Standard. In an iris, one of three inner petals or petallike structures, usually erect.

Tamper. A hand tool or power device that is used to compact soil so that it is less likely to shift or crumble.

Topsoil. The uppermost layer of soil, which is the most fertile and workable for gardeners.

Tsukubai. A stone basin, used in the traditional Japanese tea ceremony.

Turion. A bud of certain water plants, which falls to the pond bottom over winter.

Underlayment. A thick fabric placed under a liner to protect it from sharp objects in the pond excavation. Some liners have underlayment attached.

Ultraviolet sterilizer. A device that kills microscopic organisms harmful to fish by causing their cell content to explode. It causes other particles to clump so that they can be more easily removed by filtration equipment.

Wall fountain. A fountain that spills water from a decorative plaque mounted on a wall or other vertical surface.

Water table. The highest level at which the ground is completely saturated with water.

Zeolite. A silicate often used to soften water, it comes in gravel or rock sizes. Water gardeners sometimes use it in an emergency to absorb pollutants such as ammonia.

Index

Numbers in **bold italic** indicate pages
with photos or illustrations of the subject.

Credits

Illustrator: Michele Angle Farrar

page 1: Jerry Pavia **page 4:** Jerry Pavia **page 5:** *top* Mark Lohman; *bottom* Elena Elisseeva/ Dreamstime.com **page 6:** Jan Kranendonk/ Dreamstime.com **page 7:** Jerry Pavia **pages 8–9:** courtesy of the USDA **pages 10–11:** Tom Dowd/Dreamstime.com **pages 12–13:** *top center & bottom left* Northwind Pictures; *center* Redeyed/Dreamstime.com; *bottom right* Brian Vanden Brink **page 14:** P. Berger/Photo Researchers **page 15:** Steve Allen/Dreamstime.com **page 16:** Osaka Museum/Bridgeman Art Library **page 17:** Aryu/Dreamstime **page 18:** Stapleton Collection/Bridgeman Art Library **page 19:** *left* Derek Fell; *right* Villa Lante della Rovere/Bridgeman Art Library **page 20:** Derek Fell **page 21:** *top* Stapleton Collection/Bridgeman Art Library: *bottom* Jose I. Soto/Dreamstime.com **page 22:** *top* Eric Crichton/Bruce Coleman; *bottom* Derek Fell **page 23:** *left* Steve Solum/Bruce Coleman; *right* Derek Fell **page 24:** Brian Vanden Brink **page 25:** Jerry Pavia **page 26:** *left* Roger Foley; *right* Saxon Holt **page 27:** Brian Vanden Brink **pages 28–29:** Nastiakru/Dreamstime.com **page 30:** *left* Roger Foley; *right* Allan Mandell **page 31:** *left* Saxon Holt; *right* Ken Druse **page 33:** Elena Elisseeva/Dreamstime.com **page 34:** Brian Vanden Brink **page 37:** *left* Walter Chandoha; *right* carolynbates.com **page 38:** *bottom left* Jane Grushow/Grant Heilman Photography, Inc.; *top right* Roger Foley **page 39:** *top left* Ken Druse; *bottom left* judywhite/New Leaf Images; *bottom right* Roger Foley **page 40:** Ron Sutherland/Garden Picture Library **page 41:** *top* Jane Grushow/Grant Heilman Photography, Inc; *bottom right* Jacqueline Murphy/CH **page 42:** *left* Roger Foley; *right* Walter Chandoha **page 43:** *top* Walter Chandoha; *bottom* Pam Spaulding/Positive Images **page 44:** Fabio Cardano/Dreamstime.com **page 45:** Eric Crichton/Bruce Coleman **page 46:** *left* Larry Lefever/Grant Heilman Photography, Inc.; *right* judywhite/New Leaf Images **page 47:** *top* judywhite/New Leaf Images; *bottom* Photos Horticultural **page 48:** Brian Vanden Brink **page 49:** Jerry Pavia **page 50:** *all* courtesy of Beckett Corp. **page 51:** Brian Vanden Brink **page 52:** *top* Tony Giammarino/Giammarino & Dworkin; *bottom both* Derek Fell

pages 53–56: *all* Jerry Pavia **page 57:** Saxon Holt **page 59:** *both* Brian Vanden Brink **page 61:** Michael & Lois Warren/Photos Horticultural **page 62:** Tony Giammarino/Giammarino & Dworkin **page 63:** Jerry Pavia **pages 64–65:** Elena Elisseeva/Dreamstime **page 66:** Jerry Pavia **page 67:** Mark Lohman **page 68:** *left* Derek Fell; *right both* John Parsekian **page 69:** Jerry Pavia **pages 70–71:** *all* Derek Fell **pages 73–75:** *both* Jerry Pavia **page 76:** Derek Fell **pages 77–79:** Jerry Pavia **page 81:** *top* courtesy of Beckett Corp.; *bottom* Jerry Pavia **page 82:** Jerry Pavia **page 83:** *all* Derek Fell **page 85:** *top* Alan & Linda Detrick; *center & bottom* Jerry Pavia **page 87:** *top* Photos Horticultural; *bottom right* Jerry Pavia; *bottom left* Ron Sutherland/Garden Picture Library **page 88:** *top* judywhite/New Leaf Images; *bottom* Brian Nieves/CH, products courtesy of Waterford Gardens **pages 90–91:** *both* Jerry Pavia **page 93:** Photos Horticultural **page 94:** *all* courtesy of Danner Mfg. **page 95:** Brian Nieves/CH, products courtesy of Waterford Gardens **page 96–103:** *all* Jerry Pavia **pages 104–107:** *all* Harry Heit/Steve Katona's North Hill Water Gardens **page 108:** Jerry Pavia **pages 110–111:** *all* Jerry Pavia **page 113:** Walter Chandoha **page 114:** John Glover **pages 116–119:** *both* Mark Lohman **pages 120–123:** *all* Jerry Pavia **page 124:** *top* Rachelks/Dreamstime.com; *bottom* Mark Lohman **page 126:** Jan Kranendonk/Dreamstime.com **page 127:** Jerry Pavia **pages 130–131:** Olegd/Dreamstime.com **pages 132–135:** *all* Jerry Pavia **pages 136–137:** *left*

Steven Wooster/Garden Picture Library, design: Anthony Paul; *right* Photos Horticultural, design: Ashwood Nurseries **page 141:** Photo Horticultural, design: Ash Parish Garden Club **page 142:** Larry MellicHamp, University of North Carolina **page 143:** John Glover **pages 144–145:** Jerry Pavia **page 146:** M.L. Dembinski/Dembinsky Photo Associates **page 147:** *top left* Jeff Lepore/Photo Researchers; *bottom left* Dick Scott/Dembinsky Photo Associates; *right* Larry Mellichamp, University of North Carolina **page 148:** Brigitte Thomas/Garden Picture Library **page 149:** *left* Larry Mellichamp, University of North Carolina; *right* Tamara Kulikova/Dreamstime.com **page 150:** Sanjibbhatt/Dreamstime.com **page 151:** *top* Jerry Pavia; *bottom* K. Rice/H. Armstrong Roberts **page 152:** Elena Elisseeva/Dreamstime.com **page 153:** *all* Hanson Man **page 154:** *left* Crandall & Crandall; *right* Michael Elliott/Dreamstime.com **page 155:** *all* Hans Reinhard/Bruce Coleman **page 156:** *top* Gary Meszaros/Dembinsky Photo Associates; *middle* E.R. Degginger/Bruce Coleman; *bottom* Kim Taylor/Bruce Coleman **page 157:** Hupeng/Dreamstime.com **page 158:** J. Paul Moore **page 159:** Brian Nieves/CH, products courtesy of Waterford Gardens **page 160:** Photos Horticultural **page 161:** *top* Jerry Pavia; *bottom* courtesy of Danner Mfg. **page 162:** Linda Z. Ryan/Dreamstime.com **page 163:** Webitect/Dreamstime.com **page 164:** Stan Osolinski/Dembinsky Photo Associates **page 165:** *top left* Anthony Merciera/Dembinsky

**If you enjoy *Garden Ponds, Fountains & Waterfalls for Your Home*,
look for these and other fine Creative Homeowner books
wherever books are sold.**

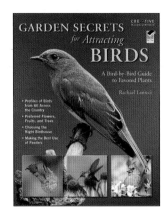

GARDEN SECRETS FOR ATTRACTING BIRDS
Provides information to turn your yard into a mecca for birds.

Over 250 photographs and illustrations.
160 pp.
8½" × 10⅝"
$14.95 (US)
ISBN: 978-1-58011-435-6

POCKET GUIDE TO HOUSEPLANTS
Secrets to growing the most popular types of houseplants.

Over 300 photographs.
312 pp.
5" × 7"
$19.99 (US)
ISBN: 978-1-58011-846-0

3 STEP VEGETABLE GARDENING
A quick and easy guide for growing your own fruit and vegetables.

Over 300 photographs.
224 pp.
8½" × 10⅞"
$19.95 (US)
ISBN: 978-1-58011-407-3

SUCCESSFUL CONTAINER GARDENING
Information to grow your own flower, fruit, and vegetable "gardens."

Over 240 photographs.
160 pp.
8½" × 10⅞"
$14.95 (US)
ISBN: 978-1-58011-456-1

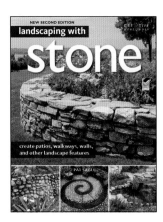

LANDSCAPING WITH STONE
Ideas for incorporating stone into the landscape.

Over 335 photographs.
224 pp.
8½" × 10⅞"
$19.95 (US)
ISBN: 978-1-58011-446-2

PLANT COMBINATIONS FOR AN ABUNDANT GARDEN
How to plan and grow the best plant combinations.

Over 900 photos and illustrations.
240 pp.
8" × 10"
$19.99 (US)
ISBN: 978-1-58011-827-9

For more information and to order direct, go to **www.creativehomeowner.com**